D0316656

Kidnapped

True Stories of
Twelve Irish Hostages

Kidnapped

True Stories of
Twelve Irish Hostages

A. J. Davidson

Gill & Macmillan

Gill & Macmillan Ltd
Hume Avenue, Park West, Dublin 12
with associated companies throughout the world
www.gillmacmillan.ie
© A. J. Davidson 2003
0 7171 3572 1
Design and print origination by Carole Lynch, Dublin
Printed and bound by Nørhaven Paperback A/S, Denmark

This book is typeset in Goudy 10.5 pt on 13.5 pt.

*The paper used in this book comes from the wood pulp of managed forests.
For every tree felled, at least one tree is planted,
thereby renewing natural resources.*

All rights reserved.
No part of this publication may be copied,
reproduced or transmitted in any form or by any means,
without permission of the publishers.

A CIP catalogue record for this book
is available from the British Library.

1 3 5 4 2

All photographs included in this book were supplied
by The Irish Times, unless otherwise noted.

For my family

Contents

Preface

The term 'kidnapping' originally referred to the abduction of children. In societies with high infant mortality, child theft was often a necessity to supplement the numbers of a group, while at the same time introducing fresh bloodlines. Families in pre-Norman Ireland would have lived with the threat of kidnap, the Vikings being particularly skilled practitioners. Indeed, history tells us that our St Patrick was stolen as a child.

By the Middle Ages the use of the word in English law had expanded to encompass the offence against adults. While kidnap is often associated with violence, it is not a prerequisite, the defining element being the deprivation of liberty. The practice reached epidemic proportions during the slave trade, though the imperative was now cheap labour rather than adding to the gene pool.

Child theft persisted up to the early twentieth century, and many favourite children's stories, such as 'Hansel and Gretel', contained a cautionary element, while misbehaving children would be admonished with threats of changelings. Perhaps the alien abduction claims so prevalent nowadays are a modern version of the Pied Piper!

The most notorious kidnap of the twentieth century was the Lindberg abduction. Its effect on the American psyche at the time was comparable to that suffered after the World Trade Centre attack. America was a different place after the Lindberg baby kidnap. Many police investigative procedures still in use today were implemented in the wake of that tragic incident.

The second half of the twentieth century saw kidnap being adopted as a terrorist tool. In Europe the Red Army Faction, the South Moluccans, the anarchist Red Brigade, Islamic fundamentalists, the INLA and the IRA are just some of the groups that used kidnap to further their struggles. Motives varied from fund-raising for the purchase of arms to exerting leverage for government concessions. While less frequent today, there are still countries where political kidnap is perceived as endemic. The Sicilians have turned it into an art form, and in some of the former states of the USSR the kidnap of foreign executives is a thriving business. Colombia has the worst record, with three-quarters of the world's ransom-related kidnaps happening there.

The breakdown of marriages, especially in pluralist societies, has sparked a resurgence in child kidnap. The opposing legal stances of the parents' respective countries can mean that some abductions will never be resolved.

Kidnap is a notoriously difficult crime for the police to investi-gate. Professional criminals, aware of the high risk of capture and consequently more unpredictable and desperate, commit the major-ity of kidnaps. Adding to the problems the police face is the fact that often they are not brought in until days afterwards, by which time the crime scene has been contaminated. Their involvement may be against the family's wishes, and the deadlines will usually be short. Ransoms can be paid in countries outside their jurisdiction. Despite the many obstacles it faces, the Garda Síochána has a good record in the successful resolution of kidnaps.

Sociologists are forever reminding us that crime does not occur in a vacuum. A crime against the person will most obviously have an effect upon the victim and the perpetrator. The victim is harmed, and the perpetrator will have to make recompense, be it judicially or conscience-inspired. Society is also damaged by crime. Like a stone dropped into a pond, a kidnap will cause a spectacular splash that fades quickly but will send ripples spreading outwards for years to come. The repercussions of the twelve kidnaps in this book have helped determine some aspects of Irish society in the twenty-first century.

1

The Curran Family and the Littlejohn Brothers

Ireland had a Cork man, Jack Lynch, as Taoiseach in October 1972. A new four-bedroom house in Clontarf, Dublin, cost £7,300. Offaly and Kerry had tied in the all-Ireland football final. Cinema audiences were flocking to see Marlon Brando in *The Godfather*, a story of intrigue and betrayal among the Cosa Nostra, the Mafia. In Dublin that autumn, another tale of intrigue and double-dealing was about to unfold.

The story had started in the North a few years earlier. Civil rights protestors had been on the march for a couple of years when, almost inevitably, sectarian violence erupted. Protestant gangs were setting fire to whole streets of Catholic houses and looting shops. Cars, buses and lorries were hijacked and burned in retaliation. Rioting became a daily occurrence, and the body count began to rise. The Stormont government introduced curfews and searches, and their rigid implementation by the RUC and the B Specials exacerbated the inter-community tension. In the cities of Belfast and Derry, Catholics were setting up civil defence committees, while the Irish Government had been asked to fund covert weapon purchases. Eventually the RUC admitted it had lost control of the streets, and British troops were sent in to keep the peace.

Soon thousands of young men in uniform were seen on the six o'clock news disembarking from the Liverpool ferries almost daily. The soldiers brought the usual camp followers. Night clubs and bars flourished, massage parlours and hot bed hotels became common sights in the grimy back streets of Belfast. One of the less conspicuous additions to Irish society, north and south, was the arrival of the intelligence services. In April 1970 Brigadier Frank Kitson was posted to Northern Ireland to take command of the 39th Infantry Brigade, the troops on the Belfast streets. An expert in counter-terrorism, he had learned his trade fighting the Mau Mau in Kenya. Although the brigadier's stay in Northern Ireland was to be a short one, his strategy for intelligence-gathering and propaganda was to be an enduring one. Kitson favoured the tactic of using counter-gangs to discredit the paramilitaries; these counter-gangs would carry out terrorist attacks that would be blamed on the enemy.

The first instance to surface of British intelligence using *agents provocateurs* in the Republic was to cause a serious rift in Anglo-Irish relations. The kidnap and hostage-taking of a respectable Dublin family would open cupboards containing skeletons both the Irish and British governments would have wished to keep hidden.

The doorbell of Noel Curran's house at Lower Kilmacud Road, Dublin, rang at 7:30 on the morning of Thursday, 12 October. Three men armed with pistols burst through the door when Curran opened it. One of them wore a mask made from a blue J-cloth. Curran knew at once what they were after; he had been prepared for something like this since taking up the post of bank manager at the start of the year. All bank managers knew it was a risk they had to live with. Curran's branch, the Royal Bank in Grafton Street, had been robbed before. The last time was in 1960, when every banknote had been taken. Head office of the Allied Irish Banks Group had drummed home what was expected of their staff in such circumstances: no resistance was to be offered, to ensure that no lives were put at risk.

The intruders quickly rounded up the occupants of the house, Mrs Mona Curran, the two children, Hugh, aged 10, and Neal, aged 4, and Curran's sister-in-law. All except Noel Curran were tied up. The bank manager was warned that if he did not do exactly as he was told it would mean unhappy consequences for his family. The men were in their early thirties. Two of them spoke with north of

England accents, while the third had a Scottish or Northern Ireland accent. The others addressed the leader, one of the Englishmen, as 'commandant'. The gunman wearing the mask was left to guard the hostages. Curran was driven in his own car to his bank in Grafton Street. On their way one of the Englishmen said, 'It's time this part of the country got a taste of its own medicine.' Talking among themselves, a comment was made about cleaning up some of the thugs that were down here in the Republic.

In Grafton Street, Curran was forced at gunpoint to open the door of the bank and deactivate the alarm system. Three other accomplices waiting nearby joined the two gunmen. One of them was carrying a large black box, later described as a carpenter's toolbox. Four of the men entered the bank, leaving one on guard outside.

As each member of the staff arrived for work, Noel Curran admitted them. They were taken downstairs by one of the gunmen and locked up in the strong-room. One male employee on his arrival thought it was an elaborate joke and poked the gunman with his umbrella. He was pushed to the floor and had a cocked pistol jammed to his head. When all twenty-two staff members were locked away, the robbers set about filling bags with notes from the vault. It was a few minutes past nine o'clock.

Some of the female staff complained of the chill in the strong-room, so the robbers ordered the bank porter, Maurice Hartigan, to make tea for them. The bank robbers were in a relaxed mood. They chatted about a recent boxing bout featuring the English boxer Joe Bugner, which had been broadcast the night before on television. They made several critical comments about the Republic's anti-quated telephone system. There was no effort to disguise their appearance, or their English accents, and they used quasi-military ranks when addressing each other, 'commandant', 'major' and 'sergeant'. One of them wore a military-style peaked cap. Despite this, the terrified staff believed the robbers were members of the Provisional IRA.

When they had finished collecting the money, the gang locked the strong-room and then the front door as they left, just before

10 a.m. They were inside the bank for two hours. The man who was left to guard the Curran family received a telephone call and, after locking his hostages in the garage, left in Mrs Curran's brown Austin Mini.

Soon afterwards, a small crowd of customers began to gather outside the front door waiting for the bank to open. Sensing that something was amiss, the Gardaí were sent for, and when they arrived at 10:30 they broke down the door and found the staff locked in the strong-room. Noel Curran quickly explained what had happened, and gardaí were sent to the Curran home to free his family. Although some members of the Curran family and the bank staff had been traumatised by their ordeal, there were no serious injuries.

Later that day the public relations officer of Allied Irish Banks, Bob Ryan, announced that the gang had stolen upwards of £30,000, £9,000 of which was in new notes. The Gardaí said that £45,000 would be a more realistic total, but no exact figure could be given until the Technical Bureau had finished its examination of the Grafton Street premises. The final tally was £67,000, which set a record as the largest bank robbery in Irish history.

Reports of the raid and the subsequent release of the Curran family made front-page headlines, with the majority of commentators blaming the robbery on the Provisional IRA. The two Curran cars were quickly found, Mrs Curran's Mini near the Green Cinema in St Stephen's Green, her husband's Hillman at Dublin Airport. Detective Chief Superintendent John Joy, who had been put in charge of the investigation, had formed an opinion that was very different from that expressed in the newspapers. He announced at a press conference that the prime suspects were a professional criminal gang from outside the state. He appealed for the owners of guesthouses and small hotels to come forward if they had any information that could help the investigation. Identikit pictures of four of the gang had been produced with the aid of twenty-five witnesses, and these were widely circulated.

The Gardaí also issued detailed descriptions of the four suspects. The 'major' was described as 6 feet 3 inches tall, of light to medium build, in his early thirties, with a tanned complexion, fair hair, and a moustache. He was dressed in a brown two-piece suit, check shirt, and brown tie. Another raider was described as 5 feet 10 inches tall, of thin build, in his late twenties, and with back-combed fair hair. The third raider was 5 feet 6 inches tall, heavily built, with a large beer belly; he had short, curly brown hair and wore a blue jacket. The fourth man was 5 feet 10 inches tall, twenty to thirty years old, and wore a dark suit with a blue shirt. One of the men was spotted by an observant traffic warden, walking along Chatham Street towards Mercer Street minutes after the gang left the bank.

Bristol police were brought in on the investigation after a member of Aer Lingus ground staff reported having seen two men fitting the descriptions boarding a flight on the morning of the robbery. The Gardaí believed that most of the cash from the robbery was still in Ireland, since its volume would have made it impossible to take on board an aeroplane.

Six days after the robbery a Garda officer travelled to London with extradition warrants for Kenneth Littlejohn, his wife, Christine, his brother Keith, and a known associate, Robert Stockman. The officer had access to first-rate intelligence, which included the current addresses of the suspects.

The next day, 19 October, Flying Squad officers arrested Kenneth Littlejohn and his brother Keith and brought them to Edgware Police Station, not the ideal place for 31-year-old Kenneth to celebrate his birthday. Stockman was soon picked up and joined them there. Littlejohn had been arrested at a house in Heather Walk, Edgware, Middlesex, and Stockman at a house in Torquay, Devon. About £31,000 of the stolen money was also recovered. Joy confirmed that £15,000 of the money had been found at the Edgware house, and another £5,000 in Torquay. He also said that £11,000 had been found in the ventilation shaft of a flat in Achill Road, Drumcondra, Dublin, five days previously. He went on to praise the media for refraining from publishing the news of the Dublin find until the Gardaí had had time to draw up extradition warrants and arrange the arrests in England.

Ten gardaí had conducted the initial investigation, and all thirty-two counties had been included. They made an early breakthrough when they received a tip-off on the Drumcondra flat. A three-day watch had been mounted, but nobody was seen entering the flat, so the decision was made to search it. The superintendent stressed that there was no political motive to the crime.

With most of the money recovered and the main culprits under arrest, the investigation was almost wrapped up. But for some, the rapid conclusion posed more questions than answers. Why would an ex-paratrooper and experienced criminal like Littlejohn allow his gang to use military ranks when addressing each other? Why had they not tried harder to disguise their accents and identities? Why had their fingerprints been left all over the bank? What was the source of the Gardaí's rapid and detailed intelligence? Some of the answers to these questions lay back in 1970, when the first Littlejohn brother set foot on Irish soil.

On 28 August 1970 a payroll robbery took place at the Midland Motor Cylinder Company near Birmingham. The snatch had been conducted like a military operation, and the gang got away with more than £35,000. The police reckoned that the thieves must have had someone on the inside, and they started their search with Brian Perks, an employee of the company who had been bound and gagged by the thieves. Background checks revealed that he had a brother-in-law called Kenneth Littlejohn, a dishonourably dis-charged ex-paratrooper who had been released from prison in 1968 after serving three years for a wages snatch in Edrington, Birmingham. The judge at that trial stated that the gang had acted with military efficiency. Perks was arrested, and a warrant was issued for Littlejohn's arrest. A series of early morning raids on thirty addresses failed to catch him. Their quarry had fled to Ireland on the advice, Littlejohn would later claim, of a corrupt detective who tipped him off in return for a percentage of the loot from the robbery.

In December 1970, Littlejohn set up a manufacturing firm called Whizz Kids (Ireland) Ltd. The principal directors were Kenneth Austen (i.e. Littlejohn) and Robert Stockman. The company announced it was to set up a factory in Co. Kerry to manufacture hot pants. The village of Cahersiveen was chosen as the site for the factory, and Littlejohn soon became a familiar figure in the surrounding area. He lived lavishly, drove a red sports car, took flying lessons, and always stood a round of drinks for the locals in the village pub. He was, as acquaintances recalled, a man in love with the good things of life and one who seemed to court danger, driving recklessly and performing stunts for small wagers. Months went by and the proposed factory faded into the Kerry mists. Littlejohn left Ireland a step ahead of many irate creditors.

Keith Littlejohn's criminal record was similar to his brother's. A petty criminal from the age of fourteen, he had served time in Borstal and Brixton Prison. During a period of attempted rehabilitation he met Lady Pamela Onslow, an official at the British Ministry of Defence and a close friend of the Minister of Defence, Lord Carrington. Lady Onslow did voluntary work for Teamwork Associates, a charity that assisted ex-Borstal boys.

Kenneth Littlejohn, with a chancer's eye for a deal, returned to England with a tale he hoped would be of interest to British security agencies. If he could convince the right people that he was of value to them, then they would provide him with immunity against the warrant for his arrest. Using Lady Onslow's influence, Littlejohn engineered a meeting at her house with a senior official of the Minister of Defence. The essence of his story was that while in Co. Kerry he had met subversives and had been shown an AK47 assault rifle, allegedly part of a shipment of arms the Provisional IRA had smuggled into Ireland. This story, though it may have had an element of truth, was greatly embellished by Littlejohn. Like any good salesman making a pitch to a customer, he told MI6 exactly what they wanted to hear. At Century House, London—head office of the Secret Intelligence Service (popularly known as MI6)—the Provisional IRA's general order no. 8, forbidding military action against the security forces of the Republic, was giving those in charge of the Irish desk many sleepless nights.

The new decade had brought serious misgivings regarding events in the North by a sympathetic Lynch Government. Lynch was perceived in London as being too soft on the Provisional IRA. It was now public knowledge that militant elements in Lynch's Government had conspired to purchase arms for Northern Catholics' self-defence. The tension between the two governments deteriorated when, after internment had been introduced, many members of the Provisional IRA fled to the south and sanctuary. If the Provisional IRA was to be defeated, this was a situation that could not be tolerated. Any political backlash in Dublin against the Provisional IRA would be welcome, and MI6 could not afford to be choosy about its origin. Subsequent meetings were arranged, and Kenneth Littlejohn was recruited by MI6 as an *agent provocateur* in Ireland.

Kenneth Littlejohn was introduced to Douglas Smythe (real name John Wyman), his handler. Smythe gave Littlejohn a phone number at which to contact a Detective-Inspector Sinclair of the Special Branch, should the police either in Ireland or Britain ever arrest him. Here was the 'get out of jail' card he had been seeking. He returned to Ireland, where his brother joined him a year later. He was given the task of infiltrating the Official IRA and provoking a feud with the Provisional IRA. The brothers and Christine moved to Smuggler's Cottage, near Clogher Head, Co. Louth, just a few miles from Dundalk, a town notorious for its strong republican support and home to many Provisional IRA men on the run. The extended family appeared prosperous and was soon well known in the area. They declared support for the republican cause, and the local Gardaí were tipped off about their criminal background, information that would undoubtedly have filtered through to local people.

Later Littlejohn was to claim that during his time in Co. Louth he met Smythe several times at various locations, both north and south of the border, at one time persuading Smythe to supply him with a gun. The weapon was picked up from the office of a Dublin solicitor. Littlejohn also claimed that he 'loaned' Smythe many Provisional IRA weapons so that they could be forensically tested and, with luck, linked to serious crimes. Many commentators on the covert intelligence operations believe that explosives were also being supplied to Littlejohn. An ex-mercenary, Leslie Aspen, who often brought money to the Littlejohns, was known to have been involved in arms-smuggling.

From February 1972 the Littlejohn brothers were members of a gang that robbed a dozen banks on both sides of the border. After one raid in the North, Kenneth was arrested by the RUC and had to play his immunity card. Despite his involvement in various bank raids, he had made limited progress with his infiltration of the Official IRA and in desperation put himself forward as a 'hit man' available for hire. He sensed, or was persuaded by Smythe, that the Official IRA was pursuing a strategy of political assassination at that time. John Taylor, a Stormont minister, was shot and wounded in the spring of 1972, but that was an isolated incident. Nothing of note developed from Littlejohn's clumsy offer. A friendship with Brian Mathers, a Newry man on the run, was Littlejohn's last-ditch attempt at covert infiltration, but it soon became apparent that Mathers' associates were not front-line troops; rather, they were petty criminals on the periphery of the IRA.

British intelligence suggested that much of what Littlejohn later claimed to have played a part in could be discounted as the lurid invention of a Billy Liar character, though there is evidence that he did petrol-bomb Garda stations in the towns of Louth and Castlebellingham, Co. Louth. He felt a compulsion to talk himself up to Smythe, not least to justify the over-generous allowance he was being paid. Century House confirmed that Littlejohn told Smythe of elaborate plans to assassinate Seán Mac Stiofáin, chief of staff of the Provisionals, and Séamus Costello and Seán Garland of the Official IRA. This was intended as the spark that would ignite a feud between the two wings of the IRA.

Littlejohn may have become a liability, but he had not taken leave of his senses. In September 1972 a car he used was stolen and left at Glassdrumman, Co. Armagh, just north of the border. Sensing a conspiracy, he requested that the British Army check it for booby-traps. He received the all-clear from them and a later second clearance from the RUC. Still suspicious, he asked Edmund Woolsley, a publican from Warrenpoint, thirty-two years old and married with six children, to pick it up for him. On 18 September, Woolsley and two customers went to retrieve the vehicle. He was killed when a booby-trap bomb exploded as he opened the door. It is not known who planted the booby-trap, but it signalled the beginning of the end for the Littlejohn brothers. If either of the IRA factions was responsible, the Englishmen's cover had been blown and they were of no further use to MI6. But could MI6 have planted the booby-trap? The Littlejohns realised that their welcome in Co. Louth had run out, and they moved back to Dublin, renting a flat in Drumcondra.

Littlejohn was not the only agent Smythe was running. He had several other contacts north and south of the border. His work load had grown so much it was decided that the handling of Kenneth Littlejohn should be transferred to a man called simply Oliver. This was the story Littlejohn was given, while the real reason for his handler's departure was kept from him.

Douglas Smythe and Detective-Sergeant Patrick Crinion of the Irish Special Branch were under investigation in Dublin. The Special Branch already knew that much of their classified material was being passed to Smythe (known as Wyman in Dublin). They allowed Crinion and Smythe their freedom to continue to conspire until they had enough evidence to convict. The trap was sprung, and Smythe was arrested in the act of receiving IRA intelligence from Crinion. It was a coup for the Garda Síochána and a huge embarrassment for the British. The Special Criminal Court gave the two men six-month prison sentences. However, the British Government was not prepared to let Smythe serve his sentence in Ireland. They wanted him back in England, where he would not cause embarrassment and where his many secrets would be preserved. But the advantage lay with the Irish Government; Britain had nothing to bargain with—at least not until the kidnap of the Curran family and the bank robbery in Grafton Street, Dublin.

It is unlikely that the Littlejohn brothers were fully briefed about their part in the deal the British Government was pursuing. Littlejohn and his new handler had not been getting along before the bank robbery, and he had been threatening to quit. He would later claim that Oliver helped plan the robbery, and had been very enthusiastic, but his attitude had changed when they talked for three hours in Trafalgar Square, London, shortly before the Littlejohns' arrest. When Littlejohn was picked up he was allowed to make one phone call. He called Detective-Inspector Sinclair at the Special Branch, his 'get out of jail' card. He explained the predicament he and his brother were in. Sinclair's response was 'So what?' Littlejohn knew then he had been set up.

The British and Irish governments struck a deal. The Littlejohns would be extradited to Ireland to face a charge of robbery, in return for Crinion and Smythe being handed over. At this stage the Irish authorities did not know that Smythe had been the Littlejohns' handler. It was vital from Britain's point of view that the exchange take place before the Irish discovered the full extent of British intelligence operations in Ireland.

The British Government had an extra bargaining chip to speed up negotiations. If the Irish failed to co-operate, Kenneth Littlejohn would be tried for the 1970 Birmingham robbery and, if convicted, jailed, making extradition impossible. The British, understandably, considered the trial of the Littlejohns as the lesser of two evils. What did it matter if two petty criminals got a long-overdue come-uppance, compared with the catastrophic exposure of Smythe as a spymaster? With Smythe safely back on English soil, it would matter little what the Littlejohns claimed at their trial.

The Irish Government was duped into agreeing to the transfer. They genuinely believed they had landed the 'bigger fish'; this belief was reinforced by the British shrewdly insisting that the Littlejohns' charges be limited to the Dublin robbery and that their trial be *in camera*. The Government conceded that the Littlejohns would not have to face any political charges. It was also agreed that witnesses with any knowledge of the brothers having acted on instructions from British intelligence would be barred from testifying.

The deal hammered out between the two governments was so uneven that it strongly suggests that the Lynch Government had secrets of its own to protect. Certainly the Arms Trial of 1970 had come close to bringing it down, and they would have been keen to avoid a further scandal.

Littlejohn, though, was not going back to Dublin without a fight. Confessing to the Birmingham robbery might have kept him in England, but that meant his brother facing extradition on his own. With this in mind, Littlejohn asked for a list of well-known names to be served with summonses to appear on his behalf at Bow Street Court, London, during a hearing opposing extradition. The charges against Christine Littlejohn were dropped, and the requested summonses to Lord Carrington, Lady Pamela Onslow, Douglas Smythe and the mysterious Oliver were never issued. The hearing was heard before Lord Widgery *in camera*. This secret hearing was a precaution taken by the Attorney-General on behalf of the British Government to prevent details of Smythe's covert activities in Ireland emerging before he was returned. Lord Widgery ruled that the Littlejohns and Robert Stockman be extradited. They were put on the next flight to Dublin, with Smythe and Crinion heading across the Irish Sea in the opposite direction. Robert Stockman was released from Portlaoise Prison a few months later, with all charges dropped.

The Littlejohn trial took place in August 1973. Anthony J. Hederman SC prosecuted for the state, while John Lovatt-Dolan SC led the defence. The odds of an acquittal were heavily stacked against the brothers from the start. The ploy of bringing charges only on the Grafton Street robbery meant that the Littlejohns' defence team could get limited mileage from claiming political grounds. Only when Kenneth Littlejohn himself took the stand to give evidence could any reference to his life as an *agent provocateur* be raised. He stuck to his story and insisted that he was not the principal of the bank robbery gang, and that he had been persuaded into doing it by the promise that outstanding charges in England would be struck off for all time. His bravado in the witness box did not help his cause. He tried to portray himself as an honourable man doing dishonourable things in order to save lives. The money, he hinted, was to be used to set up and arm a splinter group of the IRA, which he would command. Mr Lovatt-Dolan attempted to persuade the court that the fact that the Littlejohns' extradition hearing had been held *in camera* was proof enough that the British Government had something to hide.

The court disagreed, and the brothers were found guilty. Mr Justice Finlay noted that their offence carried a maximum sentence of life imprisonment. They had planned and executed a robbery that involved depriving a young wife and her children of their freedom, putting them and Mr Curran in fear of their lives. The judge handed down a sentence of fifteen years to Keith Littlejohn, who, he was satisfied, had played a subservient role. Kenneth Littlejohn was sentenced to twenty years. As he was being led from the dock to begin his sentence, Kenneth Littlejohn spoke to the public gallery: 'Thank you, England. Ask Carrington what he thinks of that.'

Over the next few months, as it became clear that the Irish Government had been 'sold a dummy' over the Littlejohn extradition, relations between London and Dublin deteriorated. Jack Lynch, a barrister by profession, felt particularly humiliated. His anger came to a head at a press interview he gave, where he suggested a suspicion that the bombings in Dublin on 2 December 1972 were the work of British intelligence. At the time the Dáil was debating tougher anti-terrorist legislation, and it appeared likely that the bill would be defeated, until the afternoon of the vote, when two car bombs exploded in Dublin, killing two people and injuring seventy-four. There was outrage in the Dáil, Fine Gael abstained from the vote, and the legislation was passed.

It was not the last time Lynch stumbled over the Littlejohns, who had almost cost him his party leadership. A report on the brothers had been seen by Lynch before being deposited with the

Department of Foreign Affairs. The Taoiseach promptly forgot about it, because of the pressures of a general election. When the intelligence aspect furore broke during the Littlejohns' trial, Lynch denied knowing about it. He was caught out when Garret FitzGerald checked up on it. Lynch was genuinely embarrassed and offered to resign as leader of the opposition. FitzGerald, quite rightly, said a resignation was unnecessary.

Wary of a complete breakdown of relations between London and Dublin, Lord Wigg, security adviser to the former prime minister Harold Wilson, called for Lord Carrington's resignation and demanded that a public inquiry be held into the Littlejohn affair. But the British Government made no official statement over the Taoiseach's comments.

Brian Mathers was later convicted for his part in the robbery and was sentenced to ten years' imprisonment. Robert Stockman was tried for a Co. Monaghan hotel robbery and relived his association with the Littlejohns in the witness box. He claimed that he and Kenneth had intended buying a restaurant in Torquay, but denied that this was what the unrecovered portion of the money from the Grafton Street robbery had been destined for. Judge Ryan acquitted Stockman, expressing deep reservations about the identification parade from which Stockman had been picked out.

Mountjoy Prison was a dangerous place to be for the Littlejohn brothers after the revelations in court. They were kept in solitary confinement in B Basement, a section of the prison reserved for inmates being punished for breaches of discipline. At first there were no other inmates, but following a prison riot in October 1973, several other cells were occupied and a truce was negotiated with Provisional IRA prisoners. Kenneth Littlejohn embarked on a hunger strike and lodged a motion in the High Court to rule their trial in the Special Criminal Court unconstitutional, but the decision went against them. An appeal to the Supreme Court against this ruling was being prepared, and their solicitor, William Blood-Smith, would have consultations with them inside the prison. The Littlejohns received a few visits from close friends and family and two visits from British Embassy officials. The second of the visits from the embassy officials was only a few hours before Kenneth abandoned his hunger strike and they made their escape attempt.

At 7 p.m. on 11 March 1974 the brothers asked to join an exercise class with other prisoners, a privilege that had been suspended since Kenneth had gone on hunger strike. Permission was granted, and at 7:40 p.m. the brothers left B Wing through a gate and a door at the north gable of the building and crossed the prison grounds diagonally to a section of the 20-foot perimeter wall. Amazingly, there were no guards on duty outside the other wings of the prison. Even more fortuitously for the Littlejohn brothers, four long planks of wood had been propped against the wall. The brothers climbed the makeshift ramp to the top of the wall but were spotted by an alert warder, who quickly raised the alarm. However, they dropped down the other side, where Keith landed badly, spraining his ankle. The Garda patrol of the outer perimeter was apparently not on duty that night. The escapers made a run for it, but Keith's ankle was causing him too much pain. He insisted that his brother leave him, and Kenneth reluctantly did so. The warder who had raised the alarm chased Kenneth along Glengarriff Parade, a cul-de-sac off the North Circular Road. The prisoner climbed into a waiting Hillman Avenger and was driven off at speed. Keith was captured, taken back inside the prison, and searched. He had a sheet of paper bearing an address in Howth and some telephone numbers. The hunt for his brother was immediately concentrated round the Howth peninsula. A report of a sighting near Binns Bridge, not far from his former flat in Drumcondra, was ignored.

The Government was extremely embarrassed by the escape, coming six months after the audacious helicopter escape of three republican prisoners from Mountjoy's exercise yard. Sinn Féin was incensed. A spokesman said, 'The escape was too simple.' The republicans raised other points. Why had the Littlejohn brothers been allowed to wear civilian clothing? How did a man who had been on hunger strike for thirty-four days have the strength to outrun a warder? One republican said, 'I've been in the basement at Mountjoy. Believe me, it is a very unpleasant place and, I should have thought, virtually escape-proof, unless of course they were helped.' In fact, as we have seen, the actual escape took place from the exercise yard.

Keith Littlejohn was taken under heavy guard to the Accident and Emergency Department at the Mater Hospital and had his injured ankle X-rayed. After an hour he was given the all-clear and was returned to Mountjoy.

Christine Littlejohn was contacted at her house on Pennsylvania Road, Torquay. She gave a short statement to the press. 'I hope he has got away for good, but I didn't expect him to make an escape bid while his Supreme Court appeal was pending.'

The day after the escape, Mr Justice Butler dismissed the Littlejohns' action in their absence, declining to hold that the provisions of section 5 of the Offences Against the State Act or the powers of the Special Criminal Court were unconstitutional.

Kenneth Littlejohn evaded recapture, probably with the aid of the unrecovered £11,000 from the Grafton Street bank robbery, thought to have been stashed somewhere in Dublin. He surfaced some months later in Amsterdam. For years afterwards he told his story to the trickle of journalists who turned up on his doorstep. His claim that he had been sold out by British intelligence was probably true, but there was little sympathy for him. It was not as though he had been exactly duped into working for MI6. He had shamelessly used and exploited a great number of people, including Lady Onslow, whose tireless work to assist ex-Borstal boys had taken a severe jolt. Littlejohn had few scruples when it came to manipulating people, including his own brother, and the unfortunate Edmund Woolsley, who paid the ultimate price. If British intelligence turned the tables on Kenneth Littlejohn, there were precious few left who cared.

Two years passed before he was once again extradited to Ireland, this time to face the charge of escaping from custody. He used the dock to repeat his allegations, but on this occasion they lacked impact. People had grown tired of Kenneth Littlejohn and his embroidered stories. He was reunited with Keith in Mountjoy Prison. Both were released in 1981 on grounds of ill health. They returned to England and laid low for a time. But less than a year had passed before Kenneth was to be in trouble again. A judge sent him to prison for six years for armed robbery.

Lady Onslow came close to paying with her life for her association with the Littlejohns. In 1982 a parcel bomb containing 2 lb of plastic explosive was sent to her home in Kensington, London, by the Provisional IRA. Fortunately, the detonator was faulty, and Lady Onslow was unhurt when she unwrapped the parcel.

2

Thomas Niedermayer— A Double Tragedy

❖❖❖

T he kidnap of Thomas Niedermayer was an attempt by the Provisional IRA to coerce the British Government into freeing the Price sisters in exchange for his release. The sisters, Marian and Dolours, had gone on hunger strike in an English prison soon after commencing their life sentences for the Old Bailey bombing of 8 March 1973 in London. A welcome bonus to the kidnapping would be the chance to seriously damage the Northern Ireland economy by discouraging foreign investment. Unfortunately, it led to two tragedies, seventeen years apart.

Thomas Niedermayer, forty-five years old, was the West German managing director of the successful Grundig plant in Dunmurry, Belfast, which produced audiocassette recorders. Originally from Nürnberg, he now lived with his wife, Ingerborg, and their two teenage daughters, Gabrielle, aged nineteen, and Renate, aged sixteen, at Glengoland Gardens, Suffolk, a suburb of Belfast, not far from the factory. He had been head of Grundig (NI) Ltd since 1961 and was awarded an honorary OBE in 1967 for his services to industry.

It had been a quiet Christmas for the Niedermayer family. Ingerborg had been taken into hospital seriously ill before the holiday break, so her husband and daughters had not felt too festive. They had spent a large part of Christmas Day at her bedside and heard the welcome news that she was on the mend. Already her husband was making plans for her return home, probably early in the new year.

Two men called at the Niedermayer home at about 11:10 p.m. on 27 December 1973. Renate answered the door. The callers, two teenage men, appeared well mannered and apologised for disturbing her at such a late hour. They said their car had been in a minor collision with her father's car, parked on the road in front of the house. After Niedermayer went to inspect the damage, he was seen by his daughter talking to the men next to the family's car and a green Hillman Hunter. Renate went back inside and so did not see what happened next. When Niedermayer turned to walk back to the house the men seized him. There was a brief struggle with the men before he was bundled into the rear of their car and driven off at high speed.

A neighbour and management colleague, Helmut Hoeck, witnessed the entire incident from the unlit living-room of his house. He was so taken aback by what he had seen that he decided to check whether any other neighbour had seen it as well, in case his eyes had been deceiving him. None of his neighbours had witnessed anything untoward, so a precious ten minutes passed before he made a 999 call. It was only when the RUC arrived at the Niedermayers' house that his daughters discovered what had happened.

The Niedermayer home was only a short distance from Andersonstown, a Provisional IRA stronghold, and the RUC detectives' first suspicions were directed there. They could not be certain whether it was the Provisional IRA or the Official IRA that was behind his abduction. Although the official RUC stance was that they were keeping an open mind about the kidnap, loyalist paramilitaries were not seriously considered as suspects.

It seemed the investigation was fated to start slowly. The British army was not informed of the abduction for seventy-four minutes, but when eventually brought in it quickly swung its vast manpower into action. Suffolk and Andersonstown were sealed off, 24-hour roadblocks were set up all over Northern Ireland, and traffic along the hundreds of border roads was subjected to constant checkpoints. It was to be the North's biggest manhunt.

Niedermayer had indeed been driven into the heart of republican Andersonstown, to a house in Hillhead Crescent. His abductors were armed with pistols, and the man in the back seat with

Niedermayer used his gun to pistol-whip him when he tried to wave at a passing army Land Rover as they were leaving Suffolk. A hand was clamped over his mouth and he was forced into the footwell of the car as it drew up at traffic lights. When the car stopped, the men checked that there were no pedestrians around before they hauled him from the vehicle and pushed him through the side door of a house. Dragged upstairs, he was taken to a small bedroom at the rear of the building. He was thrown down on a mattress and knelt on while his wrists and legs were bound. The window had been boarded up on the inside, and he was allowed only a dim bedside light. The house was supposed to be empty, his captors explained. He was to be guarded by three men, who took turns to stand watch in the room. They told him he had been taken for leverage on the British judiciary to effect the release of the Price sisters.

The Price sisters, daughters of the veteran Belfast republican Albert Price, were part of the eleven-strong team sent to bomb London. The bombings in Britain were to coincide with a plebiscite about the border being held in Northern Ireland on 8 March 1973. Dolours went to London on a reconnaissance trip a month before the attack; Marian joined her later. Four cars were stolen in Belfast, resprayed and fitted with false number-plates, loaded with explosives, and taken across to England on the Dublin-to-Liverpool ferry. Two of the car bombs were discovered and defused, the other two exploded, one at the army recruitment office in Whitehall, and the other at the Old Bailey. One hundred and eighty people were injured, and a bystander died from a heart attack. Ten of the bombing team were arrested at Heathrow Airport. Eight of them, including the Price sisters, received life sentences.

When the security forces' net failed to catch anyone in the first twenty-four hours, Superintendent William Edgar was brought in to head the investigation. Right from the start his job was complicated and plagued by the multitude of rumours that surfaced concerning the kidnapping. Almost all the paramilitary groups were blamed at one time or another. Hoeck's delay in alerting the police prompted speculation about Niedermayer's private life and financial affairs.

The eyes of the world, Superintendent Edgar knew, would be watching his every move. An international element was inevitable, because in 1971 Niedermayer had been appointed Northern Ireland Honorary Consul of the Federal Republic of Germany. The post involved fostering economic links between Northern Ireland and Germany and promoting Germany's interests in the province, together with the protection of German citizens living or visiting there. Warnings to other consuls and foreign businessmen were given, especially those linked with the Dupont tyre factory in Derry and the Hoechst electronics plant in Coleraine.

The day after the kidnap the house where the Niedermayer family had lived for eight years was besieged by the media, but they got little copy for their hours of standing around in the cold. One of the daughters was seen peeking through a venetian blind, but there was no response to telephone calls or to knocks at the front door. Later an RUC car arrived and the girls departed with the police, leaving the house in darkness. Douglas Getty, second in command at the Grundig factory, told the waiting press that the girls were with close friends and were being guarded by the RUC. He went on to say that Ingerborg Niedermayer had been informed of her husband's abduction and was being taken care of by the hospital.

A description of Niedermayer was issued and published in most of the Northern newspapers. He was said to be 5 feet 10 inches tall, with black hair going grey. When abducted he was wearing a light-brown woollen jacket over a red T-shirt, light brown trousers and slippers. Three nights after the kidnapping the RUC made a television appeal for information. A spokesman urged the Sunday night audience, 'If you know something, please let us know somehow.'

A lot of anger was felt over the kidnapping. Local people took a pride in the successful Grundig factory, and at a time when manufacturing workers in Britain were being placed on a three-day week, any successful firm in this unemployment blackspot was to be applauded, never mind having its manager kidnapped. Loyalist reprisals for the kidnapping could not be ruled out. The Vanguard Unionists warned of retaliation if Niedermayer was not released immediately. The indignation mounted steadily the longer the kidnappers remained silent.

Niedermayer was the fifth German diplomatic representative to be kidnapped while working abroad in the space of five years. Not all of these kidnaps had been resolved successfully. Count von Spreti, ambassador to Guatemala, had been kidnapped in 1970 by a group seeking the release of seventeen political prisoners and a £280,000 ransom. He was killed by his abductors after six days. In the same year, on 1 December, Eugen Beihl, honorary consul in San Sebastián, had been kidnapped and killed by Basque separatists. The day after Niedermayer's snatch a French businessman, Yves Boisset, was kidnapped in Buenos Aires. He was the manager of a car production plant.

The Secretary of State for Northern Ireland, Francis Pym, only recently appointed after a Cabinet reshuffle, said he greatly deplored and regretted Herr Niedermayer's abduction. The German businessman was highly regarded by the former Ministers of Commerce Roy Bradford and Robin Bailie, who had worked closely with him. Pym assured people in Ireland and Germany that the security forces would spare no effort in finding the missing business-man. 'Every possible step is being taken to trace Herr Niedermayer as a matter of extreme gravity and urgency,' Pym said. The German Embassy in London was being kept abreast of developments. Pym flew to London the morning after the kidnapping for a forty-minute meeting with the West German Ambassador, Gunter von Hase. It was thought that the British Government would not condone the payment of any ransom demanded, but would not try to interfere with any arrangements Grundig cared to make.

The British Army, unlike the RUC, pulled no punches when it came to naming who it thought was responsible for the kidnap-ping. Three days after Niedermayer was taken an army official con-firmed that the Provisional IRA was its prime suspect. He added that it was possible that the delay in hearing from the kidnappers was because they had been prevented from leaving Northern Ireland by the high level of army activity at the border. It was felt that no contact would be made until the Provisionals had Niedermayer safely ensconced in a safe house somewhere in the Republic.

The British army revealed that it had details a few months before of an IRA plan to kidnap twelve prominent people in the North. An army source said, 'We thought the plan had been abandoned, but it is possible that Mr Niedermayer's capture is just a trial run.'

The 1,300-strong work force at the Dunmurry plant held their managing director in high esteem, and credited him with preventing sectarianism among the mixed religions of the work force. There was a history of good labour relations at the factory, and Grundig had only recently announced plans for an expansion, with 500 new jobs in Belfast and a new factory in Newry, Co. Down, to employ 1,000 people. The Dunmurry works committee, after an emergency meeting with officials from the Irish Congress of Trade Unions, issued a statement calling for the immediate release of Thomas Niedermayer in the interests of all working people throughout Northern Ireland. 'We call upon all trade unionists to join with us in condemning this callous act. We ask them to use all their strength to show the world we will not tolerate it.'

The German consul in Liverpool, Dr Kurt Friese, and Adolf Wohlrab, head of Grundig's tape recorder production branch in Nürnberg, flew to Belfast for talks with the Northern Ireland Minister of State, William von Straubenzee, and RUC officers at Stormont. On 29 December the Grundig head office in Bonn announced that the kidnap would not stall its planned expansion in Northern Ireland. The new Newry factory would go ahead as planned.

The first contact from the kidnappers eventually came three days after the abduction. A telephone call was made to the office at the Dunmurry factory. The caller simply said that Niedermayer was alive and well. There was no mention of a ransom or a possible exchange for republican prisoners. The RUC had picked up a rumour that persevered longer than any other: that the Provisionals planned to exchange Niedermayer for the Price sisters, then on hunger strike in Winchester Prison, County Durham. The idea was preposterous, the Northern Ireland Office insisted. No exchange would ever be made.

The officers of the Garda Síochána were working long hours on the southern side of the border. They had a stroke of luck at one of their checkpoints near Ballybofey, Co. Donegal, on New Year's Eve, when the two occupants of a car were seen parking their vehicle some distance from the checkpoint and walking away across the fields. The gardaí did not approach the vehicle but left it under covert surveillance when they stood down the checkpoint. The men returned to their car after dark and were promptly arrested. The car contained 250 lb of explosives and several thousand rounds of ammunition. The arrested men were Martin McGuinness and Joseph McCallion. McGuinness was a known Provisional who had fled Derry in the wake of Operation Motorman, the introduction of internment. He had moved to Buncrana, Co. Donegal, and although he had been seen back in Derry on a few occasions, he had evaded the security forces. A Dublin court sentenced McGuinness to six months' imprisonment for membership of the IRA.

January was three days old when West Germany requested and received permission to send a special investigation unit to Northern Ireland. The RUC leadership said all the right things about international co-operation and the valuable contribution alternative policing methods and techniques could bring to the investigation. Out on the streets of Belfast and in the lee of the hedges of south Armagh, however, the ordinary constables were not so appreciative. It was felt that valuable man-hours would be wasted playing nursemaid to a bunch of German hot-shot detectives. One senior policeman expressed what most of his colleagues were thinking when he said, 'The longer the kidnappers keep quiet, the less chance there is of him being alive.'

Ingerborg Niedermayer, now recovered and discharged from hospital, made an emotional television appeal a week after her husband's abduction for his release. She had become a virtual recluse, rarely straying far from the telephone. Full-page advertisements were placed in newspapers throughout Ireland offering a £3,000 reward for information.

Ten days after the abduction the kidnappers made contact again. They phoned Grundig's London office and demanded a £250,000 ransom. There were no details about how or when the money was to be paid. Surprisingly, no threats were made against Niedermayer's life. It was assumed that this was a preliminary contact and that the caller would phone again. He did not.

When Merlyn Rees was appointed Secretary of State for Northern Ireland in March 1974, after the general election of 28 February, it emerged that for some weeks the Provisional IRA had been involved in secret discussions with the Northern Ireland Office in the wake of the Sunningdale Agreement. The Provisionals were keen to have Sinn Féin legalised in time for the election, and one of the topics under discussion was the fate of Niedermayer; but the talks broke down before any firm resolutions were agreed.

Weeks dragged by without any developments in the investigation. Understandably, keeping a large team of detectives tied up on one investigation was a luxury the RUC could not afford. Murders and other serious crimes were occurring daily, and it was not long before the Niedermayer files were put aside, to wait until some fresh information or chance discovery would shed new light on the case.

But Ingerborg and her daughters could not put it aside. Life was very different without the man of the family. They decided not to leave Northern Ireland; it was the only home the girls knew, and their father had fallen in love with the landscape and the people. He had often said that when he died he would like to be buried in Northern Ireland.

By June 1974 the Price sisters' hunger strike at Durham Prison was almost 200 days old, and the volume of adverse press the British Government was receiving encouraged the Provisional IRA to try forcing their hand regarding the sisters with another kidnapping. This time the victims were the elderly Earl and Countess of

Donoughmore, taken from their home at Knocklofty House, near
Clonmel, Co. Tipperary. Ruairí Ó Brádaigh, president of Sinn Féin,
intervened and persuaded the Provisionals not to carry through
their threat to kill the two hostages. They were released unharmed
in the Phoenix Park, Dublin, after four days of captivity. Lord
Donoughmore said that he and his wife had been treated well by
their kidnappers, being served cooked breakfasts and chops or steak
for dinner. The Prices' hunger strike was abandoned forty-eight
hours later.

A further ten months had passed when, on St Patrick's Day
1975, the Price sisters were told they were to be transferred to the
Women's Prison in Armagh. This was a concession granted by the
British Government to help prolong a ceasefire that had been agreed
during one of the periodic negotiations between the Provisional
IRA and London. During their earlier hunger strike the sisters were
controversially force-fed. The furore over this was so great that the
Home Secretary, Roy Jenkins, decided that no other prisoner would
be treated this way, a decision that would require re-examination
six years later.

The Nürnberg District Court declared Thomas Niedermayer
dead in August 1976. The primary purpose of the declaration was
to ease the financial burden the Niedermayer family had been put
under. Death-in-service benefits could now be settled by the
Grundig pension scheme and a widow's pension paid.

The Northern Ireland Office offered the family £200,000 in
compensation, and it was accepted. With all hope gone, a plot in a
Derriaghy cemetery, Co. Antrim, was reserved, and Ingerborg
Niedermayer had a granite tombstone erected in 1978. The church
was chosen because it was the one in which the family worshipped
when they first arrived in Northern Ireland. The tombstone was
engraved: 'Thomas Niedermayer. In Loving Memory. March
1928–December 1973. Thy Will Be Done.' The rector of Christ
Church, Derriaghy, Rev. Norman Barr, said, years later, 'Periodically
she would visit the cemetery to stand for a few moments beside the
empty plot.'

Almost five years later the RUC received information regarding a field in the Glens of Antrim. Under grey skies, a team of police and forensic scientists conducted a thorough search of the field, an operation that lasted for several days. They even considered the demolition of a derelict house at the edge of the field before the search was called off. Nothing was found. The RUC announced that the Niedermayer family had been informed about the search.

The first possibly truthful information to surface about Niedermayer's fate came in an American newspaper interview with Peter McMullan, a former Provisional IRA member, in September 1979. He claimed that Niedermayer had been taken to a house in Turf Lodge, Belfast, after his abduction but had died from a heart attack within hours. He was buried in a bog not far from Andersonstown.

Brian Smyth worked as a digger driver, and in the early spring of 1980 his firm had been contracted by Lisburn Borough Council to clear an unofficial dump in the wooded Colin Glen just on the south-west outskirts of Belfast. Fly-tippers had been dumping rubbish in the glen for years, and the eyesore was to be cleared as part of Lisburn's spruce-up campaign.

The 11th of March was not a particularly cold day, but a shiver ran down Smyth's back as he worked the controls of his digger. One month before, the body of Leonard Kaitcher had been found on the road above, less than 300 yards from where he was now working. Originally from Dublin, the antique dealer had been kidnapped early in the morning from his luxury home in the affluent Malone Road area of south Belfast. The men who abducted him had tied up his two sons, telling them that if they wanted to see their father again they were to raise a million-pound ransom. Their father's last words to them as he was taken away were, 'I'll hardly see you again.'

The two sons attempted to rendezvous with the kidnappers at an arranged location that evening with as much of the ransom as they could raise, but the men failed to turn up. Their father's body was found in Colin Glen Lane, not far from Andersonstown, the following morning.

Smyth tried to forget about the unfortunate Kaitcher and turned his concentration back on his work. He had been on the site for three weeks, and the borough's technical officer was anxious for him to be finished. He was working on a steep slope, 18 feet from the road. The blade of the digger bit into the rubbish and earth as if it was marshmallow. The machine gave a jerk as he raised the arm. In the disturbed earth at the base of a tree, something caught his eye. He squinted for a better look—old bones, he thought. Some farmer must have dumped one of his dead animals. Smyth realised he was wrong when he saw clothing remnants clinging to the bones. He shut off the digger and climbed down for a closer look.

Lewis McAvoy, Lisburn Borough's technical officer, alerted by the digger's engine stopping, came across for an explanation. He took one look at the bones and knew they were human. He told Smyth to leave everything as it was and went off to contact the RUC. The rotting footwear on the skeleton's leg could have been a slipper, he thought.

Thomas Niedermayer's shallow grave was less than a mile from his house in Glengoland. Detective Chief Superintendent Bill Mooney was now in command of the investigation. He supervised the body's painstaking removal and transfer to the Belfast mortuary. There was no jewellery on the body that might have provided an immediate clue to identification, though the clothes did seem to match those Niedermayer was wearing when he was last seen. The Niedermayer family were informed of the discovery of the skeletal remains.

Ingerborg Niedermayer was so certain that the body was that of her husband that she started to arrange for his funeral before receiving official confirmation from the police. Staying with friends in Belfast, she had been shown the clothing remnants taken from the badly decomposed body. The police tried to find Niedermayer's dental records, but they could not be found. Positive identification would have to wait a while longer. The funeral was put on hold.

There was some press speculation that Niedermayer's dental records had been stolen during an armed robbery at his dentist's surgery the same week the RUC announced they were digging up a field in the Glens of Antrim. A police spokesman denied this but had to admit that the records could not be traced. He was asked how many dental practices had been robbed at gunpoint during his time as a policeman. He replied that he did not have those figures to hand!

Bone marrow samples were taken for DNA identification, a 28-day procedure in the early 1980s, so a dental professor from Queen's University, Belfast, was asked if he could assist. By examining a full-face photograph of Niedermayer taken eleven months before his kidnapping as he was showing the then Secretary of State, William Whitelaw, around the Grundig factory, the professor was able to superimpose X-rays of the skeleton's skull and jaws. On 15 March a confirmed identification of the remains was made. It was indeed Thomas Niedermayer. Post-mortem forensic examination showed that the murdered man's legs and arms were bound, and his skull had two fractures, possibly made from the toe of a Browning pistol. Either fracture could have proved fatal, but death could also have been caused by asphyxiation or by a heart attack.

Niedermayer's funeral eventually went ahead on 20 March, and he was buried in the country he loved so much, in a graveyard less than a mile from Dunmurry. The Grundig factory closed as a mark of respect, and on a bitterly cold day some four hundred mourners filled the small church and the cemetery. Representatives of the RUC attended, as did members of the Bonn government, along with the German ambassador to Ireland. Niedermayer's brother Albert and sister Heria Herdig joined Ingerborg, Gabrielle and Renate at the head of the mourners.

The church service was conducted in English and German, a Lutheran minister from Dublin, Dr Kurt Prussman, assisting the rector. The Bishop of Connor, Rt Rev. Arthur Butler, referred to Niedermayer's frequently expressed wish to be buried in Northern Ireland: 'His request is in itself a tribute to the friends he made and the men and women of Grundig he worked with. He ended his life among us in a dreadful way, and we all feel the shame of it.' The

Catholic Bishop of Down and Connor, Dr William Philbin, attended the service. As the coffin was being lowered into the grave, Ingerborg plucked a red rose from a wreath and, in keeping with German tradition, placed it on the lid.

A thousand Northern Ireland workers lost their jobs in September 1980 when Grundig closed its Dunmurry factory. The closure, which had been announced at the end of June, was blamed on competition from the 'tiger' economies of the Far East. It marked the end of Grundig as a major employer in the North. A company spokesman said the future was so bleak for European manufacturers that they had to decline an offer of government assistance. He did not see why taxpayers' money should aid lame ducks when better opportunities would present themselves in other industries. The Dunmurry operation had been running at a loss for two years, and it was not feasible to switch other Grundig products to the Belfast factory. The proposed new factory in Newry had not been built; Niedermayer's abduction was probably the principal reason for the change of mind at Grundig's head office in Nürnberg. Indeed Niedermayer had been responsible for most of the negotiations. Some five thousand Grundig employees were also made redundant in Germany.

More facts about Niedermayer's death came to light in February 1981 when, in a Belfast court, John Christopher Bradley, forty-two years old, pleaded guilty to his manslaughter. A charge of murder, which he also faced, was not proceeded with by the Director of Public Prosecutions because of inconclusive medical evidence. Prosecuting counsel told Lord Justice Jones that RUC detectives had questioned a woman, referred to as Witness A, who had told them that on 26 December 1973 she and her husband were told to move out of their house at Hillhead Crescent, Andersonstown. They left immediately and returned several days later. Soon afterwards her husband redecorated one of the bedrooms and bought a new bed and mattress. The judge asked whether Witness A had known about the hostage and was told by Crown counsel that she had not. Witness A had divorced her husband, and he was no longer resident in the United Kingdom.

Bradley, a former Provisional IRA member, had been arrested a short time after Witness A made her statement. He had joined the IRA in 1971 and had eventually become a training officer. He claimed to have left the Provisional IRA in 1978, no longer being able to justify its campaign. Niedermayer, he confirmed during an interview, had been intended as an exchange for the Price sisters. The statement he had given to RUC detectives was read out in court. He was one of the men assigned to guard Niedermayer. Their prisoner had become very restless on his third day of captivity. In the early evening there had been an altercation between Niedermayer and his guards. They had to sit on him to subdue him after he tried to run down the stairs of the house at Hillhead Crescent. 'We tried to calm him down but he would not stay quiet; he kept on yelling. Someone suggested we should gag him or try to knock him out. His nerves were going and he was raving. We tied his hands behind his back and tied his legs, but he was still trying to scream and struggle. We more or less tied him for his own safety. One of the other men hit him with the butt of an automatic pistol to knock him out, but he did not stop screaming. We held his face down on the mattress. I think I had his back and legs. We held him for I don't know how long. He was still struggling, but then he went limp and somebody said the man was dead.'

The statement tallies with a lot that was known from the forensic examination of the body, but there was one glaring difference: Niedermayer's skull had two fractures. The depth of his fear at the time is something that can never be known. At the mercy of callow young thugs, he may have thought that if he was a big enough nuisance to them they might tire of it and let him go. Or he may have believed that it was only a matter of time before he would be killed. A successful businessman, used to being in charge and having his orders carried out, had been stripped of all control. Perhaps he fought like a demon, believing, if nothing else, that he could at least die at a time of his own choosing.

Bradley went on to describe how he and two others had taken Niedermayer's body to Colin Glen and dug a shallow grave. They placed his body face down and said a short prayer over it, refilled the grave, and said another prayer. 'I felt drained after what I had been through. The whole episode was not very pleasant. We had no intention of harming him at any time. We had been told to get him everything he wanted and to be as helpful as possible.'

A second accused, Eugene McManus, fifty-one years old, of Rockville Street, Belfast, admitted to being the adjutant of the Belfast brigade of the Provisionals and having arranged for the bedroom of the Hillhead Crescent house to be cleaned and redecorated, at a cost of £200. In his statement to the RUC he said that he was at home on the night of 30 December 1973 when a man called and asked to speak to a friend who was in his house. The friend left soon afterwards, returning later to inform McManus that Niedermayer was dead. Though taking no part in the kidnap, McManus claimed to have been told what had happened. His story was different, in that allegedly Niedermayer had tried to attract the attention of an army patrol as he was being driven away from his home. One of the kidnappers had been forced to pistol-whip the hostage. When the kidnappers arrived at the house they discovered that Niedermayer was dead. This version of events appears to be the most suspect of the accounts, including the one published in an American newspaper. Why would the bedroom require professional cleaning—£200 was a great deal of money in 1973—if Niedermayer had not been alive and a prisoner there?

Elements of the truth are probably to be found in all three stories. Niedermayer may have been pistol-whipped in the back of the car and again some days later. Either way, his kidnap and death were an embarrassment to the Provisional IRA and a propaganda disaster, coming so soon after Sunningdale. It is hardly surprising that they failed to issue a statement of admission.

There was to be one final sad note to the Niedermayer story. In June 1990 Niedermayer's widow flew back to Ireland. She travelled south and booked into a hotel at the seaside town of Bray, Co. Wicklow, saying she intended to swim often in the sea. The summer weather had been excellent that year, with temperatures reaching record figures. On 15 June, a week after arriving, her fully clothed body was recovered from a beach at Greystones, five miles south of Bray. Family documents were found in her hotel room. In August the inquest's verdict concluded that she had drowned accidentally. She was buried next to her husband in the Derriaghy cemetery.

3

Dr Herrema and the Siege at Monasterevin

⟨≈⟩∘⟨≈⟩

E
ddie Gallagher's response was always going to be a dramatic one. His lover, Rose Dugdale, the mother of his son, was in jail. There was no way he was going to let her rot behind bars.

They had met in England in 1971. Despite—or perhaps because of—the huge differences in their social backgrounds, their relationship quickly developed into a passionate love affair. Dugdale was from an affluent Devon family and was a committed anarchist; the 32-year-old Gallagher was a poorly educated manual worker from Ballybofey, Co. Donegal.

Small in stature, Gallagher was intelligent and charismatic, a gifted strategist who had masterminded the mass republican break-out from the high-security Portlaoise Prison in 1974. Plastic explosives had blasted holes in the perimeter walls, resulting in the biggest jail escape in the history of the Republic. Nineteen republican prisoners got away, although many were subsequently recaptured. He was also thought to have had a hand in the daring helicopter escape of three Provisional IRA leaders from the recreation yard of Mountjoy Jail in Dublin ten months earlier. Gallagher carried a Dirty Harry-style long-barrel revolver, rather than an easier-to-conceal snub-nosed gun.

In January 1974, Dugdale and Gallagher launched a daring attack on an RUC station at Strabane, Co. Tyrone, using a startlingly original tactic. They commandeered a helicopter, loaded three milk-churn bombs on board, and forced the pilot to fly towards the station. The first bomb had to be jettisoned into the sea, but the others were dropped near their target. Both missed, one landing in a school playground, the other in the garden of a house. Neither exploded.

Gallagher got away after this piece of recklessness, but Dugdale was less fortunate. She was captured and charged with her part in this raid and also with her earlier involvement in the £8 million art robbery at Russborough House, near Blessington, Co. Wicklow, home of the millionaire collector Sir Alfred Beit. She got nine years. Her son Ruairí was born soon after the start of her prison term. Martin McGuinness, destined more than twenty-five years later to be the first Minister of Education in the Northern Ireland Assembly, stood as the child's godfather.

While Dugdale was on remand awaiting trial, Gallagher's active service unit embarked on a string of lucrative robberies. Between raids he hounded the IRA leadership with plans to free her. With Gallagher rising fast on the 'most wanted' charts, the Provisional IRA leaders were naturally reluctant to risk their most dynamic volunteer on such a foolhardy venture. Admiration was soon replaced with paranoia when it became evident that not all the money was finding its way back to the Provisional IRA Army Council. Having refused to sanction any of his schemes to release Dugdale, the Provisional IRA leadership grew fearful that a resentful Gallagher was planning to form a splinter group. Within months his assassination was ordered. This was a serious miscalculation. Fearing that the RUC and the Garda Síochána were closing in on them, several of Gallagher's friends fled to the United States, and it was for this contingency that Gallagher had held back money. Only one thing was certain: he was going nowhere without Dugdale. Now he needed to find a way to free his lover and placate the Army Council.

Marian Coyle, a deeply introverted woman, was selected as Gallagher's accomplice. Their plan was an audacious one: the kidnapping of Dr Tiede Herrema, a Dutch industrialist making headlines because of his handling of a strike at the Ferenka factory in Limerick. He would subsequently be exchanged for three prisoners held in Irish jails: Rose Dugdale, Kevin Mallon (one of the nineteen Portlaoise escapers), and James Hyland. The freeing of Mallon and

Hyland would, Gallagher was certain, indemnify him from Provisional IRA reprisals. None of his regular active service unit could be involved in case their loyalty to the Provo leadership conflicted with his ultimate goal.

'Staff Captain, Killed in Action', is how Joe Coyle, Marian Coyle's uncle and one of the founders of the Provisional IRA, was described on a republican memorial mural in Derry. A teenager at the time of his death—from burns received when an incendiary bomb detonated prematurely on 26 June 1970—both she and her brother Phillip drifted into militancy after the slaughter in that city on Bloody Sunday. Kevin Mallon and Marian Coyle met frequently and had formed an alliance based on mutual respect and a common ideology. Perhaps some sense of guilt over Mallon's recapture spurred Coyle to join Gallagher in the Herrema kidnap. It was she whom Special Branch detectives were tailing when she had unwittingly led them straight to Mallon. She was accused of attempting to wound the arresting gardaí—her gun jammed—a charge of which she was acquitted after uncertain identification by witnesses.

Gallagher's agile mind was capable of constructing and presenting false cover stories for extended periods. For upwards of a year he had maintained a focus on his objective while still planning and participating in bank raids, keeping one step ahead of both the police and the Provisional IRA command. His nerves were stretched taut, and he wasn't a man to suffer fools gladly. In the young Coyle he found a trusted co-conspirator, someone he could be at ease with, and they were constant companions for months before the kidnap, eventually sharing a flat in Monasterevin, a town on the road between Kildare and Portlaoise.

Brian McGowan joined their ranks in November 1974. From Tullamore, Co. Offaly, he was twenty years of age and a skilled mechanic. His first duties were to find Dr Herrema's home, discover the make and registration number of his car, and establish his morning routine. McGowan had little difficulty fulfilling these orders.

The task of finding safe houses was given to the final member of the gang, John Vincent Walsh. These were not intended as hide-outs where Gallagher would conceal his victim but as places where Dugdale, Mallon and Hyland could lie low after their release. Like his hero, the Carthaginian general Hannibal, Gallagher planned only for success.

Two vehicles would be required: one for the initial abduction and another for transport whenever there was a need to move. McGowan and Gallagher bought a Fiat 850 coupé for cash from a garage in Newbridge, Co. Kildare. The gang stole a mark 2 Cortina from outside a house in Crumlin, a Dublin suburb. McGowan resprayed the Ford and fitted false plates. He cut through a panel behind the rear seats, thus providing direct access to the boot.

Gallagher, Coyle and McGowan met on the evening of 24 September 1975 for a penultimate briefing. The route along which Dr Herrema drove his Mercedes to work each morning was discussed at length. The Monaleen road, on the outskirts of Limerick, was little used. The high banks on each side provided good cover, and the houses were well spaced out—ideal for the initial snatch. Each member of the gang knew exactly what to do. Failure wasn't an option. All were prepared to die, but they would not have expected the kidnap to pose any real problem. McGowan had established that Herrema did not have a bodyguard, even though it was barely two years since Niedermayer's abduction, and besides, that had been in the troubled North. It was what would come in the days afterwards that preyed most on their minds that night.

McGowan was given the Fiat to look after, and Gallagher and Coyle drove away in the stolen Ford. There was still one piece of the jigsaw to put in place. Gallagher asked McGowan to find a temporary staging post for Herrema—a house where they could hide out for a few days. It has been suggested that leaving such an important consideration to the last minute showed poor planning on Gallagher's part. However, the opposite could be said to be more valid: the fewer people and the least amount of time involved meant less chance of loose tongues. Either way, it was decided that Tom Dunne of Rosenallis, Co. Laois, a sympathiser who from time to time had provided shelter for Provisional IRA volunteers on the run, was

the man for the job. The stage was set and the characters assembled
for a drama that would have the whole world as its audience.

Gallagher's gang gathered in the isolated Cumber House, a farmhouse not far from Kinnitty at the western edge of the Slieve Bloom
Mountains, Co. Offaly. They rose early on the last day of September
and were soon on the road to Limerick. Despite McGowan's careful
reconnaissance, their first attempt to seize their target was frustrated.
No Mercedes saloon drove along the quiet Monaleen road that
bright autumn morning. They had no option but to return to
Cumber House. Further attempts on the next two mornings also
failed. On the fourth day, 3 October, Coyle took up a position further along the road, from where she could observe the Herrema
house. When she saw Dr Herrema's young son open the up-and-
over garage door, it was immediately evident what had gone wrong.
For some reason the target had swapped his usual Mercedes for
a Hillman estate. When Herrema drove away, Coyle urgently
signalled Gallagher to stop the Hillman.

Gallagher, half a mile away, dressed in a makeshift Garda uniform, took up his position in the middle of the road and flagged
down the estate car with its single occupant. 'What's your name?'
he asked as the driver rolled down the window. Dr Herrema identified himself. Gallagher instantly produced his long-barrel revolver
and ordered him from the car. Herrema was unceremoniously bundled into the Ford, driven by McGowan, with Walsh in the front
passenger seat. Gallagher had slipped a blindfold over the victim's
head as he manhandled him into the rear seat. They drove towards
Herrema's house to pick up Coyle and then joined the traffic on the
Dublin road at Annacotty. The Hillman was abandoned where it
had been stopped. Dr Herrema's attaché case still rested on the
handbrake.

From the warmth of the morning sun on his face through the car
window, Dr Herrema correctly calculated that the kidnappers' car
was heading north-east. Gallagher informed his victim that he was

to be exchanged for three prisoners. He asked Herrema for names of possible contacts in the German Embassy. This blatant error by Gallagher may be put down to nerves or, more likely, an attempt to confuse Dr Herrema with misinformation. Herrema corrected Gallagher and provided him with some contact names at the Dutch Embassy in Merrion Road, Dublin.

Relief at the news that he wasn't to be murdered out of hand soon shifted to despair when Herrema's thoughts turned to his wife, Elizabeth. They had moved to Ireland from Arnhem two years previously when he was appointed managing director of the Ferenka steel-cable plant. Two of their children were studying at Dutch universities, while the younger two attended school in Limerick. He was a fit 54-year old and knew that life had prepared him better than most for the ordeal he had ahead. During the Second World War he had been interned for a time by the Germans and had witnessed appalling atrocities. He also held a master's degree in arts and philosophy and had been told that his 1,200 work force admired his no-nonsense approach and his keen sense of humour. But Elizabeth, then on a trip to the Netherlands, would have the tougher time. She would have to endure the loss of influence in important decisions. When a hostage is to be used as a pawn in negotiations with a government, the victim's family is often left out in the cold. Staff at the plant and the embassy would rally round her, and the Government would treat her with great delicacy and diplomacy. However, the cruel truth was that she could do little to speed his release. All anyone could do was pray that the ordeal would be a short one.

The kidnappers stopped briefly at Cumber House so that McGowan could pick up the Fiat, and Herrema's hands and feet were bound. Coyle took over the driving and they made for a cottage at Cloncannon, the home of Tom Dunne's uncle, David Dunne. Here Herrema was laid on a flea-infested single bed in a spare room.

Coyle then drove Walsh home to Tullamore, before travelling on to Dublin to leave the Ford at Parkgate Street, not far from

Garda headquarters in the Phoenix Park. Once again Gallagher was
intent on spreading misinformation, while at the same time raising
two fingers to the Gardaí.

While in Dublin, Coyle made four telephone calls. The first two
were to Mr Kwint, the first secretary at the Dutch Embassy; the
third was to the offices of the *Evening Press*. 'We demand the release
of three political prisoners: Dr Rose Dugdale, Mr Kevin Mallon
and Mr James Hyland, and if they are not released in 48 hours
Dr Herrema will be executed.' Demands that the Ferenka plant be
shut down for twenty-four hours and that the Gardaí should desist
from mounting roadblocks and searches were also tagged on. The
final call was made to the Gardaí in Limerick, repeating the
demands. Coyle made no reference to who had taken Dr Herrema
and ensured that the calls were kept short. She left the telephone
box at noon. The first act ended less than four hours after Herrema
had been taken by force.

Dr Herrema's abandoned Hillman, the key still in the ignition, was
discovered by his son and a Ferenka employee. Shortly after that
the Gardaí at William Street, Limerick, were informed. Chief
Superintendent Tom Kenny alerted headquarters and then all
stations throughout Ireland. Roadblocks were set up and an all-
ports warning issued. Reports of a Cortina car being spotted in the
area soon came to light, one witness reporting a garda in the rear
seat. Crime scene specialists from the Garda Technical Bureau were
sent for and a major incident investigation was initiated.

The first official Government reaction was a short statement
issued in the early part of the afternoon. The Minister for Justice,
Patrick Cooney, rejected the demands, adding, 'What the kidnappers
are asking is that we open the gates and let subversive criminals
loose in society with impunity.' Liam Gosgrave's Government made
it clear from the beginning that there would be no capitulation
to the kidnappers, a stance that was echoed by the leader of the
opposition, Jack Lynch.

Elizabeth Herrema, at a press conference on the morning of 4 October, agreed that the Government was taking the correct attitude. A spokesman for Ferenka announced that the plant would be closing for twenty-four hours. Gallagher made this apparently illogical demand to lay another false trail for the Gardaí. Production being halted for a day was hardly going to have any lasting consequence on the economy, but if the kidnappers were employees, what better way to camouflage their absence?

The next communication from the kidnappers was on the third day. A postal delivery to the Dutch Embassy brought a poorly recorded cassette tape. Dr Herrema, apparently reading from a prepared script, stated:

Mr Ferarkis, this is Herrema. This well-organised group is going to jeopardise the position of Ferenka in Limerick for ever, and you know how important Ferenka is to the development of Limerick and Ireland.

Please put pressure on the government—the Dutch and Irish governments—to let me get free and let the Irish Government answer the demands of this group, who are very serious. Seeing the situation I am in, my condition is reasonable.

Love to my wife and children through Ferenka. Workers of Ferenka, keep the factory closed till I'm free or till you hear of me. Don't put pressure on the government to save Ferenka.

There had been numerous other contacts, but this was unquestionably genuine. From the start, the Garda investigation was to be hampered by nuisance claims, false sightings, rumours and counter-rumours, and even one elaborate fake ransom demand relayed to them by a priest. Despite this, it was not long before the Gardaí, having questioned associates of Dugdale, Mallon, and Hyland, announced that their prime suspects were Eddie Gallagher and Marian Coyle.

Elizabeth Herrema returned from the Netherlands and made a television appeal for her husband's release. 'My husband is a good and kind man, devoted to his family and his work—work which is important to Ireland and particularly to Limerick. It is difficult to believe that this terrible thing has happened to us in a country which we love so dearly and have been so happy to live in.'

In Limerick, thousands marched through the city in protest and were addressed by the mayor, Thady Coughlan. A few days later Coughlan announced his intention to seek an audience with the Pope to ask him to appeal personally to the kidnappers to spare Dr Herrema's life.

Six days after the kidnap, a Father O'Reilly of Tullamore answered his phone at three o'clock in the morning and was told that a tape had been left in his letter box, which he was to deliver to Dublin to Dónal Mahony, a Capuchin priest. Father Mahony, national chaplain of the international peace organisation Pax Christi, had earlier volunteered and had been approved by the Gardaí as official mediator.

This message was again read by Dr Herrema. It contained a demand for the Ferenka factory to be shut down and a plea for Mahony to ask the International Red Cross to intercede with the Government. The message was to be broadcast on radio that night between 8 p.m. and midnight. Father Mahony found himself in the unenviable position of the kidnappers' publicist, and now it was his turn to be flooded with hoax calls.

A second volunteer mediator stepped forward, Philip Flynn, a trade union official and deputy general secretary of the Local Government and Public Service Union. He was a former member of Sinn Féin. Unknown to Flynn, Gallagher was already considering him as a mediator, having thus far been unimpressed by Father Mahony's efforts on their behalf.

Gallagher's first mistake arose indirectly from his efforts to provide better conditions for his hostage. Dr Herrema, although receiving adequate food and treatment, consistently complained about conditions at the cottage: he had been badly bitten by fleas;

the bindings on his hands and ankles were chafing his skin; and the toilet facilities were very basic. These complaints, combined with a natural prudence, prompted Gallagher to ask Tom Dunne to find a new safe house for them.

On the second Saturday of his captivity Dr Herrema was transported to a thatched cottage at Kildangan, Co. Offaly, the home of Bridie Bailey's parents. Their stay was very brief, Marian Coyle being disconcerted at the lack of a bathroom. Mrs Bailey and her husband, P. J., then suggested the home of her sister-in-law Catherine Hall at 1410 St Evin's Park, Monasterevin.

Michael and Catherine Hall were spun a story about a priest and a young woman who needed to be put up for a night. Once they saw the trio—Gallagher being dressed as a priest—arrive at their house in the early hours, they wanted nothing further to do with it but were threatened at gunpoint by both kidnappers. Catherine Hall consulted her sister-in-law and was advised to do exactly what Gallagher asked. It would only be for a day or two, she told her, adding that he was a dangerous man.

The following night Gallagher dispatched P. J. Bailey and his wife to Dublin. Their first task was to confirm Flynn's role as mediator. P. J. made the phone call, and Flynn, who recognised the voice of an old acquaintance, agreed. Bailey and his wife then dropped the tape through the letterbox of a Monkstown priest before phoning Philip Flynn a second time to let him know the tape's whereabouts and his instructions. Bridie Bailey made this call and, in a state of high agitation, failed to give the exact location of the tape. Flynn had to try the homes of several priests until he retrieved it.

Gallagher raised the stakes in this tape, threatening the amputation of Dr Herrema's foot if there was any further prevarication by the Government demanding proof of life. Flynn easily slipped into his role as mediator-cum-propagandist and at a press conference criticised both the Government's and the Garda Síochána's response. Off camera, he insisted that this was the way to play it if he was to gain Gallagher's full confidence. Commissioner Edmund

Garvey insisted that any information that could save lives would be passed along.

Five days passed before the next tape was delivered, this time to the home in Santry, Dublin, of a retired garda. That same Friday, Philip Flynn covertly received a transcript of this tape and a ransom demand for £2 million. He was asked by Gallagher to give the ransom demand as much publicity as was feasible. In consultation with AKZO (Ferenka's parent company), Flynn decided not to consent to this. An alternative plan was hastily drawn up in secret. Gallagher, Coyle and the ransom would be clandestinely flown out of the country in return for Dr Herrema's freedom. This proposal was relayed to P. J. Bailey, along with a strong recommendation that it be accepted.

Gallagher wasn't happy with some of the plan's details, and Flynn, disguised as a priest, shuttled back and forth to Monasterevin that weekend for meetings with Bailey, who would listen to the latest suggestion before taking his leave, returning after a short time with Gallagher's answer. Although Bailey could have been departing to make discreet phone calls to Gallagher, Flynn felt sure the kidnappers were nearby. He pushed for a face-to-face meeting with Gallagher, but was turned down. Dejected, he returned to Dublin. Then, late on the Sunday night, he received a message proposing a get-together with Gallagher the following night. It was a meeting destined never to take place.

Meticulous if repetitive work by detectives, combined with a stroke of sheer good luck, produced the decisive breakthrough in the case. Routine questioning of known associates of Gallagher had picked up a flaw in Brian McGowan's alibi. The inconsistency sparked enough interest for him to be questioned by Special Branch detectives on 20 October. When the Ford used in the kidnap was found in Tullamore, McGowan, in a written statement, admitted his part in the kidnap and mentioned the Baileys' parents' house at Kildangan, though maintaining that he had no knowledge of where the hostage was then being held. Bailey was arrested at his home in Canal Harbour, Monasterevin, and coincidentally the Halls were there. No-one was allowed to leave.

Meanwhile, Philip Flynn had arrived in Monasterevin and waited several hours for P. J. Bailey to arrive and bring him to Gallagher. When he didn't show up, Flynn drove back to Dublin.

The Baileys, the Halls and McGowan were transported to Naas Garda Station for further questioning. At 5:30 a.m. on 21 October, Bridie Bailey admitted that the kidnappers and their hostage were at 1410 St Evin's Park. A conference was hastily held, and it was decided not to wait for reinforcements: the failure of the Halls to return home would have alerted the kidnappers that all was not well. Detective-Sergeant Patrick Sheil of the Special Branch was given the front door key, a flak jacket, and the dubious honour of being the first man in.

Seven armed detectives raided the St Evin's Park house shortly after first light. Four kicked in the bolted front door, while three took the kitchen door at the rear. Ten snipers trained their sights on the windows and doors. The ground floor was empty.

'Gallagher, this is the Gardaí,' announced Detective-Superintendent O'Dea through a loudhailer from across the street. 'The house is surrounded by army and gardaí. Come out with your hands up!'

The reply was immediate. Gallagher blasted off all six rounds from his revolver, screaming obscenities down the stairs and threatening to kill Dr Herrema. As the echo of the shots faded, Gallagher smashed a bedroom window. 'Please stay away,' pleaded Dr Herrema from behind the broken pane. 'I'm wired up with explosives.'

The limited intelligence the gardaí had garnered of the kidnappers' armaments left them with only one option. A stalemate was not the ideal conclusion to the raid, but it was not all bad news. Nobody had been hurt, and the kidnappers were now bottled up in a small room with no water, no food, and no heat. They would be dependent on the gardaí for their most basic needs. The balance of control had swung away from the kidnappers.

The most immediate tasks for the gardaí were to secure the ground floor and to open negotiations with Gallagher. Electricity was cut off to the upstairs rooms, sensitive microphones were sent for, and sheets of bullet-proof glass were fixed to the ceiling and stairway to protect those below. A fibre-optic cable relayed images of the landing and the door of the box room, which had been barricaded from the inside. To amuse himself, Gallagher would occasionally lob items—a chess piece or an empty lemonade bottle—through a louvred window above the door, the racket as they clattered down the stairs provoking pandemonium below.

The man chosen as negotiator was Chief Superintendent Larry Wren, head of C3, the national security division. To assist him in his task he could call on advice from three psychologists. An operations room set up in the vacated house next door was filled with monitors, recording devices, and communication equipment. Wren had the gardaí and soldiers surrounding the house withdraw from sight, to add to the kidnappers' sense of isolation. Food was supplied, but never enough to satisfy their hunger. The menu was always the same: ham or tomato sandwiches, with milk served as cold as possible. A rope made from strips of nylon bedding was used to haul a basket up to the front window. At night, searchlights were directed at the house to disrupt the kidnappers' sleep, a strategy enhanced by the noisy generators used to power them.

A routine developed within days. Each morning Dr Herrema, briefed by Gallagher, would speak to the gardaí. The demand for the release of Dugdale, Mallon and Hyland was soon replaced by requests for concessions that would enable the kidnappers to avoid capture. Larry Wren would listen but delayed answering until he had consulted a higher authority. The delay was simply a way to buy time. The longer the siege went on, the less chance there would be that Dr Herrema would be killed. The kidnappers had been living day and night with their hostage for three weeks. He was no longer a faceless foreign businessman: he was a real person, one who ate and drank, slept and dreamed, made jokes and told stories just like them—a familiarity that would make it much more difficult for his captors to put a gun to his head and squeeze the trigger.

When he became exasperated with Wren's stalling or suspicious of covert signalling to Herrema, Gallagher would take over at the broken window, but time and again his participation would deteriorate into abusive ranting. On these occasions Wren would withdraw, affording Gallagher a chance to simmer down. Gallagher's suspicions of covert signalling were well founded. Envelopes with simple questions written on them were being held up by gardaí crouching at the base of the front wall, and Herrema, with an almost imperceptible nod or shake of his head, was able to provide Wren with much valuable information.

A small army of reporters had descended on Monasterevin, all desperate to get as close to the house as possible for the scoop of a lifetime. Gardaí joked afterwards that some enterprising reporters had caused them more problems than the kidnappers.

As the days passed, conditions inside the claustrophobic confines of the box room became atrocious. The sole toilet was a chamber pot, which Dr Herrema had to empty out of the window each morning. The weather was growing colder with each passing day. Coyle endured menstruation without basic sanitary requirements. To accentuate the miserable conditions in the house, Garda and army personnel would gather round roaring bonfires drinking steaming mugs of tea.

One of Wren's chief concerns was that the monotonous routine would cause a lapse in concentration that could cost a life. Danger was never far away. When the gardaí tried to remove roof tiles to facilitate a search of the attic, Gallagher fired a shot through the ceiling. The removal of glass from a rear bathroom window, allegedly to further lower the temperature inside, almost cost a Special Branch sergeant his life when Gallagher fired at him. Fortuitously, the bullet struck Sergeant Egan's index finger as he peered through the opaque glass at the moment the shot was fired, and not his forehead. A finger was a small forfeit in exchange for his life.

Two fraternal appeals were made for the kidnappers to end the stalemate. Patrick Gallagher made one, and, though never officially confirmed, Philip Coyle, brought from a Northern Ireland prison, made the other. A persistent rumour that the IRA would make a kidnap attempt on Elizabeth Herrema reached those in authority. This seemed so preposterous that it was dismissed, but Mrs Herrema was advised to leave Ireland for her own safety, and she flew to the Netherlands.

The end came on the eighteenth day of the siege, thirty-six days after Dr Herrema's kidnap, a resolution so abrupt that many of the reporters missed it: they were attending an impromptu birthday party for one of their colleagues. Late that evening Marian Coyle made a request for medication for Dr Herrema. This was refused, but she was told that Herrema and the kidnappers would receive medical attention immediately on their surrender. The microphones, on loan from the London Metropolitan Police, had given the Special Branch detectives an edge, in that they knew it was Gallagher who was in pain, and not the hostage. For days the operators had been listening to the constant chattering and shivering inside the freezing bedroom. The gardaí expected Gallagher to surrender first. He was always the more active of the two; Coyle's silence made it unlikely that she would be the one to take the initiative. The cramp in Gallagher's neck soon left after his surrender, leading medical experts to conclude that it was psychosomatic. Subconsciously, Gallagher wanted to surrender, and his body provided the excuse.

Just over an hour later, Coyle announced that they were coming down. After their weapons had been thrown out onto the concrete path below the front window, Coyle, then Dr Herrema and finally Gallagher, descended the stairs. Ever the showman, Gallagher had presented his victim with a bullet from his gun as a souvenir. Dr Herrema was pale, missing a tooth and had shed a few pounds but was composed and in remarkably good health after such a lengthy ordeal.

He spoke briefly to the press at the Dutch ambassador's residence in Dublin shortly after 5:30 a.m. Elizabeth Herrema had arrived at 4:30 to meet her husband. He described to the reporters conditions inside the bedroom—how he had to lie on bare boards, with only a thin blanket for warmth. Gallagher's bouts of aggression were directed mainly at those outside. After the first forty-eight hours Herrema no longer feared for his life. When asked about escape, he said, 'I thought along those lines, but there had been no possibility of this. My captors held my feet, and the window was too small.'

Elizabeth Herrema said her husband had taken strength from his ability to listen and from his patience. She did not know if she would stay in Ireland. There would have to be a discussion with her family. The interview ended after twenty minutes.

The Taoiseach sent telegrams of congratulations to Dr Herrema, the Garda Commissioner, and the army chief of staff, Major-General O'Carroll. Accolades for the handling of the siege flooded in. The *Sunday Times* and *Sunday Telegraph* both congratulated the Government. The Dutch Minister for Foreign Affairs, Mr Max van de Stoel, telegraphed the Minister for Foreign Affairs, Dr Garret FitzGerald: 'On behalf of the Netherlands Government I should like to express our very sincere gratitude for the skilful and persistent manner in which your Government has handled the awful abduction case of Dr Herrema. In particular, my Government highly values the attitude of the Irish authorities to give absolute priority to the well-being of Dr Herrema in every action which has been undertaken.' The American ambassador, Walter Curley, said, 'On behalf of my government I would like to convey to the Government of Ireland pleasure and satisfaction at the outcome of the Herrema kidnapping case.' Prayers in thanksgiving were offered during a Remembrance Day service in Armagh by Dr Otto Simms. The Chief Rabbi, Dr Isaac Cohen, sent a message of congratulations to Dr Herrema.

Before leaving Ireland for the Netherlands on the Saturday evening, Dr Herrema gave a second press conference at Dublin Airport. He was applauded at length by the press. Asked about his personal reactions to Gallagher and Coyle, he said that these young people had created a lot of problems for themselves, which was a pity. It was unfortunate that Eddie Gallagher would have to go to prison for a long time. 'If they were my own children,' he concluded, 'I would do the utmost to help them.'

The trial of the four main participants in the Special Criminal Court began on 12 February 1976 and lasted for twelve days. Gallagher and Coyle chose to stand down their legal team and represented themselves during the trial, with Gallagher handling the lion's share of the duties. His manner impressed many observers. There was no malice or intimidation in his cross-examination of Dr Herrema, and he even at one point shared a joke with his former hostage.

The three judges took an hour to decide their verdicts. The president of the court, Mr Justice Pringle, read out the verdicts. Gallagher was convicted on seven counts, Coyle on six. They received twenty and fifteen years' imprisonment, respectively. Walsh and McGowan were found guilty on two counts, and both received a sentence of eight years. The crowded public gallery had to be cleared when cheering and applause broke out. Gallagher and Coyle made death threats to Mr Justice Pringle.

Thirteen months later Michael Hall and P. J. Bailey both pleaded guilty and received five-year sentences. David Dunne was found guilty after a trial that lasted three-and-a-half days and received a seven-year sentence. The state entered a *nolle prosequi* on all counts against Brigid Bailey and Catherine Hall.

Marian Coyle would serve nine years before being released from Limerick Prison on 27 September 1985. Eddie Gallagher would serve fourteen years, and with Dr Herrema supporting calls for his release, he finally walked free from Portlaoise Prison on 28 March 1990.

But the story could have been much different. David Dunne, the resident of the cottage at Cloncannon, deeply troubled by the plight of the blindfolded victim and sceptical of Gallagher's assurance that no harm would come to him, reported the matter to a local priest. The priest advised Dunne to report the matter to the Gardaí. Neither he nor the priest did so.

4

Father Hugh Murphy and Killers in the Ranks

The kidnapping of Father Hugh Murphy, though short-lived, would help bring to justice two killers within the ranks of the RUC. The unmasking of Constable William McGaughey and Sergeant John Weir resulted from an all-too-familiar tit-for-tat act of revenge perpetrated by McGaughey, in response to the kidnapping of an RUC colleague.

A Provisional IRA attack on an unmarked RUC patrol car at Sturgan's Brae near Camlough Lake, south Armagh, on 17 June 1978, left one man, Constable Hugh McConnell, thirty-two years old, dead, and another, Constable William Turbitt, forth-six years old, seriously wounded. The two-man patrol had unwittingly driven into a Provisional IRA ambush on a quiet Saturday afternoon. The three gunmen had opened fire on them at near point-blank range, firing seventy-four high-velocity Armalite rounds. Constable McConnell had been riddled with bullets. Severely wounded, he was killed at close range.

There were a lot of people in the area at the time. The sun was shining, and the leisure facilities at the lake were being put to good use by swimmers, picnickers, and speedboats towing water-skiers. An angler enjoying a day's fishing on the shore of the lake heard the shooting. He threw down his rod and ran towards the fading echoes of gunfire. He found the body of McConnell, the father of two children, sprawled on the roadway next to his unmarked police car. It was clear from the blood pools and the top plate from a set of dentures lying on the passenger side of the vehicle that someone else had been hit in the hail of gunfire. Unusually for the

Provisional IRA, they had taken the wounded policeman prisoner. The steel heel-protectors on his boots had left clear parallel marks on the asphalt, showing that he had been dragged to another vehicle.

Bessbrook RUC Station, the dead man's base, received a 999 call about a car crash thirty minutes after the two men had left to start their patrol. The communications room at the station tried to raise them by radio. Ominously, there was no response. A number of RUC vehicles, backed up by a British Army detachment, were despatched to the lake, four miles from Bessbrook. They quickly found their dead colleague next to his bullet-riddled Austin Maxi. A scene-of-crime officer was able to establish that McConnell had been wounded, pulled from the car, and then dragged to the middle of the road, where he was finished off. Most of his face had been destroyed, and his colleagues identified him from the non-regulation slip-on boots that he habitually wore. A search revealed no trace of Constable Turbitt, but a 100-yard trail of blood splatters suggested that he was still alive when taken away. It was thought that in their rush to leave the scene the kidnappers might have had Turbitt hanging half out of the vehicle's door.

A quick reconnaissance of the roadside revealed the site where the ambushers had snacked on sandwiches and bottles of lemonade as they waited for their quarry. Constable McConnell's Walther pistol had been removed from its holster and taken, along with the M1 carbine carried in RUC cars. A murder inquiry was begun and a manhunt launched on both sides of the border for the missing constable. Regional Crime Squad detectives were drafted into Bessbrook to assist the local CID, and an initial sweep of republican suspects led to twenty arrests. The Chief Constable of the RUC, Sir Kenneth Newman, landed by helicopter at Bessbrook Station for a first-hand appraisal of the investigation.

Constable McConnell had been a keen footballer and had played for Newry Town football team. He was a member of the current RUC soccer squad. He had been in the RUC for four years and was the eighty-first full-time member to be killed in Northern Ireland since 1969. A local man, he lived at Derramore Crescent,

Bessbrook, with his wife and two children, nine and six years old. William Turbitt was married and had four children. Originally from Co. Monaghan, he now lived in Castleview Park in the County Armagh village of Richill with his wife, Margaret, and four children, Godfrey, aged fourteen, Rodney, twelve, Graham, ten, and Adrian, seven.

Their unmarked car had only recently been designated for the Bessbrook station, and the detectives were surprised that the Provisional IRA already had intelligence on the vehicle's identity. The RUC issued an appeal for the driver of a Morris Minor that witness reports said had been directly behind the police vehicle when it was ambushed.

The South Armagh Provisional IRA telephoned RTE to claim responsibility for the attack, saying that the police constables had been shot when they had failed to stop at a Provisional IRA checkpoint. Valuable documents and weapons had been taken from the cars, and Constable Turbitt was being interrogated. The car the gunmen had used to take Turbitt away was quickly found. There were tufts of grey hair and human tissue in the back.

Constable William McGaughey, twenty-nine years old, stationed in south Armagh, was incensed when he heard about the murder and kidnap of his fellow-constables. Something had to be done, and he felt he was the man to do it. He found a willing accomplice in Sergeant Gary Armstrong, twenty-five years old, a native of Co. Armagh who lived at Rosemount Park, Armagh. McConnell and Turbitt had been close friends of Armstrong, and he had taken their attack very badly. Like McGaughey, he was a member of the RUC Special Patrol Group. This was a front-line unit in the battle against terrorism. It was usually the first to be called on when trouble broke out, and its duties included the patrol of areas where normal RUC policing had been withdrawn. A high number of SPG officers had been killed or maimed in the execution of their duty, yet their perception was of a unit heavily criticised from all sides over some of their more controversial tactics. Daily confrontation with danger meant living on the edge for SPG members, and morale was low. The incidence of stress-related mental breakdowns and suicides was higher in their ranks than in regular RUC units. Divorce was common: few women knew how to deal with the pressure their spouses lived under.

McGaughey and Armstrong's plan was a simple one: they would fight fire with fire. A Catholic priest would be kidnapped, and it would be made public that if anything unfortunate were to happen to Constable Turbitt, the priest would be killed. Father Hugh Murphy was the target selected to be the bargaining tool. He seemed an unlikely candidate to any casual observer. A 59-year-old priest from St Mary's in the village of Ahoghill, Co. Antrim, he had been a Royal Navy chaplain during the Second World War and was chaplain of the Royal British Legion and holder of an OBE, conferred on him at Buckingham Palace in 1974. He was also the religious adviser to the Independent Broadcasting Authority and had acted as commentator on religious ceremonies for UTV.

McGaughey was born and raised in the countryside outside Ahoghill and must have been aware of the esteem in which Father Murphy was held by both sides of the community. However, the priest had been the centre of controversy on 13 November the previous year, when DUP councillors and Free Presbyterian Church leaders refused to take part in a Remembrance Day service at Ballymena because of Father Murphy's involvement. The service, organised by Ballymena District Council and the British Legion, went ahead as planned, though it was boycotted by the DUP, which held an unofficial service conducted by the then DUP mayor of the town.

Shortly after 7 a.m. on 18 June 1978 the priest heard a knock on the front door of the parochial house. There was nothing unusual in that: parishioners could call at any time in an emergency. There had been no sound of a car on the gravel outside, so perhaps his caller had left his vehicle at the end of the narrow lane that led to the parochial house. He slipped on his red dressing-gown over his pyjamas and went to open the front door. The man standing outside began to explain that there was a child who was seriously ill, but then brandished a gun. Another man, wearing a balaclava and holding a pistol, showed himself from behind a gable corner. The two gunmen grabbed the elderly priest by the arms. His glasses were knocked off as he struggled to free himself. Since an operation on a small tumour some years before, he had lost the sight in one eye and his eyesight was poor.

'Not this Sunday, no, no,' Father Murphy pleaded. That day was the thirty-fourth anniversary of his ordination to the priesthood, and he had planned to make reference to it during Mass at nearby Cullybackey, a church in his one-man parish. He believed the men were members of the Provisional IRA but had no idea why they were taking him. As they gagged him, his thoughts concerned the safety of his elderly mother, Sarah Murphy, ninety years old, and his niece, Mona Kennedy, who also lived in the house. His arms were pulled behind his back, his wrists were bound, and he was blindfolded.

He was frogmarched down the lane and bundled into the back of a car. The men told him they were the Provos and that if he went with them he would be helping to save someone's life. They made no threats against his life. They were not rough with him, but they were very determined. He was driven a short distance, less than a mile, before being taken from the car and led into a shed. After twenty minutes the priest was moved into what he assumed was a disused byre or stable. He could smell the dried manure and the mustiness of stale straw bedding. His guess was proved correct when he was tied to a steel ring set into the wall, such as a farmer would use to shackle cattle. A dusty coal-bag was placed over his head.

Sarah Murphy did not realise her son was missing for forty minutes. She had heard the knock on the door and thought someone required the services of a priest. It was when she entered her son's bedroom and discovered his dressing-gown and pyjamas missing that she knew something odd had befallen him. She contacted the RUC, and they despatched a patrol car to the parochial house. Father Murphy's glasses were found lying on the gravel. His mother's concern for her son's safety was heightened because of his heart condition, the result of a coronary attack twelve years previously.

A mammoth security operation was put in motion. Helicopters were brought in to search the farmland around Ahoghill. Vehicle checkpoints manned by UDR and RUC personnel were set up on all major roads. Teams of RUC personnel were given the task of searching farms and derelict buildings.

The first confirmation of the motive behind Father Murphy's abduction came when a man claiming to represent the outlawed Ulster Freedom Fighters, a cover name used by the Ulster Defence Association since 1973, telephoned Downtown Radio in Newtownards and read out a statement. A demand was issued to the South Armagh Provisional IRA to release the wounded policeman immediately. He said that Father Hugh Murphy had been kidnapped and would be returned in the same condition as Constable Turbitt. If the Provisional IRA killed the policeman, then Father Murphy would be killed too. The caller also contacted several prosperous Catholic businessmen in the south Armagh area, informing them that they should intervene with the Provisionals to plead for Turbitt's life. If they did not do so, selected targets would be assassinated over the next few days.

Condemnation of the priest's kidnap was swift and came from all quarters. Rev. Ian Paisley, whose political organisation, the DUP, had boycotted the Ballymena Remembrance Day service eight months before, appealed in 'the strongest possible manner to those responsible for the kidnapping of the Rev. Mr Murphy, parish priest of Ahoghill. It certainly does not become the Protestant cause or anybody claiming to be Protestant to act in the same way as the IRA has acted and I would appeal to those responsible to return this gentleman to his home in peace and quietness and in safety.' No good could be served by the kidnapping, torture or killing of any person, Paisley said.

The Archbishop of Armagh, Dr Tomás Ó Fiaich, speaking during a Mass in Keady, Co. Armagh, called for the safe return of Father Murphy and Constable Turbitt. He urged 'the men of terror to think again.' Appeals continued to be made for most of that day. The Bishop of Connor, Dr Butler, the Moderator of the Presbyterian Church, Rev. David Burke of the Methodist Church, the Unionist Party, the Orange Order and the Ulster Special Constabulary all added their voices to appeals for the release of the two men. Amnesty International said that the kidnaps and the threat of violence violated the most basic human rights.

In the afternoon a new caller rang the radio station and, after quoting a recognised code-word, said that the UFF denied involvement in the abduction, adding that it was thought to be the work of the Provisional IRA. He ended with a promise that appropriate action would be taken when they found out who had been responsible for this action.

Inside the disused byre, Father Murphy was being treated gently by his kidnappers. They kept him supplied with cups of tea and buttered scones, and one of the men talked to him about the appeals being made for his release. He told the priest that he would learn their identity from the media.

Perhaps the appeal that struck McGaughey and Armstrong most was the one from the wife of the missing Constable Turbitt. She called for no revenge to be taken in her husband's name, saying that no right would be served by another wrong.

An offer to mediate with Father Murphy's kidnappers was made by a Methodist minister, Rev. Sydney Callaghan, a friend of the priest and a founder-director of the Samaritans in the North. Together they had helped set up a Ballymena branch, and Callaghan promised that, in line with the Samaritans' policy, any information given to him in the process of mediation would not be passed on to the security forces without the consent of those involved.

Father Murphy discovered that his abductors were loyalists only when he heard it on the radio the men were listening to as they stood watch over him. The men confirmed that they were not members of the IRA. They told him he was being held as a bargaining counter for Turbitt, though they admitted that it was likely that the constable was already dead. The admission made the priest's blood run cold. For the first time he felt in genuine fear of his life, and said more prayers that Sunday than any other. Several times during his captivity he heard British Army helicopters flying at low level. On one occasion he heard a car stop nearby and could hear a muted conversation taking place. A police search team had intended to visit the farm but were assured by McGaughey's elderly father that none of his buildings were being used for illegal purposes.

At some time in the early evening (the priest had no way of knowing the time) the men led him to a car, and he was driven a short distance. The car stopped and he was lifted out of the rear seat. The priest began to pray, believing that his time had come. The ropes binding his wrists were loosened, but his captors drove off before he managed to extricate his hands and remove the hood from his head. Even if he had seen the men it was doubtful if, with his limited vision, he could ever have identified them.

Father Murphy was unfamiliar with the stretch of road on which he had been left abandoned. It was the aptly named Priestown Road, just outside the Co. Antrim village of Portglenone. He walked to the nearest house and was astonished when one of his parishioners opened the front door. He quickly explained that he had been released, and used their phone to contact the RUC. His parishioner had at first failed to recognise him because of his coal-blackened face. It had just gone 7 p.m.; he had been a hostage for twelve hours. He told the police where he was, and they said they would despatch a patrol car to pick him up. When they enquired whether he needed medical treatment, he told them it wasn't necessary and asked if they had found his glasses. If he was up to it and a doctor approved, he was advised, detectives at Ballymena RUC Station would interview him. He said he was in good heath but did not think he would have much useful information to give the detectives. He was wrong.

The Northern Ireland Secretary of State, Roy Mason, was one of the first to express relief at Murphy's release. He promised that no effort would be spared in the hunt for the wounded RUC constable.

The priest was examined at Ballymena RUC Station by Dr Hugo Simpson and pronounced to be in good health. The detectives spoke to him for an hour before he was reunited, still in his dressing-gown, with his mother and his niece. A photograph was taken by a *News Letter* photographer, which appeared on the front page the next day.

Unfortunately, there was to be no happy ending for Constable Turbitt. The following morning the South Armagh Provisional IRA issued a statement claiming that they had executed the RUC constable. The statement read: 'The south Armagh Provisionals wish to state that Constable Turbitt has been executed because of his involvement in the British war machine. In executing Constable Turbitt the IRA wishes to reaffirm its determination to force a British withdrawal by maintaining war operations on all fronts, military and economic. The RUC is a totally unacceptable police force and in recent times dastardly outrageous perpetrations have been carried out against the community, which have been high-lighted throughout the world by international jurists and Amnesty International.' The Provisional IRA made no mention of where his body could be found, and three weeks elapsed before it was dis-covered in a derelict Cullyhanna farm building. Forensic tests revealed that Constable Turbitt had probably died soon after he was taken captive and that his body had been immersed in a bog or marsh for several days before being moved to the farm building. However, the tests failed to show whether the fatal injury had been inflicted during the ambush or later.

Condemnations of the cold-blooded killing were quick in coming, and widespread. Dr Ó Fiaich said, 'This latest killing is a terrible blow to all those working for reconciliation.' The Church of Ireland Archbishop of Armagh, Dr Simms, said the news of Constable Turbitt's death underlined the risks constantly being faced by mem-bers of the security forces on behalf of the public. Gerry Fitt, leader of the SDLP, said that the abductors of Father Murphy had heeded the appeals by loyalist leaders, in particular Rev. Ian Paisley, but the Provisional IRA would listen to no-one, not even the appeal by Archbishop Ó Fiaich.

The Provisional IRA's allegation of the RUC's involvement in outrageous acts was soon to be proved correct. One phrase of Father Murphy's statement to the RUC detectives had set bells ringing. The man who had knocked on Father Murphy's door on that Sunday morning had made mention of a sick child. A year before, on 19 April 1977, William Strathearn, thirty-nine years old, a shopkeeper in Ahoghill, had leaned out of his bedroom window at 2 a.m. after a man had called out that he needed paracetamol for a sick child. He told the man to hang on and he would be right down. When Strathearn opened the door clutching the tablets, the man on his doorstep fired twice at point-blank range, killing him. Strathearn was a Catholic, and he, his wife and their seven children lived above his general store. He had been an active member of the village community and was well known in the area for his former prowess in Gaelic sports. He had played Gaelic football for Derry County sixteen years before. His football career ended when the petrol tank of a car he was working on exploded, killing his brother. Strathearn suffered serious injuries to one leg, and his face was left badly scarred. The barbarity of the Strathearn murder was widely condemned and was later to feature in a poem by Seamus Heaney.

No-one had yet been charged with the Strathearn killing. Loyalist paramilitaries had been suspected in the first instance, but with no firm evidence the investigation had stalled. There was no apparent motive for the killing, because Strathearn was regarded by the RUC as an affable, law-abiding citizen. However, in the hours before the killing a rumour had been circulating around Ahoghill RUC Station that Strathearn had hidden the rifle used by republican terrorists on an attack on the station the previous day. The scarring on Strathearn's face was the result, the rumour suggested, of the premature explosion of a bomb he had been constructing some years before.

The speed at which the reprisals had been launched for the station attack and the kidnap of Constable Turbitt suggested that someone local had to be involved. It was highly improbable that strangers to Ahoghill could have committed both crimes without the benefit of local knowledge or intelligence. Ballymena detect-ives began to take a closer look at RUC personnel from or based in Ahoghill. It was not long before Constable William McGaughey became a focus of their suspicion. McGaughey was from a strict Presbyterian family and had been brought up on a small farm out-side the village. His father, Alexander McGaughey, was an elder in the church and, though outwardly highly respectable, nursed a deep hatred for Catholics. William McGaughey belonged to the Cullybackey branch of the Apprentice Boys, an offshoot of the Orange Order. His pathological loathing of Catholics was well known, and he had been given the sobriquet of the 'Protestant Boy'. He had joined the RUC reserve in 1972 and was posted to south Armagh three years later. He and his wife, Angela, moved house to Woodlane, Lurgan, to be closer to his work, and in the next few years he received four commendations for exemplary police work. However, after his move to Lurgan, McGaughey met and befriended several Portadown loyalist paramilitaries.

McGaughey had already landed himself in trouble with the RUC. Twelve days after the kidnapping of Father Murphy, he was to appear in court to face a charge of theft. While acting as body-guard to the Unionist MP John Taylor of Armagh he had attended a party to celebrate the election of a Unionist, Elsie Kelsey, as mayor of Lisburn. During the party two items of furniture went missing from Mrs Kelsey's home, and McGaughey had eventually been charged with stealing a table. He pleaded not guilty and was acquitted after the jury failed to agree a verdict. A few days after the verdict was announced the RUC received an anonymous call from a woman claiming that McGaughey was the leader of the gang who had kidnapped the Ahoghill priest.

The detectives made no immediate move against McGaughey but kept him under discreet surveillance in an attempt to discover the identities of his fellow-kidnappers or killers. One name began to emerge as a fellow-suspect for the Strathearn murder, Sergeant John Weir, twenty-nine years old. The SPG man was a native of Castleblayney, had been a policeman for seven years, and had received five commendations for bravery. McGaughey and Weir had been observed in the company of a well-known UVF gunman, Robin Jackson, nicknamed the Jackal. As members of the SPG, McGaughey and Weir would have been aware of Jackson's history of violence.

By December 1978 the detectives had the bones of a case, but not enough to convict. Out of the blue, the same anonymous female caller provided them with information that led to some solid evidence. McGaughey, Weir and Armstrong were arrested. Father Murphy was taken to a disused byre at the McGaughey farm and from touch was able to confirm that it was the building he had been kept in. Later three other RUC men were arrested and charged.

The trial for the murder of William Strathearn opened in April 1980. Despite the detectives' best efforts, they had not been able to charge Robin Jackson. Sergeant Weir offered to give evidence against Jackson if he himself was granted immunity from prosecution, but the DPP decided that it was not in the public's interest to permit a police sergeant to escape justice for his part in such a dastardly murder. There would have been a political outcry.

Both McGaughey and Weir pleaded not guilty, but during the trial McGaughey changed his plea to guilty. In his statement he described how he and Weir had plotted the Strathearn murder during a drinking bout in a pub in Armagh. He told Weir that he would supply the .45 pistol, but a friend of his would do the actual shooting. Weir was concerned about the high level of police activity around Ahoghill after the attack on the village's RUC station the previous day. McGaughey told him it would be taken care of.

The two policemen left the pub and drove to a house in Lurgan. Weir remained in the car until Jackson beckoned him to come inside. There was a fourth man inside the house—a known loyalist gunman. It was quickly agreed that the policemen would rendezvous with the loyalists at the Moira roundabout on the M1 motorway, who would follow them to Ahoghill in their own vehicle. McGaughey had a contact who would supply him with details of checkpoints scheduled for the roads leading to Ahoghill. The loyalists would leave their vehicle a few miles from Ahoghill and travel on in the RUC men's car. If stopped, the presence of two policemen would deter any detailed questioning about the identities of the rear-seat passengers.

Weir drove McGaughey to his home in Lurgan to pick up the pistol, which McGaughey assured him had not been used in any other terrorist attack. The killing went exactly as planned, with Jackson firing the fatal shots. The two loyalists were driven back to their vehicle and waved off. McGaughey and Weir went to the McGaughey farm and hid the pistol.

Sergeant Weir was convicted of murder, and both he and McGaughey were sentenced to life imprisonment. Much speculation came from nationalists over McGaughey's failure to testify against his loyalist accomplices. How many lives could have been saved if he had spoken out? His silence proved collusion between the RUC and loyalist terrorists, the nationalists insisted. The determination of the men not to testify against the loyalists may have been from misplaced allegiance but was more likely because of the fear of reprisals in prison. An attempt had already been made to poison McGaughey while he was on remand awaiting trial.

Weir launched a legal challenge to his sentence, stating that his confessions made in custody had been beaten out of him. He claimed that his confinement in Castlereagh holding centre had driven him mad. He felt the walls were closing in on him, he had trouble breathing, and he had been violently sick. His challenge was unsuccessful.

McGaughey was back in Belfast Crown Court a couple of months later. In the dock with him were three other policemen from his SPG unit: Reserve Constable Laurence McClure from Glenanne and Constables Ian Mitchell and David Wilson from Armagh. They were on trial with McGaughey for attempting to cause an explosion at a Catholic-owned pub in south Armagh, the Rock Bar, in Keady, on 5 June 1978.

Sergeant Armstrong and McGaughey's father, Alexander McGaughey, sixty years old, were also accused with McGaughey of the kidnapping of Father Murphy. All three pleaded guilty in this case. Defence counsel rose and asked that he might delay making a mitigation plea until the other trial had been heard. The judge agreed. Alexander McGaughey was released on bail, pending the conclusion of the other trial.

It emerged during the trial that a bomb had been left at the door of the mainly Catholic bar, and then shots were fired blindly through the window. The shooting was a strategy of McGaughey's to keep the customers inside the bar until the bomb went off, thus ensuring maximum carnage. He had heard from the Special Branch that the Provisional IRA gunman Dessie O'Hare was to be in the bar that Saturday evening. As the masked and armed policemen arrived, a customer leaving the bar grappled with McGaughey when he saw what was happening. McGaughey shot him twice in the stomach. The bomb, 10 lb of gelignite, failed to explode after the detonator burnt out.

McGaughey and his accomplices fled in a car that McClure had stolen some days earlier from the car park of the Ritz Cinema, Armagh, while the policemen were on patrol. They left the pistol used in the attack in the vehicle before it was set on fire. The policemen returned to Armagh in an RUC car driven by Mitchell, who used its radio to check for British Army and RUC checkpoints. The attack had been committed during a meal break, and the policemen went immediately back on duty. Wilson had been asked to join the bombers, but he declined. His failure to report what was planned landed him in court.

The RUC men were found guilty, and in mitigation, Andrew Donaldson, a member of their legal team, criticised the RUC for allowing young men to be exposed to risk and attack for such long periods. He went on: 'Even the army only asks men to do a tour of duty of not more than twelve months' duration. Some of these men have spent their entire police service on the border under attack.'

McGaughey received a further seven-year sentence, while the other four policemen received suspended sentences. Before announcing sentence, Lord Chief Justice Lowry paid tribute to the detectives, in particular Detective Chief Superintendent Bill Mooney, head of the CID, who had carried out the unwelcome task of bringing former comrades to trial. Lord Lowry said: 'Anyone who thought I would look lightly on offences committed by members of the RUC would be making a gross mistake.'

When handing down sentences for the kidnap, the judge told McGaughey and Armstrong that he understood the harrowing compulsion that had made them carry out the crime. Father Murphy's ordeal was terrifying but was nothing compared with the plight of Constable Turbitt. Armstrong, a holder of the Queen's Gallantry Medal for the rescue of a soldier wounded in an ambush, was given a two-year sentence, suspended for three years. He later went on to become an evangelist preacher and to found Prison Challenge, a charity that works with prisoners and their families.

Alexander McGaughey also received a suspended sentence after he pleaded guilty to hiding the weapon that had killed Strathearn and for his role in the false imprisonment of Father Murphy. The judge took into account the fact that McGaughey, who had known nothing of the kidnapping until the victim was brought to his farm, had encouraged his son to release Father Murphy. Lord Justice Lowry had a few words for Alexander McGaughey: 'Your real punishment has been to find out what terrible deeds were done and to have first the apprehension and then the grief of knowing the situation in which your son had put himself. I am satisfied you are most unlikely to do this again, that your punishment is greater than I could impose on you, and that you yielded to the natural temptations that would beset any father in the same position.'

Nationalist politicians criticised Lord Justice Lowry for handing down such lenient sentences. They felt that suspending the sentences detracted from what could have been a bloody massacre at the Rock Bar. It seemed, nationalists argued, that the judge had placed undue weight on the statement by the defence barrister, Desmond Boal QC, in mitigation, which cited the records of the highly decorated policemen who daily had to cope with danger and stress such as most people in Northern Ireland could not imagine.

Boal had also said during his mitigation plea that his clients faced a day-to-day struggle for survival and that they saw the Provisional IRA as men lurking in the darkness intent on killing them.

The nationalists' fury was added to when in August 1980 McGaughey presented a banner to his branch of the Apprentice Boys. Appeals were made to the organisation not to display the banner during their annual march through Derry, but they went unheeded. His wife, who started divorce proceedings soon after his arrest, publicly condemned him and asked the prison authorities to prevent her husband from contacting her or her children. When the Northern Ireland Secretary, Tom King, visited the Maze prison in 1987, McGaughey called him a traitor and led chants of 'Ulster says no', a slogan coined by Unionists in protest against the 1985 Anglo-Irish Agreement. While in prison, McGaughey completed an Open University degree in English and social science. On his release, having served sixteen years, the 'born again' Christian McGaughey played a prominent role in the loyalist picketing of Ballymena Catholics attending Mass. It seemed that prison had done little to temper his hatred of Catholics. More recently, McGaughey has been active in protesting against the possible participation by Sinn Féin in the policing board set up to run the new Police Service of Northern Ireland.

Robin Jackson died of cancer in 1998 at the age of fifty-one. He was suspected of having killed upwards of two dozen Catholics but had never been successfully prosecuted for a single one. The identity of his loyalist accomplice has never been ascertained.

No-one has ever been convicted of the ambush at Camlough Lake. Years later, an informer gave his British Army handler three names and information that the real target that day was to have been Chief Inspector Harry Breen, whose head of swept-back grey hair gave him more than a passing resemblance to Constable Turbitt. The chief inspector, commander of Bessbrook RUC Station, also drove a similar car. He was killed in an ambush close to the border eleven years later. In 1990 a British Army search near Cullyhanna, Co. Armagh, uncovered two Armalite rifles hidden in a stone wall. Ballistic testing showed that these weapons had been used in the Camlough ambush. They had also been used in the Tullyvallen Orange Hall and Kingsmill massacres. A Cullyhanna Provisional IRA member, Séamus Moley, has been linked to Turbitt's death by the informer Éamon Collins. Collins later retracted, but he was abducted and bludgeoned to death in 1999.

With the endless circle of violence at that time in Northern Ireland as a backdrop, it is well nigh impossible to resist asking the 'what if' question. What if the attempted bombing of the Rock Bar provoked the ambush of Constables McConnell and Turbitt, which in turn brought about the kidnap of Father Murphy? Was the kidnap of Father Murphy an attempt by McGaughey to salvage something from a nightmare of his own making?

5

Ben Dunne's Kidnap and His Subsequent Fall from Grace

❖❖❖

When Ben Dunne was kidnapped he was a multimillionaire businessman at the top of his game. The nightmare he came through, apparently unscathed, left a legacy that was to surface years later. His kidnap was an ordeal that brought traumatic and lasting changes to Dunne himself and also altered Irish public life for ever.

For the Dunne family, opening a store in the divided town of Portadown, Co. Armagh, was always going to be problematical. Although Dunnes Stores had eight retail outlets in Northern Ireland, with a turnover of £15 million, it was still seen by the majority of northern Protestants as an Irish company. That the paternal grandparents of the family had come from the seaside village of Rostrevor, Co. Down, made little difference. Shops in Catholic-dominated west Belfast, Newry, Derry and Armagh thrived, but Portadown would be a tougher nut to crack. The Dunnes' latest venture was the anchor store of the revamped Magowan Buildings Shopping Centre in Portadown.

On the morning of 16 October 1981 Ben Dunne was alone at the wheel of his distinctive black Mercedes 500 SEL as he drove north for the heavily advertised official opening of the Portadown branch. He was a director of Dunnes Stores, started by his father, Ben Dunne Senior and already the seventh-largest company in Ireland, and with ambitious plans for further expansion. Ben Junior was the fifth of six children. Only Therese was younger, and she was the closest to Ben. When they were growing up in the 1960s the four older children would accompany their parents on holidays to the French Riviera, while Ben and Therese remained at home. Ben worshipped his father and constantly sought his approval and respect. One of the few times he had deliberately gone against his father was when he married Mary Godwin in 1972, but then Ben Senior had also disapproved of matches his other children had made. Ben Junior was keen that his children would have a more normal childhood than he had, when home had been a succession of hotels. Ben and Mary bought a house in Castleknock, Co. Dublin, where they lived with their four children. It was from there that Ben had set off an hour and a half earlier on that autumn morning.

As Ben Dunne reached Killeen, just south of the border crossing on the N1 road, travelling fairly fast, he saw a green Opel Ascona approaching from the opposite direction. The Opel was suddenly swung across the road, blocking the northern lane. Dunne stood on the brakes, and the heavy Mercedes slewed onto the hard shoulder, missing the other car by inches, before coming to a halt in a cloud of dust and tyre-rubber smoke. The Opel drove towards the stationary Mercedes. Dunne assumed the driver intended to apologise for his dangerous manoeuvre; instead, four armed and masked men sprang from the car, and one of them threw open the door of the Mercedes. The astonished Ben Dunne had no time to react. Before he had time to realise what was happening, he was hauled unceremoniously from his vehicle and brought to the rear door of the gunmen's car.

'Get in!' ordered one of the gunmen. 'Are you going to shoot me?' Dunne asked as two men sat on either side of him in the back seat. 'Put this on,' one of them said, handing Dunne a cloth hood. 'Keep your head down. Don't ask questions and you won't be shot.' A lorry driver who had witnessed the abduction drove to the nearby Customs post and alerted the Gardaí.

Dunne had an imposing stature. He was tall and well built but had rarely felt any need to make use of his physical advantage. The gunmen, one armed with an Armalite, were taking no chances. A handgun was jammed into his ribs as the car sped away in a northerly direction. It was to be a drive of twenty minutes. Dunne was taken from the car and ushered into what his sense of smell told him was a disused building or pigsty. He could feel mud squelching under his feet and a rough stone wall against his back when he was given a wooden crate to sit on. The abductors tied his hands behind his back and asked for the private telephone numbers of his father and his wife. Dunne, a pragmatic man, saw no point in holding back the information. If, as seemed likely, he had been kidnapped for ransom purposes, then the sooner that was put in motion the better.

It seemed as though his abductors were reading his mind when they asked, 'What do think you're worth?' 'Nothing. You'll get nothing from me,' Dunne answered. The men made no comment and withdrew, leaving him alone.

After several hours had passed he was pulled to his feet and taken outside. He was walked, still hooded, across some fields. His captors appeared nervous, remarking that the 'Brits' were close, too close. Dunne was grabbed under his arms and made to run. The multimillionaire took little exercise other than a round of golf and was soon out of breath and sweating profusely.

'Take it easy, lads. Go easy,' he pleaded. His captors ignored his pleas and kept up the hurried pace. They came to a deep ditch, and Dunne was made to lie in it for a couple of hours. They moved again and appeared to be walking in the lee of a hedge next to a road. Each time a vehicle approached, a gun was stuck in his neck or his ribs and he was told to keep his head down.

Eventually the group arrived at a waiting car, and he was driven to a second building. He was made to lie on the car's floor during the half-hour trip, his head still hooded. His captors were probably Provisional IRA, he surmised, or perhaps one of the splinter groups that emerged from time to time. He wondered how much they would demand for his safe return. A million pounds seemed like a nice round figure. How many Armalites or kilograms of Semtex would that buy? His firm had dealt with extortion before. It was a way of life in Northern Ireland, where protection money paid to various terrorist groups was considered a legitimate business expense and an allowable deduction by the Inland Revenue.

This second building was to be Dunne's home until his release. He was made to lie on the hard floor for most of the daylight hours, his hood firmly in place. At night he was led to a bed. He formed an impression of his captors as rough and serious men who clearly meant business. They appeared to be well-trained paramilitaries, and he had no doubt that they would have killed him if he tried to escape. He was allowed to raise the front of his hood to eat but was warned that he would be shot if he saw their faces. Dunne was not very worried for himself but felt deep concern for his wife and children and for his extended family.

The first news of her husband's kidnapping reached Mary Dunne when a friend flagged her car down as she was returning from a shopping trip. 'They've taken Ben at the border,' the woman told her. Mary Dunne's first thought was that Customs officials had detained Ben for some minor excise irregularity pertaining to the family business. Then she heard the news bulletin about the empty car and that no contact had yet been made. She immediately picked up her two eldest children from school, to prevent them hearing the news indirectly. She gave the children a hastily thought-up excuse and hurried home, her mind flooding with dark images. She hoped that focusing her mind on the care of her two youngest children—one a toddler and the other an infant—would help keep her from dwelling on the ordeal her husband was going through. But she knew she was fooling herself.

Mary Dunne's mother heard the news and left her home in Kilkenny for Castleknock to be at her daughter's side. She was one of a number of people to take up residence in the Dunne house that day; Father Dermod McCarthy, a family friend, also arrived. They tried their best to console Mary as she anxiously awaited contact from the kidnappers.

A huge manhunt was quickly launched on both sides of the border. It soon emerged that a car with Special Branch detectives had arrived at the scene within minutes of the abduction. All they could do was help initiate what would be a difficult search. The drumlin-dotted countryside was notorious for being a favoured terrorist terrain. The small fields with their high hedges on the hilly countryside were laced with minor roads skirting round the numerous tiny bogs and forests. The landscape would be a logistical nightmare to search.

South Armagh had been a no-go area for the British security forces' vehicles for more than a decade. Army outposts and observation towers were manned, but all movement of soldiers and equipment—even their refuse—had to be done by helicopter, making the Bessbrook-to-Crossmaglen helicopter flight path the busiest in the world. Acutely aware that the area lacked any real policing, the RUC issued an appeal for farmers in south Armagh to search their outhouses and farm buildings, paying particular attention to outlying buildings. The local people were friendly enough, but wary of strangers. An influx of military or police personnel would antagonise the residents, and co-operation would be quickly withdrawn.

Chief Superintendent Dick Cottrell of Drogheda, heading the hunt south of the border, had the easier job. The men under his command could travel freely and without too much fear of their lives. Although no terrorist group had yet claimed responsibility for the kidnap, most thought it bore the hallmark of the Provisional IRA. If so, it was felt that the active service unit and their captive would almost certainly be holed up on the northern side of the border.

The Gardaí were critical of the lack of properly co-ordinated roadblocks and searches north of the border, and the Taoiseach, Garret FitzGerald, called on the British ambassador, Sir Leonard Figgs, to express his concern. One direct result of this meeting was that the Chief Constable of the RUC, Jack Hermon, took personal charge of RUC operations in the manhunt. Shortly after Hermon's direct intervention a large number of extra police were brought into the search area, with a corresponding increase in Special Air

Service personnel. Two vehicles, the Opel car and a blue Transit van, were found burnt out near Forkhill on the northern side of the border. A motorcycle in the rear of the van had also been destroyed.

The business world, north and south, was outraged by the kidnap. Dunne was an influential man in a company that had brought long-term jobs to many of the employment blackspots of Northern Ireland. The family that had shunned publicity in the past was now in the limelight. The company's structure was being discussed in every pub in Ireland. Ben Dunne Senior had placed the firm he created in a trust, to keep the business a family one and to ensure that the Revenue Commissioners did not claim too large an inheritance tax bill on his death. Five of his six children (Anne was in residential care) were directors, but Ben Junior was the one most involved with the day-to-day operations of the retail giant.

A special Mass was said in the Pro-Cathedral, Dublin, at the request of Dunnes Stores employees. Ben's sister, Elizabeth McMahon, represented the Dunne family. Auxiliary Bishop James Lennon issued an appeal for Ben's release, saying, 'Kidnapping is a vicious crime, using as it does an innocent man to hold up to ransom and put intolerable pressure on his wife and young family to extort money. Such an act moves the society we live in frighteningly close to barbarism.'

Both the Irish and British governments saw the kidnapping as a humiliating and provocative attack on their authority. It was incredible that a man could be kidnapped in broad daylight along one of the world's most heavily patrolled stretches of road. The Minister for Justice, Jim Mitchell, made it clear from the start that the Government would not permit a ransom to be paid. This started a battle of wits between the Gardaí, the RUC, and the Dunne family. Ben Dunne Senior, seventy-four years old, was a brusque man, used to getting his own way, no matter what the cost.

The gang made contact with the Dunne family through a go-between. Father Dermod McCarthy, the family friend who had officiated at Ben and Mary's wedding, covertly met masked men in Co. Louth. The amount demanded was £500,000, only half what the victim thought might have been asked for, but the kidnappers were willing to negotiate if paid quickly.

The first attempt by the Dunne family to pay the ransom came to nothing when their courier, with £300,000 in cash, was stopped near Dundalk. The Gardaí knew that a large sum of money had been withdrawn from a bank and followed the courier's vehicle. They hoped to swoop during the handing over, but when darkness came a decision was made to abandon the plan rather than risk losing the money. The courier, Noel Fox, a family friend and a trustee of Dunnes Stores, was escorted to Dublin for questioning. He claimed he was acting as a decoy, trying to lure out the kidnappers.

The next thwarted attempt came on the third night, when Father Dermod McCarthy was discovered in a shed near the border during a follow-up search after a shoot-out between gardaí of the Security Task Force and three gunmen at Roche Castle, a ruin just south of the border from Forkhill. It was not thought that any of the gunmen had been wounded. Knowing the lengths the Dunne family would go to in their efforts to free Ben, the gardaí took the unprecedented step of forcing Dunnes Stores branches throughout the Republic to put the takings in the bank each evening, though denying claims that the Dunnes' assets in Britain had been frozen.

The third attempt to pay a ransom was foiled when the RUC, acting on a Garda tip-off, stopped two cars between Newry and Banbridge. A 'large sum of money' was recovered. The Minister for Justice, Jim Mitchell, announced that the Government would be undertaking a complete review of the law as it related to this sort of crime. Among changes that would be considered, he said, would be the possibility of making it a crime to pay a ransom to kidnappers.

While this hide-and-seek game was being played along the border, Dunne was being treated well by his captors. On one occasion he asked for a beer. One of the men shouted to a colleague that the 'big fella' wanted a beer. The man shouted back that Dunne should be given one, because he was a 'paying guest'.

The Gardaí believe that a fourth attempt made by the family to deliver a ransom was probably successful. Father McCarthy made a radio plea to the kidnappers on the sixth day, and it was suspected by the Gardaí that a code-word to the abductors had been included in the broadcast. That evening Tottenham Hotspur football club was playing a European Cup tie against Dundalk. The Co. Louth roads were busy with soccer fans travelling to the match, and traffic tailed back as gardaí and soldiers checked all cars. In the confusion the gardaí failed to find the white Escort they were interested in. It was known to have left Dublin's north side earlier in the day with a large sum of money.

Ben Dunne had been allowed to listen to a radio during his captivity. The news bulletins he heard kept him in touch with what was happening. He knew by Saturday night that the authorities were not going to allow a ransom to be paid. His captors delivered a note to Dunne from Father McCarthy. When McCarthy was caught in the shed on the third night by the gardaí, the kidnappers demanded from Dunne the name of a substitute intermediary. He was told his life depended on it and that the ransom would now be £750,000.

Dunne also heard McCarthy's Wednesday appeal on the 1:30 RTE radio news. His captors had told him that things were heating up and he was to be moved that night. They listened in silence when it was repeated on television that evening on the 9 o'clock news. Half an hour later one of the men returned and said, 'We've good news for you. You won't have to sleep in the fields. You're being released.'

Dunne was taken from his hiding place and driven at speed to Cullyhanna in south Armagh. Later he said, 'I was more frightened then than at any stage, because I knew they were bringing me to my freedom and I had the hidden fear we were going to be ambushed by the army or someone and have a shoot-out.'

Dunne was deposited at the gates of St Michael's Church. His kidnappers handed him three bullets as mementoes. One came from an Armalite and another from a revolver. The third, an Armalite round, was to be given to McCarthy. Dunne ran into the adjacent graveyard and sought cover in an open grave, terrified that his release was a ruse and that he was about to be killed. Éamon

Mallie, a political journalist for Downtown Radio and a native of south Armagh, had been tipped off about Dunne's release. He drove to Cullyhanna, stopped his car, and started shouting out for the hostage. Dunne showed himself, and Mallie took him to the parochial house. Dunne used Father Hugh O'Neill's telephone to let an intermediary know he was safe and free. Why he did not call his wife at this time has been the cause of much speculation. Dunne explained that he did not want to alert his wife until he was sure he would be coming home. There was still a long way to drive, and he thought they could have been stopped at a checkpoint and delayed for hours.

Dunne warmed himself at the fire and drank a bottle of Macardle's ale, but he was keen to be on the move. They left the house soon after 1 a.m. and drove across the border towards Dublin. Their car was indeed stopped at a Garda checkpoint, where the young garda failed to recognise the most sought-after man in Ireland. 'There's a boy for demotion,' Dunne said wryly to Mallie as they drove off.

On the Dublin side of Drogheda they stopped again, and Dunne phoned his wife to let her know he was safe. The family has always maintained that no ransom was handed over, but it is generally accepted that the £750,000 was paid. It seems highly unlikely that Dunne would have been freed so quickly if a ransom had not been delivered to the Provisionals. The Minister for Justice said, 'My belief is that no money has been paid.' He went on: 'In the nature of things, one cannot be one hundred per cent certain. There are many ways of transferring money. Money can be exchanged outside this state, outside this island.'

Dunne arrived back in Castleknock for an emotional home-coming. He had six days' of stubble on his face, he had shed a little weight, and his blue suit was the worse for wear. It was only after his release that the two eldest Dunne children were informed of their father's kidnap.

Unwisely, he was to admit later, Dunne refused any form of counselling after his ordeal and was back at work just twenty-four hours later. In an interview given on the twentieth anniversary of the kidnap he recalled how his mind coped with the trauma of it: 'I remember at the time thinking I had a direct link to him [God]. One minute I would be giving out, the next I would be begging him to allow me see my wife and family again. Funnily enough, he kept talking back to me. It's been like that right through my life. I always thought he kept a watchful eye on me.'

Dunne still insisted that no ransom was ever paid. He said that the first person he went to was his father, because 'I knew if someone paid, it would have been him.' Ben Dunne Senior said that nothing had been paid. He was seventy-four when his son was kidnapped but still a force to be reckoned with. He was not a man to permit political expediency to prevent him freeing his son. Noel Fox was given the responsibility of negotiating, with the assistance of Father Dermod McCarthy. There is no doubt that the kidnap placed Dunne Senior under enormous stress. The founder of Dunnes Stores suffered a heart attack two years after his son's kidnap and died a fortnight later in St Vincent's Hospital, Dublin.

At the time of his death, Dunnes Stores had seventy-seven branches with an annual turnover of £300 million. Ben Junior was appointed joint managing director with his elder brother Frank. In practice, Ben Junior was given a free rein to guide the family fortunes, and for the next decade he turned in a first-rate performance. He worked long hours, forging a reputation as a tough negotiator both with competitors and trade unions. Turnover was almost tripled to £850 million with the addition of a mere twenty new outlets.

Going by the balance sheets, it seemed that the 'big fella' had put the kidnap behind him and was prospering. But all was not as it seemed. His marriage was going through a rocky patch, and Dunne was frequently seen in the company of a woman who was separated from her husband. She introduced Dunne to her circle of friends and their habits. Rumours of drug abuse were whispered, in particular cocaine. The extent of Dunne's drug abuse was confirmed in the most dramatic fashion on a golf trip he took to Orlando, Florida.

Ben Dunne enjoyed entertaining his friends. Unlike Dunne Senior with his parsimonious ways, his son spent lavishly, frequently picking up the bill for golf trips to the United States. On 15 February 1992 Dunne and ten friends—including a taxi-driver from Jersey—flew first-class to Orlando for a few days of golf in the sun. They checked in to the Stouffers Resort Hotel: ten single rooms and a $500-a-night suite for Dunne.

That evening Dunne asked the concierge to fix him up with some female company and a supply of cocaine. The concierge was accustomed to such requests from guests and had developed the right contacts to ensure the satisfaction of his clients. An hour later, 32-year-old Cindy Mitchell presented herself at the door of suite 1044. She spent some time with Dunne and was asked to return two nights later and to bring a friend.

The group played golf the next day at the Barnett Creek course. The weather stayed fine, and the golf was enjoyable. That evening they had dinner and a few drinks and retired to their rooms in preparation for the next day's golf.

Monday evening brought Cindy Mitchell's return with her friend, Andrea Nathanson. A large bag of cocaine had been procured, and Dunne was snorting copious amounts. He was talkative and told the two women about his life as one of Ireland's leading business-men. The facts were embroidered a little, but he did also mention his kidnapping, describing it as a horrible experience. The women thought him a nervous man, pacing the room with his long strides, muttering to himself and acting slightly paranoid. This assessment was vindicated when Dunne asked Nathanson to leave. Mitchell advised him to lay off the white stuff before she too departed.

Tuesday was again spent at the Barnett Creek course, and after dinner Dunne told Mitchell to call round. As on the previous evening, he was high on cocaine. There was a visitor in the room, a man with blonde hair and wearing a Russian wedding ring on the little finger of his right hand. Mitchell did not stay long, and when she left she took, clandestinely, an imprinted slip of Dunne's credit card as a souvenir.

After Wednesday's golf the party returned to the Grand Cypress Hotel, the most expensive in Orlando. Dunne had arranged the move the night before. This time his seventeenth-floor suite was costing $1,200 plus sales tax. Late that evening he was feeling lonely, and he telephoned an escort agency, asking for a woman to be sent over to his suite. A representative from the agency, 'Eric the Enforcer', called at Dunne's suite and collected the $300 fee. The agency contacted Denise Wojcik and told her to go to the hotel. It was after 1 a.m. when she knocked on the door of suite 1708. She was greeted with a glass of vintage champagne and a line of cocaine. Line after line followed; she told the police later that they must have consumed more than fifty. She ran a bath while Dunne laid out lines of cocaine with his K Club membership card. Four hours later, Dunne felt the need of a second female companion. Cherie Rudulski was told by the agency to get over to suite 1708 at the Grand Cypress Hotel.

Needing cash to pay 'Eric the Enforcer', Dunne went to his security room safe but in his befuddled state could not open it. Inside the safe was £4,000 in Irish pounds and almost $9,000. He made repeated attempts to open the safe, growing increasingly frustrated with each failed attempt. He refused Wojcik's offers of assistance but took her advice to call hotel security and seek their help. He began to terrify Wojcik. He roared at her to get out and began to swing a piece of wood around his head. She described him as acting like 'some crazed King Kong' but bravely stayed in the room to try to calm him down.

The doorbell of the suite rang. Dunne opened the door and saw a man dressed in a black boiler-suit. The standard dress for a member of a Provisional IRA active service unit is a dark-coloured one-piece boiler-suit. Worn to prevent the transfer of trace material to a crime scene, it would be burned after the job. Reminded of his kidnap, Dunne panicked.

'Get the police, get the police!' he yelled. He retreated across the room and cowered in a corner of the balcony, which overlooked a white grand piano in the lobby sixteen floors below. Dressed only in boxer shorts, he was screaming and roaring threats. It was just a few minutes past 8 a.m., and many guests were making their way to the restaurant for breakfast, while tour groups were assembling in the lobby. It was the worst time of the day for any regrettable spectacle to intrude on the quiet calm of the five-star hotel.

The maintenance man and a chambermaid contacted the hotel's security manager and reported the Irishman's psychotic behaviour. Rick de Treville, the security manager, assumed that the Irishman throwing a fit was a member of U2, who were guests of the hotel and coincidently had suites on the seventeenth floor. He asked for two of the rock group's security staff to accompany him to the seventeenth floor. When he discovered the true identity of the troublemaker, he contacted the police.

Howard Wright, Sam Spanich and Chris Ford were among the Orange County Sheriff's Department deputies who responded to the call. The lobby was cleared of guests, and Spanich began to talk to Dunne. He genuinely thought that Dunne intended to jump, and he was not about to be taken with him.

It was then that Cherie Rudulski arrived by taxi outside the hotel. She realised there was no way she would be allowed near the suite, so she crossed the road and phoned the hotel. She asked to be put through to suite 1708 and was immediately connected. Her friend Denise Wojcik answered the call. Wojcik explained what had happened and advised Rudulski to stay put. The unfortunate Rudulski did not have enough money on her to pay for a taxi home.

On the balcony Sam Spanich continued to talk softly to Dunne, reassuring him that he was safe and that nobody was trying to get him or his money. When the lobby had been cleared, several policemen up to that moment hidden from Dunne's sight rushed him and bundled him off the balcony. He was thrown onto the bed and handcuffed. His ankles were also tied, and he had to be carried unceremoniously to a waiting ambulance. A small bag of cocaine was found in the pocket of his shorts.

Ben Dunne's wife, Mary, phoned the hotel during the fracas and asked to speak to her husband. The call was put through to the hotel's assistant manager, Courtney Torreyson, who told her that her husband was unavailable at that moment. Later, a policeman contacted her to explain what had happened, telling her about the escort and the cocaine.

Denise Wojcik made a deal with the police, offering them information in return for dropping any possible charges against her. She told them about a black bag that contained a large amount of cash and cocaine. Detective Chris Ford searched the suite and found the items Wojcik had mentioned. There were 32.5 grammes of cocaine and almost $10,000 in cash. It was the legality of this search that would be debated later at great length and that ultimately saved Dunne from a spell in the Orange County Prison.

The rest of the golfing party were unaware that anything untoward had happened to their benevolent sponsor. They were on the golf course when they eventually heard the news. Noel Fox, a family friend of long standing and a trustee of Dunnes Stores, left the golf course to telephone the Irish Embassy in Washington and was eventually given the name of leading defence attorneys in Florida.

Dunne had regained some composure in the ambulance but lost it again when the medics donned surgical gloves before examining him. The Provisional IRA used latex gloves to avoid leaving fingerprints at crime scenes. Once again the events of October 1981 were bringing flashbacks to Dunne's drug-addled mind. After examination at Sand Lake Hospital he was discharged and taken to the county jail. Butch Slaughter, his newly assigned lawyer, turned up at six o'clock to confer with his newest multimillionaire client. Bail was arranged, and Dunne was released.

The *Sunday Tribune* broke the story in Ireland and when Dunne flew into Dublin on Sunday morning the press laid siege to his home in Castleknock. His solicitor, Noel Smyth, arrived at the house that afternoon for a consultation with his client. On Smyth's advice, Dunne called a press conference at Castleknock that evening. He publicly admitted what he had done and said he was sorry for the considerable heartache he had caused his wife and family. In a televised interview for RTE News he was particularly frank, blaming only himself for the Orlando incident. One observation he made would come back to haunt him. He said that, like any manager in Dunnes Stores, he had put his career in jeopardy by taking illegal drugs.

Admitting guilt to the Irish people was one thing: a stretch of imprisonment in Orlando was something else entirely. Butch Slaughter managed to have the trafficking charges scrapped: Dunne had apparently paid the concierge considerably in excess of the street value for the cocaine, and the search of his room was deemed illegal. Noel Smyth flew to Florida for the plea negotiations. He took with him character references from a wide range of Irish business people, sports personalities, and Dunne's employees, including a letter from John Small, a Northern Ireland octogenarian and longest-serving employee of the company. Smyth recounted the facts of Dunne's kidnap and how his refusal to accept counselling may have exacerbated symptoms of post-traumatic stress disorder. He pledged that his client would enter a London clinic for the treatment of drug addiction. Dunne pleaded guilty to possession and was fined $5,000. He was also to undergo a period of treatment at the clinic and remain under the supervision of its doctor for a year.

Ben Dunne's siblings and fellow-directors were outraged. Margaret Heffernan rebuked Noel Smyth for arranging such lenient punishment for her brother. She was of the opinion that six months in prison would have done him more good. The most private of families, they had eschewed publicity in the past, but now the errant Ben had dragged them firmly into in the spotlight. On 16 July, while Ben and his family were on holiday, Frank Dunne proposed a new set of rules for running the company. Seconded by Margaret Heffernan, the plan met with little opposition from Therese and Elizabeth. The writing was on the wall for Ben; and one year after the Orlando incident he was removed as chairman. Only Elizabeth remained loyal to him, but her vote was not enough. An offer of £10 million to buy him out was a non-starter, and when Elizabeth died suddenly, Ben Dunne began to feel the icy wind of exclusion blow over him. An accomplished boardroom fighter, he and Noel Smyth started a campaign of litigation to break the family trust. Their statement of claim was that the trust was never intended to be 'a bona fide discretionary trust' and that certain family members used the assets as and when they wished.

The opening volley of shots fired by Ben brought quick retaliation from the family. Dunnes Stores commissioned Price Waterhouse to examine and report on Ben's financial transactions when he was running the company. He had goaded Margaret Heffernan over payments he claimed to have made to Charles Haughey, a man she disliked intensely. She had even visited the former Taoiseach at his home, Abbeville, near Malahide, to see if this was true. Haughey had been charming but evasive, which made Heffernan all the more determined to discover the truth. She paid a visit to Des Traynor, Haughey's financial guru, but the wily accountant denied knowing about any payments.

The trust that Ben Dunne was challenging had been initiated in 1964. The six children of Ben Dunne Senior would be entitled to their share of the assets in twenty-one years. When 1985 eventually came round, a distribution of the accumulated assets would have incurred a £40 million tax bill. Quite reasonably, it was decided to continue the trust under the guardianship of four trustees, who could distribute the assets at a time of their choosing, or when all six siblings were deceased.

Ben Dunne lodged his claim in the High Court on 22 September 1994. According to his argument, the trust was a hollow sham. He claimed that some of his fellow-directors had requested money to be lodged in overseas banks, and that payments had been occasionally made to directors using fictitious names. Many in the business community saw this as a blow below the belt. But there were no Queensberry rules in this fight. Dunnes Stores dismissed many of the executives who would have been Ben's allies. He made an inflated bid to buy out the rest of the family, thereby establishing a greater value to his shares. For months dirty tactics were utilised by both sides.

Some of the family blamed Noel Smyth's Svengali-like influence on Ben for many of the internecine tactics, and it wasn't long before litigation was begun between them and Smyth. Both parties made accusations that money was outstanding. It was thought that if Smyth was out of the picture, Ben would be more amenable, blood being thicker than water, after all. If the family's perception of Smyth was that he would roll over easily, they had seriously underestimated him.

Ben's claim was settled on the steps of the Four Courts in November 1994 for a reputed £125 million. The Price Waterhouse report, which was to have been the mainstay of Dunnes Stores' defence against Ben's claim, turned out to be a double-edged sword. Unusual payments to a politician did surface, but not to the man Heffernan suspected, nor was he even from the same party. The Fine Gael minister Michael Lowry had received payments from Dunnes Stores, including the renovation costs of his home. Inevitably the story was leaked, and the Dáil opposition, scenting blood, demanded Lowry's resignation. On 29 October 1996, Lowry stood down.

The Revenue Commissioners had followed every move of the Dunne family's falling out. It was thought that Ben Dunne had paid £30 million to settle with them, a record amount. Now it was Lowry's turn to have his tax affairs put under the microscope. Leinster House, a rumour mill at the best of times, went into overdrive. The Government had to act, and it did just that. The Committee on Procedure and Privileges appointed a retired judge, Gerard Buchanan, to report on payments by Dunnes Stores to politicians. Before Buchanan had time to deliver his report, the Dáil set up a tribunal of inquiry under the chairmanship of Mr Justice Brian McCracken. The issues under investigation were much the same as Buchanan had been charged with, but the tribunal would have greater powers, in that it could subpoena witnesses.

The McCracken Tribunal sat in public for the first time on 24 February 1997. The first witness to be called was Ben Dunne, on 21 April 1997. His evidence contained three points of immense significance. All were pure dynamite. Yes, he had donated money to numerous political parties, apparently not asking for or receiving any political favours. He had given a total of £1.3 million to Charles Haughey. Three £70,000 bank drafts had been handed personally to Haughey at the former Taoiseach's home in north Co. Dublin with the words 'Look, this is something for yourself.'

Haughey was caught out. No longer could he hide behind the tangled web spun by his financial guru, Des Traynor, who had died in May 1994. The tribunal's legal team already knew much about the destination of the funds donated to Haughey and had visited the Cayman Islands even before hearing the Dunne testimony. Ben Dunne had scratched the surface; it would take many more years of investigation and legal wrangling to fully expose the strata of deceit and chicanery underlying Irish society.

During that time the Dunne family, the disgraced politicians Charles Haughey and Michael Lowry and the Ansbacher account-holders must have wished more than once that the Provisional IRA kidnap gang had chosen a different target.

6

Shergar and the Fossett's Ponies

Shergar was a wonder horse, loved by everyone but the book-makers. Bred in Ireland by the Aga Khan, he won six of his eight races. Lester Piggott rode him to a four-length victory in the Irish Derby. The King George VI and Queen Elizabeth Stakes were notched up by the same margin. He won the 1981 Epsom Derby by a record ten lengths. Michael Stoute was the trainer and Walter Swinburn was the jockey on that memorable day. Voted European horse of the year in 1981, Shergar remains the last odds-on favourite to win the Epsom Derby. When he was retired to stud he was seen as a money-making machine, but not just by the syndicate selling his services at £80,000 a time. He had caught the attention of others—men lacking respect for the blue-blooded prince of an equine monarchy. Plans were set in motion that would result in Shergar becoming the Lord Lucan of the flat-racing world.

Co. Kildare is the centre of the Irish racehorse industry. Stud farms dot the fertile countryside bordering the broad plain of the Curragh. Visitors can take guided tours of the National Stud near Kildare and marvel at the astronomical sums of money this business commands. The breeding season begins in the middle of February, but in 1983 it seemed as if adverse weather might delay the start. Co. Kildare was in the grip of hailstorms and marrow-chilling winds sweeping off the Curragh.

In his loose box at Ballymany Stud, Shergar was restless. It was to be his second season of standing. Like the champion he was, he was champing at the bit to get on with things. He was expected to cover fifty-five mares over the next few months. His fertility rate was excellent, with forty-two mares in foal from the previous season. His first offspring had been born just a week before.

For the first time in days, the wind died and a thick fog descended. At mid-afternoon on Wednesday 8 February, Jim Fitzgerald, head groom, turned on the infra-red heat lamp hanging above Shergar's broad bay back. There would be hell to pay if the cold got into these £10 million bones.

Jim Fitzgerald had been a stable hand all his life. It was in his blood. He had started at fourteen and forty-four years later still loved his work. He needed to; if it had been just for the money he would have quit decades before. Earlier he had watched as his most valuable charge was given a run-out in the five-acre paddock. Shergar had shown little enthusiasm for the wintry outdoors, and Liam Foley, the stallion man, had ordered him inside.

Darkness closed round the stud yard soon after four. Fitzgerald whispered a few soothing words into Shergar's ears and ran a hand over the stallion's white forehead blaze. He bolted the inner door of the box and looked across at Nishapour in the neighbouring box— a fine horse, but the even-tempered Shergar was Fitzgerald's favourite. There was a world of trust in the stallion's big black eyes. Fitzgerald shut and bolted the outer door.

Pulling his jacket tight across his chest, he hurried across the yard to his home. His wife would have the tea ready. They had no plans to go out that evening—perhaps Friday night, if the weather eased. What was to happen in the next few hours would bring sorrow into his life, something he would never totally get over.

When the Aga Khan retired Shergar to stud he assembled a 34-member syndicate of investors to capitalise on the horse's immense value. Members included himself, Sheikh al-Maktum, Stavros Niarchos, and Robert Sangster. Each share of the syndicate had cost £250,000. Underwriters from Lloyd's of London carried the £10 million insurance risk, but the expected returns would be much higher, as high as £100 million, possibly more if the stallion's off-spring inherited some of their sire's character and started winning classics. The person chosen to run the stud and protect the syndicate's investment was Ghislain Drion, a Frenchman of first-rate experi-ence who was at ease in the world of the aristocracy and the super-rich, owners and trainers.

With hindsight, it is easy to be critical of the slack security of the Ballymany Stud. There were no full-time security guards and no alarms on the doors of the loose boxes, and the closed-circuit cameras were not working, though their value in the blanketing fog would have been minimal. The five-barred gate on the drive was closed, but not fitted with a lock.

There were few out and about that February night. People stayed at home, threw an extra log on the fire and settled down for a night in front of the television. Outside was no place for man or beast. But it was a perfect night for mischief. No-one saw the Ford Granada towing a horsebox pull off the main Dublin road at about 8:30 that evening. The car and a van stopped near the gate while a second car, probably a Vauxhall, carried on up the drive. As it approached the stud's yard its lights were switched off. The fog helped to muffle the crunch of the wheels on the gravel.

Inside his house, Jim Fitzgerald thought he heard a car in the yard. He listened, heard nothing more, and forgot about it. If Liam Foley or the boss wanted him, they knew where he was. So when there was a knock on the door he wasn't unduly concerned. His son Bernard rose to answer it.

The caller, silhouetted against the grey fog, was dressed in a makeshift Garda uniform. The balaclava the man was wearing didn't strike Bernard as incongruous on such a bitter night. 'Is he in?' the man asked. Bernard turned to fetch his father. A heavy blow landed in the small of his back, sending him sprawling. Jim Fitzgerald came out of the sitting-room to see his son on the floor. The next thing he saw was a pistol pointed at him. Three men pushed their way into the small house. The last one carried a sub-machine gun. They half-pushed, half-hauled Bernard and Jim into the kitchen, where Madge, Jim's wife, stood terror-stricken.

'What do you want with us?' Jim asked them. 'We haven't done anything.'

The man who had hit Bernard answered, 'We've come for Shergar, and we want two million quid for him. Call the police and he's dead.' Fitzgerald was not sure if the threat was directed at his son or Shergar. The intruders signalled for Jim to put his coat on. Two of them took him outside. With his family being held at the point of a gun, Shergar's groom had no option but to guide them to the stallion.

A strong musk of straw and warm horse hit them when Fitzgerald opened the outer door. The only light was the diffused red glow from the heat lamp above Shergar. Fitzgerald was ordered to put a bridle on the horse. A radio was used to summon the Granada and horsebox up to the yard. Four more men were in the car. The ramp of the horsebox was lowered and straw scattered over the wooden slats. One of the gang knew enough about horses to don an old jacket belonging to Fitzgerald that was hanging in the stable. The stallion nuzzled the jacket and recognised the familiar scent. Fitzgerald was forced to watch as Shergar was led out into the yard and into the horsebox without any fuss. The ramp was raised and the catches fastened. Fitzgerald remembers thinking how the shabby horsebox contrasted with the stylish transport Shergar was used to. A short nervous whinny was heard from inside. The wonder horse was starting to experience unease. Fitzgerald knew the stallion would require very careful handling if it was to survive the rigours of the kidnap and the stress of an unfamiliar routine. The next forty-eight hours would be critical. This was not some clapped-out hunter these men were about to drive off with but a stallion at its peak at the start of the season, a winter of equine testosterone in its bloodstream. He was like a loaded gun with a hair trigger. With luck the kidnappers would have a vet on standby, somebody to administer tranquillisers until the ransom was paid.

Some of the men were ready to leave. They climbed into the Granada and drove out of the yard, the horsebox disappearing into the fog. The others took Fitzgerald back into his house, where he and his family were subjected to a barrage of threats. Should any of them contact the Gardaí, they would be signing their own death warrants. They had to be Provisional IRA, Jim thought. An active service unit of the Provisional IRA had to be taken seriously. The cosy days of the seventies were long gone. Back then the Government had turned a blind eye to the republican terrorists as long as they behaved themselves south of the border. But the 1980s had seen a change in Provisional IRA policy. Margaret Thatcher had been returned to power on the back of the Falklands War, and the Provisionals were determined to take the fight to her doorstep. They needed money, even if that meant operations in the Republic.

The Fitzgeralds were held in one room for three hours, a long time to brood on what was being done to Shergar, time enough to allow the Granada and its horsebox to get well away. There had been one last chilling threat before the kidnappers left. 'Call the police and you die.'

Fitzgerald was taken outside and manhandled into the van, still parked near the gates. A man armed with a rifle stepped out of the fog. Fitzgerald was made to lie on the floor as the van was started and driven off. He could not put a time on how long it was before the van stopped and he was thrown out on a deserted road. He began to walk. Eventually he reached the outskirts of Kilcock, a market town twenty miles from the stud. A Chinese restaurant was still open, and from there he rang his brother to come and collect him. He had his brother drop him at the gates of Ballymany Stud. Not knowing what awaited him, he walked the quarter-mile through the fog and approached his house with caution.

His wife, fearful of the fate that could have befallen him, phoned a friend around midnight. The friend rang the Gardaí. It was just about then that her husband pushed open the back door and walked in. There was enormous relief that Jim had returned safely.

Later, Fitzgerald phoned Ghislain Drion. He explained what had happened and stressed that the Gardaí should be kept out of it. But they had already been in contact with Drion and had arranged to meet him at Ballymany. Drion told Fitzgerald that before he left he had phoned the syndicate's vet, Stan Cosgrove, and after some delay also managed to contact the Aga Khan in Switzerland.

The Frenchman's command of English was not perfect, and when he eventually arrived at the stud's yard and spoke to the local gardaí he had difficulty clarifying the exact purpose and composition of the syndicate. Someone in authority was needed. Drion phoned the Minister for Finance, Alan Dukes, who in turn got in touch with the Minister for Justice. The call went out for Chief Superintendent James Murphy of the Kildare district. Known as Jazzier to his men, he was the detective who had put Rose Dugdale behind bars. Murphy dressed quickly, donned his trademark trilby, scraped the frost off the windscreen of his car, and made for Ballymany Stud.

A man with an Irish accent telephoned Drion's home the next morning. Drion's wife informed the anonymous caller that her husband was at Ballymany Stud. But several hours were to pass before Drion was contacted at Ballymany. Whatever the reason for the delay, the same man did ring Drion several times over the next few days.

Chief Superintendent Murphy had little to work on and felt that a quick arrest was most unlikely. The kidnappers who vanished into the fog had picked their time well. With the breeding season about to start, the syndicate would want Shergar returned as soon as possible. Time was money, big money. With this as a background, Murphy sensed a reluctance from the syndicate to co-operate fully with the investigation. These were wealthy men, used to things being done their way. There was scepticism over the ability of the Gardaí to find the kidnappers. Some of the syndicate members were English and harboured suspicions about the Gardaí having pro-IRA sympathies. Nothing could be further from the truth, but years of reporting the Troubles by the English press had shaped opinions. Murphy had reservations of his own. He wouldn't have been greatly surprised if vital information was being withheld. He advised Drion that it would be a mistake to pay the ransom.

Jim Fitzgerald was taking time to recover. The morning after his ordeal he was still visibly shaken, and his recollections remained vague. The more questions that were put to him, the more confused he became. He had no way of assessing how much of this was due to genuine ill effects, the threats the kidnappers had made, or the fact that Drion had advised him to be circumspect. The unfortunate head groom suspected he would have to bear the blame. He was fearful that both his boss and the gardaí would think the kidnappers must have had a man 'on the inside'.

Word of Shergar's kidnap reached the media by midday. A pack of reporters and news crews began to book into local hotels. Reluctantly, the chief superintendent held an impromptu press conference on the steps of Newbridge Garda Station. The horse had been missing for just sixteen hours, yet Murphy had never witnessed anything remotely like the frenzy of the media. It was as though some member of a royal family had been abducted. Which, of course, was exactly what had happened, Murphy admitted to himself. In Ireland the love of horses runs deep. On top of everything was the prospect of worried owners taking horses out of training yards all over Ireland. It could cost the country millions in lost revenue. Murphy needed a breakthrough.

Twenty-four hours passed with no leads. Then forty-eight, and still nothing. The trail was stone cold. The gardaí and the syndicate were working along parallel lines, but driven by different priorities. The Aga Khan asked a member of the syndicate committee, Sir Jake Astor, to represent their interests. An ex-SAS soldier was employed to negotiate with the kidnappers. Astor explained, 'We were going to negotiate, but we were not going to pay.'

Proof of life was demanded. Polaroid pictures were duly delivered showing a horse next to the front page of a newspaper published on 11 February. This was not good enough, the negotiator insisted when next contacted. 'If you're not satisfied,' said the caller, 'that's it!' The 12 February telephone conversation was the final contact.

Speculation began to mount about what really happened. There was no definite proof that the Provisional IRA was involved, no code-worded statement claiming responsibility. A radio station reported a ransom demand they had received, but it proved to be a hoax. There was no shortage of sightings, all of them false. As the days passed, conspiracy theories were formulated and refined, and the sightings came from further away. Libya and Saudi Arabia were mentioned, Marseilles and the Channel Islands. The FBI was searching racing stables in the bluegrass state of Kentucky.

Murphy was disconsolate. It would have been a great case to crack as the end of his career drew near. Now he found himself being mocked by the press. He had been tagged 'Inspector O'Clouseau', and at one televised press conference a bunch of journalists mocked him by donning identical trilbies.

The story gradually faded from the front pages. Owners quickly booked alternative stallions for their mares. Security at Ballymany Stud was stepped up. Local people joked about stable doors and bolting horses. Every pub in Ireland had its 'expert' on the case. For the price of a pint, anyone still interested would be let in on the latest gossip; Shergar's sperm could be bought on the black market; the horse had been skilfully disguised and was racing again under another name; and a vet with a grudge against the Jockey Club had gelded the stallion.

Captain Seán Berry of the Equine Research Centre at Johnstown made a plea on behalf of the Irish Breeders' Council for the return of the horse. Thereafter, for several months he and his staff were flooded with crank calls from around the world.

The syndicate's vet, Stan Cosgrove, was contacted by a Co. Clare horse dealer, Denis Minogue, who claimed to have been taken blindfolded twice to the horse's hiding place. Requests for money were turned down. Rumours that a £100,000 advance was eventually paid and subsequently stolen have been strenuously denied.

The Shergar stud syndicate issued a statement blaming the IRA for the kidnap. Apparently the Provisionals were desperate to buy a supply of American Stinger missiles for deployment in south Armagh. The syndicate claimed that it had never seriously entertained paying any ransom. To have done so would have set a precedent and placed every stallion in Europe at risk.

Lloyd's, carrying the insurance on the horse, at first refused to pay, claiming that Shergar might still be alive; or if he was dead, he could have died after the policy had expired. Eventually a settlement was reached. The amount was not disclosed, but increased premiums were to cause problems for the horse-racing industry for years.

A television drama was produced in 1985, starring Stephen Rea and Niall Tóibín. Later on a feature film was made, *Shergar*, starring Mickey Rourke and Ian Holm. Both supplied their audiences with fictionalised accounts of what became of the horse.

A book was written by Colin Turner, racing correspondent of a London radio station. His premise was that the kidnap had been carried out by the Provisional IRA at the behest of Colonel Ghadafi of Libya, a sworn enemy of the Aga Khan. Turner expounded his theory when he was a guest on 'The Late Late Show'.

The death of a French bloodstock agent, Jean-Michel Gambet, gave rise to yet another theory. He was found with a gunshot wound to his head in a burning car in Kentucky. It appeared to be suicide, but forensic tests proved he had been murdered. The Mafia were suspected of killing Gambet for not repaying a loan he had taken to buy the Champion Stakes winner Vayrann from the Aga Khan. But would the Mafia have also sought revenge on this side of the Atlantic?

The truth may be more mundane. In 1992 Seán O'Callaghan, a leading Provisional-turned-informer and former chief of the Provisional IRA's southern command, claimed knowledge of what really happened. Speaking from inside Maghaberry Prison, Co. Antrim, he admitted that Shergar had indeed been kidnapped by the Provisional IRA. Kevin Mallon, a horse-racing enthusiast, was one of the team. It was he who had donned Jim Fitzgerald's old jacket in the stable block that cold February night. Coincidentally, Mallon was one of the three prisoners whose release Eddie Gallagher had demanded after the kidnap of Dr Tiede Herrema (chapter 3). According to O'Callaghan, Shergar quickly became distressed after leaving Ballymany Stud. He threshed about inside the horsebox, kicking and stamping. He became uncontrollable, a huge mass of sweating horseflesh, lashing hooves and snapping teeth. Inevitably, one of his legs was injured. The gang members panicked. No amount of soothing could calm the huge stallion. A decision was taken to shoot him. Photographs of the horse eating a carrot, his head next to a current edition of the *Irish Times*, were taken just before the unfortunate animal was killed. A pit was dug in the desolate mountains near Ballinamore, Co. Leitrim. The body was dragged into the pit and quickly covered over. No markers were left at the grave. While it is true that the Provisional IRA never claimed responsibility for stealing Shergar, it would be foolhardy to discount it. The innocent animal became just another name in the IRA's long list of missing victims.

Not everyone believes O'Callaghan's version of events, but some facts do lend credibility to it. The kidnappers insisted that the ransom be paid in £100 sterling notes. As no such denomination of note is printed by the Bank of England, many theorists argued this proved foreign involvement. But the £100 note is widely available in Northern Ireland, being printed by all four of the authorised banks. It is also difficult to accept that Shergar could have been smuggled out of Ireland. Not surprisingly, for months after the kidnap, any racehorse leaving Ireland for whatever purpose was subjected to a thorough inspection. Stories of the horse being taken to France aboard a fishing boat have to be discounted as unrealistic.

Forensic science perhaps provides the best basis for a verifiable conclusion to the Shergar story. In 1996 a laboratory took DNA samples from a dead horse suspected of being the missing stallion. The DNA profile was compared with that of hair samples taken from Shergar by two trophy-hunting veterinary students. There was no match.

In April 2000 Tommy Foley, a local councillor, found the remains of a large animal in a glen near Tralee, Co. Kerry. Two bullet holes in the skull prompted speculation that the remains could be those of Shergar. Des Leadon, head of clinical pathology at the Equine Centre, Co. Kildare, said that tests showed it was a horse, but not Shergar. The skull was that of a younger animal.

Shergar's racing prowess is still a barometer for greatness today. His Derby victory earned him a spot in the *Observer*'s 100 Most

Memorable Sporting Moments of the Twentieth Century. The Shergar Cup was inaugurated at Goodwood in 1999. Now run at Ascot, it is an annual contest between European jockeys and those from the rest of the world, the Ryder Cup of horse racing. Twenty years later, visitors to Ballymany Stud still ask which loose box was Shergar's—gone but not forgotten.

Seventeen years after the Shergar kidnap, there was to be another equine abduction in Ireland. This story failed to make as many headlines as that of the Derby winner, but it had a happier ending. In September 2000 two Shetland ponies were taken from their stable at Fossett's Circus grounds at Greenpark, Limerick. A ransom of £200 was demanded.

The ponies were taken on a Monday night, but following good work by the Roxboro gardaí the animals were found less than twenty-four hours later. During an investigation into criminal damage along the Hyde road, detectives questioned two men. An angry confrontation ensued, and the men started to hurl bricks at the gardaí. Superintendent William Keane gave a statement saying that both detectives had been injured during the disturbance. 'One of them sustained a serious shoulder injury after the cap of a pillar was thrown at him from an elevated position. The culprits fled. During a follow-up search, the missing ponies were discovered at the rear of the house.'

Marian Fossett expressed her gratitude to the people of Limerick who supported her family throughout their ordeal, saying, 'We're very thankful to everyone who helped us and we'd like to wish the two injured members a speedy recovery. We're deeply upset over the incident, but as always the show must go on.'

7

The Kirkpatricks, Richard Hill, and a Supergrass Trial

❖❖

The Irish National Liberation Army (INLA) was having a few problems in 1983. The new year was only five days old when the organisation was outlawed in the Republic. The proscription was in response to the pre-Christmas bomb attack of the Droppin' Well bar in Ballykelly, Co. Derry, when eleven British soldiers and six civilians were killed. It had already been declared an illegal organisation in the United Kingdom after the killing in 1979 of Airey Neave MP in the Houses of Parliament's underground car park in London.

Worse was to come. The organisation was being hit particularly hard by the use of supergrass witnesses in trials in Northern Ireland. Always a contentious strategy, the offer of immunity from prosecution in return for testimony against former comrades caused further controversy when Harry Kirkpatrick, twenty-five years old, the INLA second in command, turned supergrass informer.

Kirkpatrick, known as Harry-O, had himself been in custody since February 1982 on foot of evidence given by other INLA supergrasses, Jackie Grimley and Jackie Goodman. Originally arrested in connection with the murder of an RUC man in 1981 and for membership of the INLA, a list of other charges was soon to follow. He was eventually also charged with the murder of three soldiers from the Ulster Defence Regiment, a Territorial Army member, and William McCullough, the former commander of west Belfast UDA, shot dead outside his home in the Shankill Road in October 1981.

Such was the barrage of the seventy-plus charges against Kirkpatrick that it was widely assumed he would not be in a position to turn Queen's evidence, as other INLA members had done before him. So it came as a hammer-blow to the INLA leaders when in early May 1983 Kirkpatrick withdrew instructions from his defence solicitor, P. J. McGrory, who was representing most of the men accused on Grimley's evidence. At the same time he sent a letter to his wife informing her that she, along with his mother, should stop visiting him at Crumlin Road Jail, that he no longer wished to see them. The sudden reversal was the result of intense behind-the-scenes negotiations between the RUC, Northern Ireland's Director of Public Prosecutions, and the British Attorney-General. A deal had been struck: Kirkpatrick would still have to stand trial for his crimes, but the court would hand down a non-recommended life sentence, to be served in an English prison. He could expect to serve only a small fraction of his sentence before being a free man. Contributing to his decision to turn supergrass was Kirkpatrick's hatred of Goodman.

There was nothing extraordinary about the use of supergrasses. The London Metropolitan Police had used them for years to great effect, locking away many of the crime figures left after the Kray Twins era. Indeed in the early 1980s Belfast had seen a dramatic reduction in murders and sectarian crime following the first supergrass arrests. But not everyone was happy. The Provisional IRA were incensed and offered amnesty to informers who retracted, though few availed of their disingenuous offer. As more and more supergrass cases made the headlines, some members of the judiciary expressed concerns: the backlog of cases meant that those charged spent too long on remand—up to five years in one case; and the strategy was demeaning proud legal traditions. Some senior judges claimed that convicting on uncorroborated testimony reduced their role to little more than rubber-stamping the RUC's latest tactic in its war against terrorism.

The INLA's chief of staff, Dominic 'Mad Dog' McGlinchey, realised that Kirkpatrick's evidence would be catastrophic to the group. He was aware that treachery was a debilitating cancer eating away at the organisation, and he caustically described informers as 'supertouts' or paid perjurers and swore vengeance on any who betrayed him. However, Kirkpatrick was not some minor foot-soldier, considered expendable and to be used as cannon-fodder. He had been on murder sprees with some of the INLA's top gunmen, including the notorious 'Doctor Death' Gerard Steenson and Thomas 'Ta' Power. Upwards of thirty INLA men were facing hefty prison sentences because of Kirkpatrick. He had been the Belfast brigade's quartermaster and had conspired to plant a bomb on the route of the royal wedding of Charles and Diana. The INLA needed to apply serious leverage to make Kirkpatrick retract, while at the same time setting an example to other members who might be tempted to follow his lead.

On 12 May 1983 four armed and masked men knocked at the back door of the house of Harry Kirkpatrick's in-laws, Henry and Margaret Meenan, in Ballymurphy, west Belfast. When the door was opened they pushed their way in and seized Elizabeth (Liz) Kirkpatrick, the wife of the INLA supergrass, and dragged her outside to a waiting car. Only Liz and her sister Susan were at home when the men burst in.

Liz Neenan had married Harry Kirkpatrick in September 1981, and the INLA gunman Gerard Steenson had been one of the groom's guests. When her husband of four months was arrested in February 1982, Liz left the marital home at St Brendan's Walk in Divis Flats on the Lower Falls Road and moved back with her parents.

Liz was blindfolded and taken to an unidentified address, the first of several places where she was held captive. Several days passed before the INLA admitted it was holding Kirkpatrick's wife. In a statement the group said that the RUC and the British Attorney-General were responsible for the safety and well-being of Liz Kirkpatrick. They added: 'The INLA will not hesitate if the ultimate action is necessary against Mrs Kirkpatrick, in order to put an end to this practice.'

There was a precedent for the kidnapping of a close member of a supergrass's family. Patrick Gilmour, father of the Derry informer Raymond Gilmour, had been kidnapped on 18 November 1982 and was still missing. Years later it would emerge that Gilmour had been working for British intelligence. The RUC arrested thirteen people in sweeps connected to the kidnapping. Included were the chairman of the Irish Republican Socialist Party, Jimmy Brown, and the vice-chairman, Kevin McQuillan.

The preliminary hearing of those accused on Kirkpatrick's evidence, held two days after Elizabeth Kirkpatrick's abduction, collapsed in a courtroom riot. Kirkpatrick gave an obscene two-finger gesture to the accused and was overheard muttering threats to them. P. J. McGrory, defence solicitor of one of the accused, complained to the presiding magistrate, Maurice McHugh. The magistrate gave Kirkpatrick a stern rebuke.

The INLA issued a second statement in connection with the kidnapping: 'In this context we demand 1. That the RUC allow Harry Kirkpatrick to contact a solicitor. 2. That the authorities allow Harry Kirkpatrick out of solitary confinement and to mix with other Republican Socialist Prisoners.' The objective was clear: they wanted access to Kirkpatrick to make him retract.

Liz Kirkpatrick was soon on the move again. Two men drove her to a second house, where she was put in a bare room with a mattress on the floor. She had no idea where she was, but it had taken a considerable time to reach the new location. Her abductors did not tie her up, but they did keep a constant watch on her. She was given a change of clothing and some novels. Harold Robbins was the favoured author of her abductors.

Harry Kirkpatrick's mother visited her son at Crumlin Road Jail and asked him to retract statements accusing former INLA colleagues. He said only a few words to her and refused to give her a direct answer concerning any renunciation. Eileen Hill (formerly Eileen Kirkpatrick) had been an active member of the Relatives for Justice campaign, composed of the families of those accused by supergrasses. She had had to resign when her son became an informer.

Kirkpatrick was being held in the isolation annex of the prison, sharing open-cell accommodation with other republicans and loyalists waiting to give evidence. Kept together like this, they were able to offer support to each other at what was a very lonely time. The men in the annex enjoyed a relatively comfortable regime, with such perks as alcohol, television, and videotapes, conjugal visits and escorted trips outside the prison. Visits from family and friends were strictly supervised, and in some cases refused. The approval and support of his wife was often the deciding factor in a supergrass's commitment to see it through. If a wife did not approve, then her visiting rights were suspended.

Eleven days after the abduction, Liz Kirkpatrick's parents made a television appeal for the release of their daughter. Margaret Meenan, sixty-five years old, said that she had not been eating or sleeping properly since her daughter had been taken. Several other appeals were made to the kidnappers, including one from the parish priest who had officiated at the Kirkpatricks' wedding.

On 25 May, as the initial hearing was nearing completion, there was a mini-riot in the courtroom, begun by the accused. The RUC was forced to make several baton charges to quell the disturbance and restore order. Twelve police and seventeen of the accused were injured. All but two of the defence lawyers withdrew in protest. The two who remained claimed that the magistrate had acted improperly by accepting Kirkpatrick's signature on his deposition while the defendants were absent. The magistrate had ordered them to be locked in cells.

One week later the magistrate agreed with the lawyers' submission and stood down. A fresh hearing was bypassed when the Director of Public Prosecutions brought in a voluntary bill of indictment. The move infuriated the legal team for the defence. The Association of Socialist Lawyers issued a statement through P. J. McGrory, warning that 'respect for the legal system, which is the foundation of an ordered society, will be diminished.' The RUC was keen to prolong the effectiveness of the supergrass system. Deputy Chief Constable Charles Rodgers said that paramilitary organisations were 'in turmoil and very worried.' Not all the supergrasses were republicans, but the ranks of the IRA and the INLA had been particularly badly hit.

On 3 June, Kirkpatrick pleaded guilty to the charges against him, and Mr Justice McDermot's sentencing confirmed that a deal had indeed been struck with the Director of Public Prosecutions. Kirkpatrick received five life sentences, ten twenty-year sentences, thirty-five fifteen-year sentences, and twenty-seven lesser terms, all to run concurrently but without any minimum recommended term. His testimony had helped bring charges against eighteen people, and charges were pending against a further twenty. The authorities were expected any day to approve his move to an English prison. The threat to his life was a real one. Kirkpatrick frequently took communion inside the prison chapel, and a non-political prisoner was paid to slip the officiating priest a poisoned Eucharist wafer. The plan failed, as did the attempt to have Kirkpatrick shot with a gun smuggled into Crumlin Road Jail.

At a Relatives for Justice meeting, Susanne Bunting, widow of the IRSP member Ronnie Bunting, a notorious gunman from a staunchly loyalist family, claimed that she had been told by the RUC in Castlereagh holding centre that Harry Kirkpatrick would serve only seven years of his 1,000-year cumulative sentence.

The INLA was to raise the ante further. On 1 August it kidnapped Harry Kirkpatrick's sister, Diane, thirteen years old, and her stepfather, the Englishman Richard Hill, fifty years old. The kidnappers used Hill's car to transport the frightened victims. They were taken from their summer holiday cottage before dawn, though it was forty-eight hours before a telephone caller contacted the *News Letter* in Belfast and, quoting a recognised code-word, confirmed that the INLA had abducted them. The two-bedroom cottage was near Kilcummin, Co. Mayo, and overlooked Killala Bay. Richard Hill was well known in the area, because he had worked and lived in Crossmolina before moving to Belfast. The family would make return visits two or three times a year. Richard and Diane had been there for six days before their abduction.

Kenneth Littlejohn

Thomas Niedermayer

Dr Tiede Herrema

Press conference after the release of Dr Herrema

Father Hugh Murphy (left)

Ben Dunne

Ben Dunne with his solicitor, Noel Smyth

Shergar (Inpho)

Liz Kirkpatrick with her father, Henry Meenan

Don Tidey at the time of his rescue (Photocall Ireland)

*Don Tidey some years
following his ordeal
(Photocall Ireland)*

Dominic McGlinchey

Dominic McGlinchey's wife, Mary, and their two sons. She was murdered in 1987 in the course of a feud between the INLA and a breakaway faction called the IPLO.

The body of Dominic McGlinchey following his murder in Drogheda

Bernadette McAliskey attending the funeral of Dominic McGlinchey

The scene in Waterloo Road, Dublin, following the rescue of Jennifer Guinness

Jennifer Guinness and her husband, John, being driven away following her release

Jennifer Guinness and family members

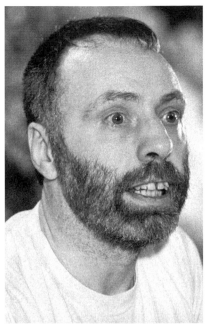

Brian Keenan

Brian Keenan's sisters,
Brenda and Elaine

John O'Grady

John O'Grady's luxurious house in south Co. Dublin

*Dessie O'Hare
(Photocall
Ireland)*

Chris Crowley

The morning after their removal, villagers noticed a broken pane of glass in the front door, which was lying ajar. There was no sign of a struggle or of the cottage having been ransacked. Hill's Ford Cortina was missing. No alarm was raised, as he had spoken to neighbours the night before and told them he intended going to Dublin the next day. The Gardaí were eventually alerted when RUC detectives contacted the local station in response to the tele-phone call to the newspaper. The Gardaí at first issued a denial that any kidnap had taken place. There were a lot of red faces in the local Garda station when they finally admitted that Diane Kirkpatrick and Richard Hill were missing. To add to the embarrassment, Superintendent Daniel Kennedy confirmed that the RUC had had previous contact with the Garda Síochána to apprise it of Richard Hill being a possible target of the INLA. A team of detectives was brought from Dublin, and forensic technicians examined the house. A thorough but belated search of the Killala area was made by forty gardaí, assisted by an Air Corps helicopter, but it was thought that the kidnappers would have left the area almost immediately.

Police north of the border stepped up their hunt for the missing teenager and her stepfather. When Liz Kirkpatrick was kidnapped there was a feeling among the security forces that her disappearance may not have been genuine. She was thought to have had strong republican sympathies and had vowed to divorce her husband when he had made it public that he was becoming the latest supergrass. But the kidnapping of a teenage girl was a heinous crime and one that the security forces were determined to resolve.

The INLA's snatch of Diane and her stepfather was partly in response to Harry Kirkpatrick's unfazed reaction to his wife's abduction. Dominic McGlinchey was certain that the RUC had convinced Kirkpatrick that Liz was in no danger. Kirkpatrick told a visitor that he suspected her of having an affair with one of the men he believed was behind it.

Diane Kirkpatrick and Richard Hill's initial fear that they were going to be killed slowly diminished as time passed, but they still remained very frightened. Diane suffered most; the stress of events in Belfast had already brought on a speech impediment. Her step-father had taken her off for a few weeks' holiday in the hope that her speech might recover away from the strain of living in Belfast. Any chance of that happening now had been well and truly dashed. Their captors had taken them some distance, and for one stage of the journey they had travelled in the boot of a car. They were being treated well enough, though tied up a lot of the time and under strict surveillance. Diane felt that most of the captors treated her considerately, except for one who she thought was nasty. They were not physically abused, though they soon found being locked up twenty-four hours a day very boring. There was little conversation between the prisoners and their captors.

Father Declan Caulfield, a Co. Mayo priest and family friend, appealed to the kidnappers to release the girl and her step-father. Richard Hill had worked at a power station in Co. Mayo, and Diane had been born and started school there. They had moved to Belfast when Richard Hill had sought employment as a theatre manager.

A week after the Mayo kidnap, a Provisional IRA unit attempted to kidnap the millionaire businessman Galen Weston from his home at Roundwood, Co. Wicklow (chapter 8). Three days later a Dublin solicitor, William Somerville, was kidnapped from his home in Enniskerry, Co. Wicklow. He spent twenty-four hours chained to a tree before being found by the gardaí. 1983 would prove a record year for kidnappings, north and south of the border, causing the resources of the RUC and the Garda Síochána to be stretched to their limit.

Ten days after the Mayo abduction the two hostages were moved to another location. That night they were allowed to take a short walk in the fresh air under close guard. The INLA had rented a holiday home in Gortahork, Co. Donegal, from a local business-man, Tony Kelly. Three men and a woman had paid a deposit of £30 to Kelly two weeks previously, and the day they took up residence they paid the balance.

Kelly had no reason to suspect that his property was being used as a safe house for the kidnap gang. Nothing about the men's behaviour caused him any anxiety. They were sometimes seen in off-licences, and local people noticed lights on in the house very late at night, though they thought nothing of it. An armed robbery at the Beach Hotel, Downings, Co. Donegal, was later attributed to the INLA kidnap gang.

At another secret location, Liz Kirkpatrick was having her waist-length hair cut short by her abductors. They claimed it would be too easily identified. Her freshly cut hair was then dyed. She was still being treated well, even being granted the opportunity to sunbathe. There were few luxuries, however, and little news of her husband.

The INLA continued to carry out terrorist operations during the summer. Gunmen attacked RUC checkpoints in Markethill, Co. Armagh, and Dungannon, Co. Tyrone. The Tyrone attack went badly wrong for them, and two INLA members, Brendan Convery and James Gerald Mallon, were killed during a shoot-out with the RUC. Dominic McGlinchey sent wreaths to both funerals.

With Diane and Richard settled into the house in Co. Donegal, the INLA, through their political wing, the Irish Republican Socialist Party (IRSP), issued a further statement to the *Irish Times*. The statement read: 'The INLA are engaged in a war of liberation against the crown forces. Those who inform betray this struggle and those who fight for freedom. If the only way that pressure can be put on these informers is by putting pressure on their families, so be it. Obviously we would prefer to be dealing with Kirkpatrick himself.' The statement went on to allege that the information provided by Kirkpatrick had been fabricated.

On 17 August, the sixteenth day of their ordeal, a chilling third statement was issued by the INLA, through a Belfast journalist, claiming that Diane Kirkpatrick and Richard Hill were to be executed 'in the very near future' if Harry Kirkpatrick did not immediately retract. Diane and Richard by chance overheard news of the death threat on the kidnappers' radio, and it caused them tremendous anxiety. Hill did what he could to comfort his step-daughter, telling her that the men could not be that brutal. He tried to remain positive, to keep both their spirits up.

Eileen Hill, Diane's mother, from the St James district of west Belfast, made an appeal on radio that evening for the release of her daughter and husband. She told a journalist afterwards that she had visited her son the previous week and that he had told her he thought the INLA was bluffing. She did not ask her son to retract his evidence, and he did not refer to it.

Diane and her stepfather were rescued in peculiar circumstances in the early hours of 18 August. When gardaí raided the Gortahork house, seven men fled out the back into the surrounding country-side. The gardaí did not give chase—fortuitously, it seemed, because the rear garden of the house had been booby-trapped with two blast bombs. Inside the house the gardaí found bomb-making equipment, timers, a rifle, and a machine gun. The INLA kidnappers hijacked four cars to make their escape. One car was stopped after a chase, during which shots were fired at pursuing gardaí, and two men were apprehended. They were taken to Letterkenny Garda Station for questioning. Later the same day a further four men were arrested outside Milford.

Richard Hill and Diane Kirkpatrick were kept at Letterkenny Garda Station from 5 a.m. to 9 p.m. They were interviewed at length, remaining inside the station all that time. A local GP, Dr Maureen Bonner-Skelly, examined the two kidnap victims, who were in reasonably good health after their seventeen days in captivity. The gardaí remained tight-lipped about the exact circum-stances of the early morning raid. They refused to talk to the press, and the door of the station was kept closed all day.

Diane and Richard were smuggled out of the Garda station and, accompanied by a party of journalists from Independent Television News, the Press Association, and Downtown Radio, taken to the nearby Three Ways Motel. Eileen Hill, who first heard the good news on a radio news bulletin, joined them there. After a short reunion they recorded a television interview.

Richard Hill, in fresh clothes and relishing a pint of lager, said that he and his stepdaughter had been treated well during their captivity and had not been physically abused, although they were locked up for twenty-three hours a day, which soon became very wearing. Diane said, 'I am just very tired and want to go home to bed. I was frightened most of the time.' Eileen Hill referred to how she had taken the news of their release when she said, 'I couldn't believe it. I thought they had got it wrong.' Due to celebrate her forty-sixth birthday the next day, Eileen Hill added, 'What a marvellous, marvellous birthday present!' After making a further appeal for the release of her daughter-in-law, she concluded, 'I do not understand why people do these things. Do they realise the hell they put people through? I have been living through hell, sheer hell.' The Hill family returned to Belfast and moved to a secret location so they could recuperate in private, away from the attention of the media.

The Gardaí, led by Chief Superintendent Pat O'Connor, continued their search of Co. Donegal for the remaining kidnappers. Seven further arrests were made, including that of John O'Hara, brother of the INLA hunger-striker Patsy O'Hara.

Two days after the Hills were released the INLA temporarily withdrew their threat on Liz Kirkpatrick's life after her father-in-law, Ronnie Kirkpatrick, made an appeal for her life to be spared. Harry Kirkpatrick's mother again visited Harry in Crumlin Road Jail. Her son had been refusing to see her for ten days but then sent word to her through another visitor. She thought this change of attitude meant he might be ready to retract. She admitted she lost her temper with him when it emerged that he had no such plans. He had lost a lot of weight and seemed very worried, she said.

The Meenans made another television appeal for the release of their daughter and called on their son-in-law to retract. Later that night Liz Kirkpatrick walked through the door of the house from which she had been abducted. Her captivity had lasted for thirteen weeks. She had been collected from a house by a Catholic priest, Father Denis Faul of Dungannon, Co. Tyrone, and driven to her parents' home in Ballymurphy, west Belfast. She was unharmed.

After a joyful reunion her father said, 'God has answered our prayers.'

Father Faul, who had played a prominent role in negotiating an end to the Maze hunger strikes in 1981, kept secret the exact circumstances of Liz Kirkpatrick's release. He did admit that he had had limited contact with her abductors. It was believed that he had driven through the night to a location he had been given, and where he found the missing woman in a bedroom. He asked her, 'Do you want to go home?' Neither Father Faul nor Liz Kirkpatrick offered any information about why she had been released. It is commonly supposed that after the liberation of her father-in-law and niece the INLA had lost their most powerful bargaining advantage. A statement telephoned to the *Irish Times* the day after Liz Kirkpatrick's return said: 'The Irish National Liberation Army released Liz Kirkpatrick, wife of informer Harry Kirkpatrick. It did so at the request of the Ard Comhairle of the IRSP.'

The Hill family decided in September that they had suffered enough stress and harassment, and they left Belfast, saying they would never be back.

The Gilmour family saw Liz Kirkpatrick's release as an optimistic sign that Patrick Gilmour might soon be free. Patrick, father of supergrass Raymond Gilmour, had been missing for nine months. He was eventually returned home, unharmed, on 26 September 1983.

The RUC had a brief interview with Liz Kirkpatrick over what it termed her alleged abduction. The RUC's stance of suspected duplicity appeared to be vindicated from comments made in an interview given to a radio news reporter. Liz Kirkpatrick condemned the actions of her husband and restated her determination to divorce him if he did not retract evidence given against other INLA members. She said she had gone willingly with her kidnappers, because she was scared. Claiming not to have noticed if they were armed, she also maintained that she had not formed any sort of relationship with them during her thirteen weeks of captivity. 'I was made to feel happy enough,' she commented.

Father Faul thought the kidnappers had tried to brainwash Liz

Kirkpatrick. He said, 'I heard the interviews she gave, but she would never have said anything like this before the kidnap. I believe they put things into her head.'

The welter of contradictory statements issued by the INLA over the summer—one claimed that Liz Kirkpatrick had been executed—proved that they were being pressed hard by the supergrass strategy. The rounding up of INLA men had left the group barely operational in Belfast and Derry, though still active in the rural areas of Cos. Armagh and Louth. Dominic McGlinchey had always been paranoid about informers and double-agents within the ranks of the INLA, and his suspicions were well founded. Although the Gardaí claimed to have rescued Diane Kirkpatrick and Richard Hill, the truth emerged later. Paddy Ward, one of the INLA men entrusted with guarding the couple, was working for British intelligence and had been instrumental in securing their freedom.

Ward had been a Provisional IRA volunteer until he was twenty-four, when he became disillusioned with their tactics and resigned. The Provisional IRA had tortured his brother, and his sister lost the baby she was carrying after being threatened at gunpoint. To protect his family, the young Ward needed access to arms and the protective shielding of belonging to a paramilitary force. The INLA could provide both. He was further encouraged to join their ranks by a British Army handler, persuaded that any intelligence he could provide would help to undermine the Provisional IRA.

By August 1983, Ward was the commander of the Derry brigade and a member of the INLA's Army Council. His rapid rise was a case of filling the shoes of men on the run or arrested on evidence supplied by supergrass testimony. In his two years in the INLA, Ward became close to Dominic McGlinchey. The chief of staff, also on the run after the Droppin' Well bombing, trusted nobody, but his organisation was being assailed from all directions and he could not do everything on his own. Ward was summoned to Co. Donegal to assist in guarding Diane Kirkpatrick and Richard Hill.

At first Ward was not too concerned with the safety of the two captives. He expected Kirkpatrick to be discredited, and ultimately

they would be set free. Although he managed to contact his handler on a few occasions, there was little the British could do in Co.
Donegal to free the captives. To have alerted the Gardaí would
have meant compromising his cover.

Then, on 17 August, McGlinchey called a meeting of the INLA
Army Council. Mary McGlinchey, his wife, was also in attendance,
and it was she who proposed that the two hostages held in Co.
Donegal should be killed. Her husband agreed, but Ward argued
against this. He said that killing a thirteen-year-old girl would generate too much bad publicity. Mary McGlinchey suggested, only partly
in humour, that the girl be drowned, so her death could be put down
to misadventure. Ward countered this by pointing out that Mary
McGlinchey was not a member of the Army Council and had no
right to be there. She silenced all debate by pulling out a gun and
firing a round into the ceiling. The vote for the hostages' execution
was carried by seven to two. The killing was to be carried out the
following morning; sleeping bags were to be prepared to receive the
bodies before dumping them at the border.

Ward contacted his handler and told him of the decision. It was
quickly agreed that during his next stint on guard he would take the
two hostages to a Garda station, asking them to pretend they had
escaped and to keep to that story no matter what. The 'escape' did
not go exactly according to plan. Ward waited until his six comrades were asleep before he led the hostages from the house. He had
earlier warned them to be dressed and ready to move quickly. He
drove them twenty miles to Letterkenny Garda Station. An alert
Garda patrol car followed Ward's Peugeot back to the bungalow at
Gortahork. Reinforcements arrived, and after a fifteen-minute gun
battle the INLA men escaped out the back. Presumably, Ward had
told the hostages to warn the gardaí about the booby traps at the
rear of the house.

Ward and another INLA man were picked up a couple of days
later and questioned at Letterkenny Garda Station. The Special
Branch detectives let it slip that the hostages had been assisted in
their escape. If the remaining members of the INLA gang were to

discover this, which seemed inevitable, then Ward was a dead man. Ward was not charged, and he retreated to Derry, where, surrounded by his closest allies, he felt beyond McGlinchey's reach.

McGlinchey sought revenge on another man he suspected of helping to free the hostages. Gerard Barkley's naked body was found near Redhills, Co. Cavan, on 26 October 1983. He had been shot in the head. Detectives believe that McGlinchey had personally fired the fatal round. He suspected Barkley because Kirkpatrick had not provided any testimony against him, although there would have been ample evidence to do so. 'Sparky' Barkley had been very close to Kirkpatrick, and any possibility of Kirkpatrick having a last-minute change of heart ended with Barkley's cold-blooded murder.

Two days later, when Ward was attending a brother-in-law's wedding in Co. Donegal, four INLA men abducted him from the White Strand Motor Inn. He was taken in the boot of a car to Bailieborough, Co. Cavan. The McGlinchey husband-and-wife team tortured him for three days. He was beaten badly about the head, his fingers smashed, his ribs broken, and he was held down on a hot stove, burning his back, buttocks, and feet. Ward admitted nothing but was sentenced to death after a speedy 'court-martial'. McGlinchey told Ward in an offhand manner that he was probably innocent—no-one could have held out against so much pain—but he would still have to die, since he might seek revenge if he was allowed to live.

Later that night Ward managed to overpower a sleeping guard and made his escape. He went straight to Bailieborough Garda Station and confessed to the kidnapping of Diane Kirkpatrick and Richard Hill. He knew that the only safe place would be in custody. Sentenced to three years' imprisonment, he declined to use his role in the hostages' escape in mitigation, as members of his family were now being held by the INLA to discourage him from turning supergrass. He served a little over two years, in solitary confinement at his own request. On his release, Detective-Sergeant Kevin Carty arranged a passport for him, and the prison chaplain provided a plane ticket to Canada. He built a new life for himself there, until the Canadian authorities found out about his terrorist history. For a while Ward was something of a *cause célèbre* in Canada as he fought deportation, but eventually he was returned to Ireland. He now lives outside Ireland.

The trial of the INLA men and one woman, Michelle Dorrien, Kirkpatrick's sister, charged on information supplied by him, finally went ahead in April 1985. The defence team tried to destroy Kirkpatrick's credibility rather than challenge his evidence. It proved to be the weaker strategy. They also tried to show that Kirkpatrick cared for no-one but himself. Desmond Boal QC probed Kirkpatrick during cross-examination about why he had chosen to give evidence against his sister. 'Is there any other social or human relationship that exists at the moment that you value?' Boal asked.

'I don't understand the question, my lord,' Kirkpatrick said.

'I'm sorry if it appears to be a difficult one,' Boal mocked.

Sentencing was pronounced on 16, 17 and 18 December. The Crown Court was crowded with the twenty-seven accused, mostly from Belfast and Armagh, and more than seventy prison officers as Mr Justice Carswell read his judgment. There were two hundred charges in all relating to forty-two terrorist incidents. During the second day of the judgment the court was cleared after noisy outbursts from the accused and their relatives in the public gallery. In the lunch-hour recess, relatives of the accused staged a demonstration in front of the court, chanting slogans and blocking traffic. All but two of the twenty-seven were found guilty and received sentences varying from five life sentences to a suspended two years. Mr Justice Carswell described the task of dealing with the case as an onerous one, given the multiplicity of the charges and the volume of the evidence. He found Kirkpatrick to have been a cool, composed and courteous man and a credible witness. He had been in the witness box for twenty-six days of the 100-day trial. Of Steenson the judge said, 'Of all those who have appeared before me he is undoubtedly the most dangerous and sinister terrorist—a ruthless and highly dedicated, resourceful and indefatigable planner of criminal exploits, who did not hesitate to take a leading part in assassinations and other crimes.'

The convicted men served only a year of their sentences. Kirkpatrick was the thirtieth supergrass, the last in a queue of informers who had seen three hundred people charged with terrorist offences. The death-knell of the supergrass strategy was sounded two days before Christmas 1986 when twenty-four of the men sent to prison on Kirkpatrick's testimony were released by the Court of Appeal. The Lord Chief Justice made it clear that most of the men he was freeing were probably far from innocent, but the justice system had been ill served by the scramble for convictions. Thomas 'Ta' Power would be murdered a month later in the first wave of a power struggle and revenge killings sparked by the supergrasses. Steenson was killed two months after that. The INLA had split into two camps, and there were a lot of old scores to settle (see chapter 11). Another ten men would be killed before a truce was called.

The Special Criminal Court in Dublin tried Mary McGlinchey in 1986 for her part in the kidnapping. Despite the fact that her fingerprints were discovered at the Gortahork house, she was acquitted. She was shot dead on 31 January 1987. Her husband survived a gun attack in 1993 but was killed in February 1994. Bernadette McAliskey spoke at his funeral and described McGlinchey, who had admitted to more than thirty murders, as 'the finest republican of them all.'

On 20 February 2002 Colm Peake, originally from Andersonstown, Belfast, who had been given a life sentence in the Kirkpatrick supergrass trial only to be released a year later, walked into Fitzgibbon Street Garda Station, Dublin, and, in front of a garda and a civilian, shot himself in the head. He had been on the run from theft charges and had been drinking heavily beforehand. Rushed to the Mater Hospital, he was placed on a life-support machine but died thirty-six hours later.

8

Don Tidey and the Murders at Derrada Wood

For the forces of law and order there can be a slim margin of chance between the successful resolution of a kidnap and having it go disastrously wrong. Don Tidey's kidnap was one of the latter. The sequence of events that make up the Tidey kidnap story started well enough for the Garda Síochána but ended with a double tragedy.

Galen Weston was one of the wealthiest businessmen in the world. A Canadian resident in Ireland, he was the head of the supermarket giant Associated British Foods, which owned Quinnsworth in Ireland. Other Irish interests of Weston's were the Penney's fashion chain and the Brown Thomas department store. His name had been on the Provisional IRA kidnap list for years. They made their move in August 1983 at Weston's home in Roundwood, Co. Wicklow.

The attempted abduction proved catastrophic for the active service unit that had been handed the task. Since the kidnapping of Shergar the Gardaí had been keeping round-the-clock surveillance on known members of the Provisional IRA. They soon discovered that something big was being planned. Solid facts were hard to come by—a scrap of information here, a whisper heard somewhere else. Then came a lucky break. An informer provided the final pieces of the intelligence jigsaw when he supplied vital details of the planned Weston kidnap.

On the evening of the chosen day, thirteen armed Special Branch detectives took up their positions at the Weston house. When the terrorists entered the courtyard the trap was sprung and an order was given for the subversives to lay their guns on the ground. Who fired the first shot is not known, but in seconds the courtyard was being raked with gunfire. Four IRA men were wounded and captured. Three others escaped. (One of those captured and sentenced was Nicky Kehoe. Almost twenty years later, in the 2002 general election, Kehoe, now a member of Dublin City Council, was to stand as a Sinn Féin candidate in the Taoiseach's constituency of Dublin Central, narrowly failing to win a seat.) Weston and his wife, Hilary, were in London at the time, attending a polo match at Windsor.

The Shergar débâcle and the Roundwood ambush had left the Provisional IRA smarting. It was decided that Quinnsworth was going to have to pay. A second kidnap was sanctioned, and on the morning of 24 November 1983 they made their move.

Don Tidey was the target. A 49-year-old Englishman of Scottish origin who had come to live and work in Ireland in the late 1970s, he was chief executive of the Quinnsworth supermarket chain and Galen Weston's right-hand man. He lived in Rathfarnham, Co. Dublin, with his thirteen-year-old daughter Susan and two sons, Andrew, aged twenty-two, and Alistair, nineteen. His wife had died from leukaemia some years previously.

It was still dark when Tidey and his daughter left their dormer bungalow that morning. He slid behind the wheel of his Daimler saloon and switched on the headlights to start his regular school run to his daughter's school, Alexandra College in Milltown. They had travelled only a short distance when they saw that the entrance of their cul-de-sac was blocked. Two cars, an Escort and a Cortina, one with a revolving blue light, formed a roadblock at the junction of Woodtown Way and Stocking Lane. A man dressed as a garda flagged down Tidey's car. Forewarned to be vigilant after the failed abduction of Weston, Tidey sensed that something was not quite right and tried to reverse away. But his son Alistair, who had been following his father from their home in his Fiat, was blocking his path.

The man in Garda uniform approached the Daimler and levelled a sub-machine gun at Tidey's head. Two male accomplices pulled Susan and Alistair from the cars, firing a number of shots into the air. Susan started to scream. Tidey was manhandled into the Cortina and whisked away at high speed. His car was also driven off but soon abandoned, its tyres slashed. The kidnappers drove at high speed along the steep and twisty Oldcourt Road towards the junction at Bridget Bourke's Old Bawn Tavern, Tallaght. They clipped another car but did not stop. They skirted the rush-hour traffic and headed towards Maynooth.

Alistair and Susan lost little time in raising the alarm. Chief Superintendent Patrick Culligan headed the hunt. The Special Branch had their suspicions right from the start about who was involved. The main suspects were members of the gang suspected of snatching Shergar and the three gang members who had escaped from the ambush at Roundwood. It was also thought that some of those involved might be from those still on the run after the mass escape of thirty-eight prisoners from the Maze Prison, Co. Antrim in September. The army was called in, and a nationwide manhunt was launched.

A number of Dublin pirate radio stations broke the news of the kidnap, thus making a news blackout futile. It was the eighth kidnap in Ireland that year, only two of which had been carried out by subversive organisations. The Gardaí successfully resolved five of them, the ransom was paid in another two and the victims released, and a Co. Louth butcher managed to escape his kidnappers. Although not a common crime in Ireland, the cost of underwriting kidnap and ransom policies was being reviewed by Lloyd's at the time of Tidey's abduction.

The task force set up a few years previously to handle such events as hijacking and kidnapping was overstretched, as the notorious INLA leader Dominic McGlinchey was also being hunted. McGlinchey had admitted supplying the weapons used for the triple murders at the Mountain Lodge gospel hall in Darkley, Co. Armagh, a few days before the Tidey kidnap. He had jumped bail and gone on the run a year previously, shortly before the Supreme Court had ordered his extradition to the North to face charges of murdering an elderly woman in Co. Antrim. The task force had recently been slimmed down in response to budget constraints, though Dr Michael Woods, the Fianna Fáil opposition spokesman on justice, had demanded that it be restored to its full complement.

Throughout Ireland houses were raided, derelict buildings checked, and cars and lorries stopped. Isolated farm buildings were searched, and surveillance on known activists was stepped up. An all-ports warning meant delays for travellers. It seemed that the country was being turned inside out.

The cars used in the kidnapping were quickly found at Connolly's Folly, Maynooth. The Escort had been burnt out, but the beige Cortina, stolen the night before in Newcastle West, Co. Limerick, was unscathed. Attention was now switched to three other vehicles: a yellow Mini, a red Transit van, and a brown Renault

The Minister for Justice, Michael Noonan, told the Dáil that the Government was opposed to the payment of any ransom. He said: 'The payment of ransom would be likely to encourage others to resort to the same tactic. The level of money usually sought by way of ransom is such that the Government could not acquiesce in the idea of it falling into the hands of paramilitary or other subversive groups. The probable cost in terms of human life and suffering does not need to be spelled out.'

The early focus of the hunt was Tralee, Co. Kerry. A man and a woman were arrested and held for questioning under the Offences Against the State Act. They were released without charge after seventy-two hours. Two Navan men were also arrested and released without charge. Speculation mounted that the Provisional IRA were in negotiations with Associated British Foods in England. Ray McSherry, the security manager of Quinnsworth, was about to board a chartered Avair plane to England when gardaí intercepted him. It emerged that he had been under surveillance since the kidnap. The gardaí questioned him for twelve-and-a-half hours at Whitehall Garda Station, Dublin, after which McSherry drove to the head office of Quinnsworth in Dún Laoghaire. The Gardaí had made strenuous efforts to prevent the payment of any ransom in both the Ben Dunne and Shergar kidnaps.

On 1 December the three Tidey children made a heartfelt television appeal for the safe release of their father. Andrew Tidey said: 'We have now had to live a week without my father, and the strain has been quite terrible. The greatest worry is the silence. Every time the phone rings, your hopes are raised, and then when it isn't the kidnappers, they are dashed.' Their father, it was revealed, was a health and fitness enthusiast and would have been able to cope well with a period of captivity. Susan was, with the help of her friends, making a full recovery from the shock she had suffered.

Days passed without any significant progress in the hunt for the kidnappers. The Gardaí, painfully aware of criticism of ineptitude, stepped up the number of searches. No city, town or village escaped their scrutiny. Arrests continued to be made throughout the country, but more often than not the people would later be released without charge. William Kelly, a forty-year-old painter from Tralee, Co. Kerry, was not so fortunate. He had been arrested soon after the attempted hijacking of a Mercedes car and during questioning admitted his part in falsely imprisoning Tidey early in the abduction. Detectives charged him, but unfortunately he could not or would not supply any information on Tidey's whereabouts. An attempt to extract money as a result of the abduction was made in Dublin, but it was a hoax and was quickly discounted by the Gardaí.

On 2 December, Garry Weston, Galen's brother and chairman of Associated British Foods, confirmed that a £5 million ransom had been demanded, the same amount the Provisional IRA had intended to ask for Galen Weston's release in its failed kidnap attempt. Garry Weston said that no ransom would be paid. A Special Branch officer had travelled to London to help in co-ordinating the search in Britain that Scotland Yard had initiated. The rules for this involvement were established in 1973 when West German police and the RUC helped monitor a London suburb where it was suspected that a ransom was to be handed over.

Almost inevitably, the hunts for Dominic McGlinchey and

Tidey were to cross. The INLA leader overpowered two gardaí in Carrigtohill, Co. Cork, and left them bound and gagged. The gardaí had called to a house as part of the search for Don Tidey. The next day Jack Marrinan, secretary of the Garda Representative Association, said that gardaí were ill equipped and poorly trained for the searches they were undertaking. His demand for more bullet-proof vests and better radio communications was an attempt to publicise the inadequate equipment and protocols within the Garda Síochána, a shortcoming that would end in tragedy only days later.

A fortnight after the kidnap the Church of Ireland Archbishop of Dublin, Dr Henry McAdoo, appealed for the release of Tidey. The appeal was made during a special service of communion at Alexandra College. The Catholic Archbishop of Dublin, Dr Dermot Ryan, requested prayers for his safe return. A nightly vigil was being held at Tidey's own place of worship in Whitechurch, Co. Dublin. Rev. Horace McKinley described Tidey as a devout member of his congregation and a weekly communicant. Members of the kidnapped man's family regularly attended the vigil.

Appeals were being made to the kidnappers almost daily. Dr Tiede Herrema broadcast an appeal on the evening television news. He and his wife had recently returned to Ireland and were living in Dublin. The Irish Congress of Trade Unions called on those holding Tidey to release him unharmed. Séamus Brennan, a Fianna Fáil deputy for Mr Tidey's constituency, put down a special notice question in the Dáil asking for reassurances from the Government that everything possible was being done to secure his release.

Fresh appeals came soon after a second demand for the ransom had been made. No details were revealed about the new contact, but the Gardaí revealed at the same time that a Polaroid picture of the victim holding up a recent edition of an evening newspaper had been delivered to the head office of Associated British Foods a few days after the kidnap. The *Evening Herald* that Tidey was holding was taken as evidence that he was still in Ireland.

It was small wonder the security forces kept coming up empty-handed in their searches. The Provisional IRA, learning from

previous experiences, had made ingenious and meticulous prepar-
ations to conceal their hostage. Tidey was in fact being held captive
in Derrada Wood, a plantation of young trees spread across a slope
three miles north-west of Ballinamore, Co. Leitrim. Set in a wild
and desolate landscape, Derrada Wood was less than twelve miles
south of the border.

Co. Leitrim's population had never recovered from the twin evils
of the Great Famine and emigration. There had been little investment, and unemployment was high. Population density was low, and
the area was filled with abandoned cottages. The region was much
favoured by the Provisional IRA as a training ground, not least because
of a core of diehard republican supporters among the local population.

Deep in the wood a pit had been dug, measuring 5 feet by
14 feet and 5 feet deep. The floor was covered with a carpet of twigs,
briars, and bracken. A section of a polythene silage cover provided
shelter from the all-too-frequent rain in that county. Brambles and
ferns camouflaged the polythene from casual observation. This den
was Tidey's home for three weeks. The site had been well chosen: he
could have yelled his head off and no-one would have heard him.
Too overgrown to be a favourite of dog-walkers, the wood was visited
from time to time by Customs and Excise officers checking for poitín
stills. Garda manpower was minimal in the area, the only patrol
vehicle having been withdrawn because of budget cutbacks a few
days before the Tidey kidnap.

Comfort was not a priority for the kidnappers. No lighting or
heat was supplied. A bale of hay was the only seating, but basic provisions were supplied. There was a small cardboard box containing
canned food, tinned vegetables, drinking water, and a few cans of
beer. Tidey was made to wear a blindfold, incorporating makeshift
earplugs, at all times, a blue boiler-suit, and a balaclava. He had not
been allowed to shave since his snatch. His kidnappers held their
conversations out of earshot, and Tidey had not spoken in anything
louder than a whisper for days.

In early December the Gardaí received intelligence from the
RUC Special Branch that Tidey was being held in the vicinity of

Ballinamore. Extra manpower was brought in and increased surveillance of known sympathisers ordered, a strategy that was to pay immediate dividends. A leading Provisional IRA figure was spotted in the district. The sighting of a second activist not far from the area seemed to corroborate the RUC intelligence. The theory was that the two might have been bringing provisions to the gang holding Tidey.

Chief Superintendent McNally was highly experienced in the cat-and-mouse tactics involved when hunting terrorists in the border counties. He consulted Commissioner Larry Wren, chief negotiator during the Monasterevin siege, and 'Operation Santa Claus' was drawn up. It was approved on Tuesday 13 December, allowing a mere forty-eight hours for hectic logistical fine-tuning before the commissioner himself travelled to Co. Leitrim to witness its commencement on Friday morning.

The scale of Operation Santa Claus was unprecedented—an intensive search of a ten-mile radius of countryside around Ballinamore, an area greater than three hundred square miles. Ten search teams would be involved. Each consisted of an inspector, two sergeants, a local garda, two Special Branch detectives with knowledge of border intelligence, seven detectives armed with Uzi submachine guns, and a group of ten cadet gardaí temporarily seconded from the Garda Training College at Templemore, Co. Tipperary. A soldier armed with a rifle would accompany each group as an extra safeguard. McNally was taking no chances. The men they were going up against would not hesitate to shoot their way out if they were cornered. He wanted the kidnap resolved without loss of life.

In line with the festive title of the operation, the search units were code-named Rudolf 1 to 10. Their task was daunting: to search upwards of 200,000 acres of the wildest woodland and deepest bog in Ireland. Ballinamore Garda Station was the base and each unit would be in constant radio contact. The men making up these search units were bussed in on Thursday night and Friday morning, 15 and 16 December.

Among the eager recruits was Peter Gary Sheehan, an unmarried 23-year old from Co. Monaghan, the son of Detective-Garda Jim

Sheehan, who was stationed in Carrickmacross. Cadet Garda Sheehan was to be part of Rudolf 5. The military escort of the unit was Private Patrick Kelly from Moate, Co. Westmeath. An experienced soldier, the 36-year-old married man served with the 6th Infantry Battalion and had recently completed his fourth tour with the United Nations peace-keeping force in Lebanon. The youngest of his four children was just eleven weeks old.

It was hard for Gary Sheehan to hide his enthusiasm. Five weeks from graduating at Templemore, he was being given the chance to do some real police work. It would be a relief to leave the classroom and breathe some fresh air for a change.

A pre-emptive round-up of known republicans around Ballinamore on the Friday morning signalled the start of Operation Santa Claus. One of the first Special Branch raids was on a public house. The publican was John Joe McGirl, a committed republican and vice-president of Provisional Sinn Féin. One of the founder-members of the Provisionals' Army Council in 1969, he had served several prison terms, including one for transporting munitions in a hearse. He was taken to Castleblayney Garda Station, where three other Ballinamore republicans were soon to join him.

By this time Rudolf 5, under the command of Detective-Inspector Bill Somers, had completed its first sweep and was about to begin its second. The countryside around Derrada Wood had few inhabitants, but the Priors were one of the families resident in the area. Bernie Prior ran a joinery workshop; his brother Hugh was a farmer from Drumdowna Lane; and Joseph McGirl, a nephew of the publican John Joe, did casual work at the joinery.

A man answering Joseph McGirl's description was seen running from a field within the Rudolf 5 search area. He was spotted again at lunchtime and was arrested. A short time later, a line of armed gardaí stopped Hugh Prior's car, and he too was arrested under section 30 of the Offences Against the State Act. The gardaí decided to use Prior's own vehicle, a blue Cortina, to transport him to Ballinamore Garda Station by way of the road that skirted Derrada Wood.

At about 2 p.m. the men in Rudolf 5 began their sweep of Derrada Wood. The going was tough, the searchers having to hack their way through dense undergrowth. The young trees had not had their lower branches removed, nor had any trees been felled for the purposes of thinning the plantation. Two gardaí and a soldier on the western flank came upon a huddled figure. Before they could call for reinforcements, Gary Sheehan appeared from the opposite direction. The garda cadet came to a low ridge of earth some fifteen yards in front of him. A man dressed in military camouflage and boots was hunkered down next to the low ridge, apparently cleaning dirt from his rifle, which was similar to the army's FN self-loading weapon.

Patrick Kelly, next in line to Sheehan, heard the cadet challenge the crouching figure. A Garda sergeant was the first to react and called for assistance when he saw that the crouching man was not a soldier. His challenge unanswered, Sheehan turned towards Kelly, and both were mown down by a burst of automatic fire. Sheehan was struck in the head and died instantly. The armed members of Rudolf 5 took cover and returned fire. Another cadet, Joseph O'Connor, heard what sounded ominously like a death rattle come from his colleague. Private Kelly had fallen next to a clump of saplings. He too was dead.

A civilian witness, Peter Fee, cycling to Derrada Post Office, heard the gunfire and noticed a flurry of military activity. He reported hearing a loud bang a few seconds after the sound of the gunfire had faded. What he had heard was a stun-grenade, which had been pitched towards the nearest members of Rudolf 5. The four Provisional IRA kidnappers made the most of the opportunity and ran off in two directions. Two of them seized three members of the search team, two gardaí and a soldier, and, pushing the new hostages ahead of them, disappeared into the thick undergrowth. The other two men ran to a nearby house, where they found a blue Opel Kadett with the keys in the ignition.

Garda Cadet O'Connor spotted a bearded man in combat dress wriggling on his stomach on the earth in some undergrowth. He was signalling frantically and hissing, 'Tidey—hostage.'

When the kidnappers reached the edge of the wood they dis-
armed their three hostages and released them. Breaking cover, they
quickly overpowered two soldiers who had been providing extra
support for Rudolf 5. From the crown of the small hill the fleeing
duo now had a clear view of the road skirting it. The first vehicle to
come along was the blue Opel Kadett driven by their comrades. It
was waved down, and the two clambered in. Further along the road
an alert garda realised what was happening and drove his patrol car
across the road to form a roadblock.

Don Tidey had just risen cautiously to his feet when a garda and
a soldier seized him. They were certain they had caught one of the
kidnappers. He was roughly forced to the ground and made to put
his hands on the back of his neck. Body-searched and stripped of
his shoes, he was then marched out of the wood to be presented to
Bill Somers, the inspector in command of Rudolf 5. Detective-
Garda Dónal Kelleher was standing next to the inspector.

Nearby, the Opel slewed to a halt at the makeshift roadblock,
and there was a volley of shots from the car. Detective-Garda
Kelleher, realising who the barefoot prisoner was, threw himself in
front of Tidey. Bullets ripped into the courageous detective's legs.
The gardaí and soldiers returned fire.

It was at that moment that Prior's blue Cortina came along the
road. In the confusion there was a 'friendly fire' incident. Bullets
fired by gardaí and soldiers raked the car. Hugh Prior's neck was
grazed by a round that shattered the rear window of his vehicle. 'I'm
shot! I'm shot!' he shrieked. 'Don't fire. There are gardaí and
a prisoner in this car,' yelled one of the escorts from inside the
vehicle. The shooting slackened off. The kidnappers abandoned
their vehicle and ran off, pinning down pursuers with sprays of
automatic fire. Chief Superintendent McNally realised that, with
his men spread over a wide area in their different units, it would be
a couple of hours before the area could be effectively sealed off and
an organised pursuit mounted—time he did not have. The kidnap
gang would be long gone.

As the dust settled, the Garda command began to take stock of the situation. It was far from their finest hour. On the plus side, Don Tidey had been freed; but at what cost? Two men were dead, another shot and a civilian wounded while in Garda custody. Several of the Garda cadets were displaying symptoms of post-traumatic stress disorder. The few days in the fresh air, so eagerly anticipated, had become a nightmare.

McNally spoke to Don Tidey in Cavan later that afternoon. A local doctor had already examined him. Apart from shock, nervous exhaustion, and superficial cuts and bruises sustained when he had been wrestled to the ground, the freed man was unharmed after twenty-three days of captivity. Tidey and McNally talked at length in an upstairs room.

The British Prime Minister, Margaret Thatcher, congratulated the Taoiseach on the rescue of Don Tidey. She added: 'I understand that great gallantry was displayed by those who released Mr Tidey. I offer my congratulations to all concerned. At the same time I am deeply saddened to hear that two members of the Irish security forces have been killed and others injured in the course of the operation. I would like to convey my deepest sympathy, through you, to the families and colleagues of those killed. I send, to the injured, my best wishes for their early recovery.'

Shortly after 1 a.m. on Saturday morning another accidental wounding near Ballinamore added to the Gardaí's woes. John Wrynne, twenty-seven years old, was returning home with his wife when he was struck in the head by a single bullet fired by a soldier after Wrynne had passed through an army checkpoint. Six rounds were fired. His car went out of control and crashed. He was rushed to Richmond Hospital, Dublin, where he underwent emergency three-hour surgery to save his life.

Don Tidey, flanked by his three children, held a press conference on Saturday afternoon, close to the scene of his abduction. He explained how he had coped with the ordeal. 'The only thing you can do is what I learned to do: to take account of my circumstances and count my blessings. The one thing you do not do is anticipate, since looking forward only made you more aware of the uncertainty.'

Deprived of most sensory stimulation, he concentrated on whether it was warmer than the day before or less wet than the day before that. He paid tribute to the Gardaí and the army and said that any feelings of elation he had at the moment were tinged with sadness for those who on this beautiful day were saddened by the loss of their loved ones. He did not take questions from reporters. On Sunday the six men arrested on the pre-emptive sweep were released without charge.

Patrick Kelly was the first soldier to be killed in action in the Republic since the foundation of the state. He was buried in his home town, Moate. A cold wind blew across the Tobber graveyard as a unit of soldiers shouldered their weapons and came to attention. The coffin was draped in the Tricolour. At the request of the young soldier's widow, Cathrina, no volley of shots was fired. The Bishop of Ardagh and Clonmacnoise, Dr Colm O'Reilly, told the congregation: 'It is Patrick and those like him, who served and who continue to serve the cause of peace, who are entitled to be called the great patriots of our own time.'

Gary Sheehan was laid to rest at St Joseph's in Carrickmacross. The Christmas lights were turned off as a mark of respect. Thousands attended the funeral. Gary's parents, Jim and Margaret, together with their other children, Gráinne, David, and Jennifer, sat in front of the altar next to the coffin. A tiny posy of carnations and freesias in a small wicker basket was placed next to Sheehan's coffin. A note read: 'To Gary from your wee girl, Gráinne Hunt.' President Hillery and the Taoiseach, Dr FitzGerald, attended the funeral.

'What is happening in our country', asked the Bishop of Clogher, Dr Duffy, 'when human life is so expendable?' He told the congregation that the use of guns had been glamourised in Irish history, but guns were wasteful instruments of hatred, and all acts of violence delayed the coming of peace.

For days afterwards the area around Ballinamore and Ardmoneen was the scene of intense army and Garda activity. The army's Rangers unit was brought in to assist, their blackened faces bringing a surreal look to the countryside. Hopes for an early capture were raised when a pool of blood was found near a bridge at Cornlea, near Derrada. The mood was ugly among the men on patrol. If any of the gang were to be caught, they could not expect any kid-glove treatment. Some of the gardaí directed their aggression towards the press in the wake of the damning criticism of the Garda Síochana.

Six days after Tidey was freed, three armed men managed to escape from a house in Claremorris, Co. Mayo. The focus of the hunt had been switched to the surrounding area after an incident on the Tuesday night near Ballycroy, forty miles west of Ballina. Three gardaí stopped a Mercedes at Ballyveeney bridge. A woman was driving, and there was another female passenger and three men in the car. The gardaí were overpowered and tied up by the three armed men, who then escaped in Sergeant O'Rourke's car. It took the gardaí three hours to free themselves and emerge from the bushes where they had been concealed. Their car was quickly found, its tyres slashed. Checkpoints and house searches were swiftly begun, and it was during a search of nearby houses the next day that the three men, carrying automatic rifles, fled from what was thought to be an unoccupied bungalow. Shots were fired in the air, but the men escaped into the fields. They did not return fire. Gardaí believe that the three had been tipped off about the searches, and they arrested the owner of the bungalow. Soldiers from Mellows Barracks, Galway, and Custume Barracks, Athlone, were drafted into the area, and gardaí were confident that the gunmen would not escape the cordon that had been established. Meanwhile the searches and checkpoints in the Ballinamore area were relaxed.

The Mercedes was found in Charlestown, sixty miles away, at the house of its owner. She was taken in for questioning but was later released. Unfortunately for the searching gardaí, there were no further sightings or reports of car hijackings or car thefts in the following days. The conclusion drawn was that the gunmen had access to another vehicle, in which they fled the area. Countless searches and checkpoints produced no results. It would be Christmas Eve before the Gardaí publicly admitted defeat. 'We are bitterly disappointed that they have got away,' said Superintendent Vincent Smyth, co-ordinator of the manhunt.

In the new year, after meticulous forensic examination of Derrada Wood, the Gardaí released the names of four men they wanted to interview in relation to the kidnapping of Don Tidey. Three of them were escapers from the Maze Prison. Brendan McFarlane was the most notable, because it was he, as officer commanding the Provisional IRA prisoners, who had led the mass escape.

Heavy pressure was brought to bear on the Government to proscribe Sinn Féin after what happened in Derrada Wood. Charles Haughey, the Fianna Fáil leader, pledged support for a ban, as did the Northern Unionists and the main church groups. James Prior, the Northern Ireland Secretary of State, was against proscription, preferring a withdrawal of government co-operation at all levels with Sinn Féin. Gerry Adams, MP for West Belfast and president of Sinn Féin, refused in an interview to condemn the actions of the Provisional IRA gunmen in Derrada Wood. He said, 'You have to set it against the background of what happened at Roundwood.' He added, 'There was only one other incident in which a garda was shot dead by the IRA. You can't represent that as an attack upon the institutions of the state, or as a premeditated, deliberately planned attack upon the Free State forces.' Joe McGirl, a veteran republican and former Sinn Féin TD, said in an interview with the *Leitrim Observer*, 'I regret the death of two Irishmen over an Englishman, but I'm certainly not going to join the bandwagon of condemnations.'

It would be two years before the first arrest, and it was not one in which the Gardaí could take much pride. Michael Burke, a leading Provisional IRA member from Cork, gave himself up at Tralee Garda Station. A witness to the early-morning snatch of Don Tidey near his home identified Burke as one of the men involved. In June 1986 he was sentenced to twelve years' imprisonment for the false imprisonment of Don Tidey. The owner of Derrada Wood, John Curnan, aged fifty-nine, of Dromcroman, Co. Leitrim, was sentenced to seven years for the false imprisonment of Tidey; the last five years were suspended because of ill health. William Kelly, aged forty-one, of Tralee, Co. Kerry, was sentenced to three years for helping to provide transport used in the kidnapping.

McFarlane fled to the Netherlands but was traced by the RUC, extradited, and returned to the Maze Prison in December 1986. He was paroled in 1997. A few weeks later a tip-off that he was on a bus travelling north enabled the Dundalk gardaí to arrest him before he left the Republic's jurisdiction. He was charged with the false imprisonment of Don Tidey. Subsequently he was released on £100,000 bail pending trial. Four-and-a-half-years later, his trial has yet to begin.

Hugh Prior sued and was awarded £30,000 for his neck wound. John Wrynne survived his gunshot wound. Twenty years later, no-one has yet been charged with the unlawful killing of Gary Sheehan or Patrick Kelly.

Although Tidey's employer, Associated British Foods, denied the payment of any ransom, it later emerged that a payment of £2 million had been made. The money was credited to a numbered account at the Swiss Bank Corporation in Zürich, subsequently transferred to Ireland through the Bank of Ireland's New York branch. The Government introduced emergency legislation in 1985 that allowed it to seize £1.75 million held in an account with the Bank of Ireland in Navan. The chairman of Associated British Foods denied that this money was in any way connected with Tidey's kidnap. Two men, Alan Clancy and David McCartney, claimed that the money was theirs and instituted High Court proceedings for its return. The action failed.

The Navan money had been earmarked for Sinn Féin's local government election campaign of May 1985. The loss of the funds almost brought down Gerry Adams, when hardliners opposed to his ballot-box approach tried to oust him. He clung on tenaciously and managed to turn the tables on the hardliners; four militants were expelled, and Adams's position was secured.

An attempt to recoup the money was made in 1988 when the Bank of Ireland was the subject of an extortion demand of £2 million.

Although no money was paid on that occasion, the Provisional IRA resumed an earlier strategy of kidnaps and extortions, primarily against the families of bank managers, which more than compensated them for the loss of the Navan money. In 1995 Deputy Willie O'Dea raised the matter in the Dáil with the Minister for Justice, Nora Owen, after a newspaper reported that the Provisional IRA had been receiving more than £1 million a year for up to ten years from kidnap-threat extortion.

Controversy over the Derrada Wood killings was rekindled in 2000 with the broadcast of a documentary on the Discovery Channel, 'Fighting Hatred'. In it, Seán O'Callaghan, the Provisional IRA informer who claimed to know what became of Shergar, was revealed as the source who tipped off the Gardaí about the plan to kidnap Galen Weston. It was also alleged that he had been involved in the planning of the Tidey kidnap and was the supplier of intelligence, which the RUC relayed to the Gardaí, on Tidey's Ballinamore location. Why then had the Garda C3 security section not alerted Tidey? Was it to protect their most valuable source of information within the Provisional IRA? If so, it was a decision that cost the lives of Gary Sheehan and Patrick Kelly. O'Callaghan gave himself up to the British police in 1988 and was sentenced to a total of 539 years' imprisonment for two murders and forty-two other crimes. He served eight years and was released in 1996 after receiving a royal pardon.

9

Jennifer Guinness— Four Houses and a Hostage

<⟨⟩⟩⟨⟨⟩⟩>

Bearing the name Guinness in Ireland is a double-edged sword. It certainly ensures invitations to the most fashionable social events, but it can also draw disparagement from society's malcontents. Acutely aware of this, Jennifer Guinness, a deeply private person, had always maintained a low profile—at least until the day she found herself unwillingly thrust into the spotlight. Her story was one of courage and determination and would earn her the respect of all who heard it. It started with a fishing party.

Olive Marron from Carrickmacross, Co. Monaghan, owned a small bungalow in the countryside near Drumconrath, Co. Meath, which she would rent out to fishermen visiting the region. On 28 March 1986 she took a phone call from a man who asked if he could rent the bungalow for a couple of weeks, starting on 1 April. They agreed a rent of £120 per week. Only after the man had hung up did Marron realise she had not asked him for his name.

Marron's mother called at her daughter's bungalow on the arranged day, and one of the three men there paid her the £240 as agreed. At the weekend Marron and her mother visited the bungalow to check that all was well and had a casual conversation with the two men in the kitchen. There was a lot of fishing tackle lying around the house, and the men seemed to be having an enjoyable break and were well acquainted with the best fishing in the area. When she asked their names the men changed the subject, and she left still in the dark about their identities. On 8 April one of the fishing party called to see Marron at her home in Carrickmacross and asked if they could stay on for a couple of extra days. She agreed, and he paid her £40 sterling.

The three men posing as fishermen were members of a criminal gang. John Cunningham, thirty-five years old, from Ballyfermot, Dublin, was the gang leader. His older brother Mickey, a year older, and Anthony Kelly, forty-three years old, were his henchmen. It was Kelly, a sometime stall trader from Tallaght, who had arranged to rent the bungalow. They were prominent Dublin criminals and associates of Ireland's most infamous criminal, Martin Cahill, dubbed by journalists the 'General'. Crime had paid for their lavish life-styles, meals at the most expensive restaurants, vintage wines, and exotic holidays. They enjoyed spending money, especially other people's.

Renting the cottage was the first step in a plan they had hatched. Time was running out for them, and a desperate course of action was called for. All three were wanted for questioning by the West Yorkshire police in connection with a series of armed robberies in the Leeds area. Kelly was also suspected of the murder of Sergeant John Speed and the attempted murder of Constable John Thorpe. In February the West Yorkshire police had attempted to extradite Kelly, but the warrant had failed on a legal technicality. It was only a matter of time before they tried again, and they would not botch it a second time. So the trio needed one big job to provide them with enough funds to leave Ireland and make a new life for themselves in Spain. They had decided that a kidnapping for ransom would be the most rewarding, and from a short list of potential female victims they made their selection. The gang believed that if they abducted the wife of a rich man, the anxious husband would pay up without hesitation.

At 1 p.m. on 8 April 1986 the three men, armed with handguns, a live grenade, two fake bombs, a radio signal transmitter, and a replica Uzi machine gun, parked an antiquated beige Toyota car near John and Jennifer Guinness's home. The Howth property was in a secluded cul-de-sac off Ceanchor Road on the Howth peninsula in north Co. Dublin. They watched the house and front courtyard for a couple of hours, deciding on a plan of entry, when they saw Jennifer Guinness take her dogs for a walk. Mickey Cunningham and Kelly would hide under a sheet in the rear of the car while John Cunningham waited behind the wheel for her to return.

Jennifer Guinness, forty-eight years old, loved walking; having her dogs at her side made it an even greater pleasure. On this occasion, however, she could not be long, because Simon Nelson, a dealer in rare books, was expected to call at the house to pick up some sailing literature. She had told her daughter Gillian, twenty-three years old, and the housekeeper, Patricia Coogan, to welcome him if he arrived before she returned. At four o'clock she started the return leg of her walk. Jennifer Guinness was of slight stature, though stronger than she appeared. She had shoulder-length grey hair and was wearing a light-blue sweatshirt and cream trousers. Her love of yachting had left her with a tanned, almost weather-beaten complexion.

As she approached her front door, Cunningham started the battered Toyota and drove into the courtyard. Guinness assumed it was Nelson who was pulling up. Cunningham got out of the car and approached her. She used her key to open the door and walked over to a hall table, where the sailing directories had been left. She turned to greet her visitor, who had followed her in, and saw that he had a gun in his hand.

'Don't be stupid,' she said. 'No, it's not a joke,' the man replied. He told her to put her hands on the hall table and asked if there were any panic alarm buttons in the house. Guinness assured him there were none. She was afraid to shout out in case it would bring her daughter running. She took a closer look at the intruder, who spoke with an educated Dublin accent. He was about 5 feet 11 inches in height, of medium build with a beer belly, a deep complexion, and dark eyes. He was dressed in a navy-blue jacket, trousers and jumper and wore grey driving-gloves. He had pulled a balaclava over his head.

The nightmare that Jennifer Guinness found herself in grew a great deal worse when two masked and armed accomplices pushed into the house. The second raider was a six-footer, well built and with shoulder-length grey hair. He was wearing denim jeans, a green bomber jacket, and white trainers. He too wore leather driving-gloves. The third man was two or three inches shorter than his accomplices and of a slighter build. He wore a blue corduroy jacket with denim jeans and white trainers. They pushed past her into the kitchen to round up the other occupants. Patricia Coogan was made to fetch her fifteen-year-old daughter from a staff apartment. The women were brought through to the hall where Jennifer Guinness was being held. The men addressed the man with the beer belly as 'Colonel'. All four women were brought to a television room off the entrance hall. The men ripped the telephone lines from the junction boxes.

Jennifer Guinness tried to explain that the gang must have the wrong house, and that there was nothing for them there. 'Oh, no, that's not true,' Cunningham said. He forced her to show him where the safe was. When she opened it, he pocketed cash and some valuable pieces of jewellery worth £56,000. He wanted to know which paintings were the most valuable. She showed him one valuable portrait but made it clear that the painting was too well known in the art world to be sold.

John Cunningham told her they had come for her daughter, Gillian, and if she and her husband wanted to see her again they had best co-operate and pay up. The ransom for her release would be £2 million—for the organisation, he added. She asked him if they looked like people who had an enormous amount of money. The two other raiders continued to ransack the house, and Mickey Cunningham found her passport. 'We don't shoot Irish people,' he said, trying to underline his brother's reference to a paramilitary organisation.

There was panic when the doorbell rang unexpectedly. John Cunningham was the first to act. He hauled Jennifer Guinness towards the door, and with a gun in her side and an arm twisted up her back, she was instructed to open the door. It was Simon Nelson, the book dealer. The petrified man was brought in and interrogated by Cunningham. He was told that he and his family would be killed by the 'organisation' if he ever talked about what he had seen. The pillaging was interrupted a second time when the doorbell rang again. A female census enumerator had called to deliver a form. Guinness, again with a gun held to her side to ensure that she did not try anything, put her head round the door to speak to the woman, who left without realising anything untoward was happening. She thought that Guinness had only opened the door a fraction so that her dogs could not get out.

When John Guinness, fifty-one years old on 10 April, arrived home at 5:30 p.m. he had no idea of the drama that awaited him. He found the front door locked and so walked round to the kitchen door. The raiders pounced on him as he entered and took him through to the hall. He was told to sit on the sofa as Mickey Cunningham set about priming the two 'bombs'. Believing that he and the others were to be killed, Guinness made a lunge for John Cunningham's fake Uzi. There was a short struggle before the gang overpowered him. 'You're a clever bugger,' Cunningham taunted. He put his gun against Guinness's head and pulled the trigger. Nothing happened, of course. Guinness was punched in the face, and the trigger of another gun was pulled. This time a shot was discharged, which embedded itself harmlessly in the dining-room wall. John Guinness's nose had borne the brunt of the punch and bled profusely, though he was not seriously hurt. Cunningham said he would show John Guinness what happened to people who crossed him. He had decided to take Gillian and her mother as hostages in return for a £2 million ransom. The ransom was to be paid in sterling or dollars, or a combination of both. Asked how long it would take him to raise the cash, Guinness said one week. Cunningham seemed satisfied, but warned him to expect a phone call with further instructions. 'Jackal' would be the code-word.

The high ransom demand was obviously set because of John Guinness's position as chairman of Guinness Mahon Bank. There was no doubt that he was a wealthy man, but close friends knew that he was far from the super-wealthy bracket. Jennifer Guinness had been born Jennifer Hollwey in England, the daughter of a former British Army lieutenant-colonel. Her brother, George Hollwey, was chief executive of the Bell Shipping Group, the largest in Ireland. The couple had been married for twenty-six years, the next day being their wedding anniversary.

When Gillian was separated from the rest she broke down in tears. Jennifer Guinness pleaded with the gang not to take her daughter but to take only her. 'John will pay more for me,' she argued. It was eventually agreed that Jennifer Guinness would be taken, but in return the kidnappers demanded a shorter deadline for the ransom payment. Pressing home on the concession, Jennifer also bargained to be allowed to take some extra clothes. Cunningham nodded and told her to be quick. Watched by one of the men, she grabbed two shirts, two pairs of trousers, and two pairs of pants. Before the raiders left they tied up the other five with ties. No specific threats were made about the consequences should the ransom not be paid, but the trussed-up prisoners were warned not to contact the Gardaí. Jennifer Guinness was bundled into the rear seat of the Toyota, hooded with a pillowcase, and covered with a rug. One of the men sat on her legs, while the other two sat in the front.

Those left behind heard the car drive off, but could not be sure which direction the kidnappers had taken. It was assumed that if they left the peninsula by car they would have taken the most direct route, Carrickbrack Road, which skirted the southern edge of Howth, across the isthmus and through Sutton Cross. John Guinness thought the kidnappers could possibly have had a boat moored somewhere nearby.

The Toyota was driven for about an hour through the northern suburbs of Dublin. After leaving Sutton, Guinness was allowed to sit up. She was able to take furtive peeks from beneath the hood and knew the roads well enough to hazard a guess at the car's route. At some point the car was stopped and one of the gang got out.

Later on the car was stopped again, the men swapped vehicles, and another gang member joined them. Their new car was a five-door model. Guinness, still hooded, was placed in the rear compartment of the hatchback and covered with the parcel shelf. She rummaged around in the darkness and found a wheel brace, which she concealed under her jacket. The car was heading north, she thought, almost certainly along the Ashbourne Road. The men in front did not talk during the journey.

Back in Howth, John Guinness managed to untie himself after twenty minutes, then quickly freed the others. He spent fifteen minutes consoling the distressed women, then he and Gillian drove to a neighbour's house. Liam McGonigle, a solicitor, listened in amazement to the incredible story. It was decided that John Guinness should do exactly as the kidnappers had commanded and refrain from contacting the Gardaí, but when John and his daughter left, McGonigle telephoned them.

The Garda Commissioner, Larry Wren, was informed of events at 9 p.m., just as he was about to address the annual conference of the Association of Garda Sergeants and Inspectors in Limerick. The Gardaí requested a news blackout from the media, so the kidnappers would not know the police had been brought in. It was a policy the Garda Síochána had adopted since the abduction and murder of a London woman, Muriel McKay, by a criminal gang in 1969. Later the Gardaí denied that John Guinness had contacted them, refusing to say how they had learnt of the kidnapping.

Commissioner Wren asked his deputy, Éamon Doherty, also attending the conference in Limerick, to co-ordinate the investigation. The now all-too-familiar Garda kidnap response was initiated. An incident centre was established at Raheny Garda Station. The national cordon plan, which virtually sealed off the country, was activated. Roadblocks were set up throughout the country and an all-ports warning issued. The RUC was alerted. House-to-house inquiries around the Howth area were ordered. The Special Branch would look at any possible terrorist angle. The whereabouts and movements of several notorious Dublin criminals were to be checked by a team of Serious Crime Squad and Special Branch detectives, led by Detective-Inspector Gerry McCarrick.

The kidnappers arrived at the rented bungalow at Drumconrath, Co. Meath. They took Jennifer Guinness from the rear of the car and led her into the house. During the uncomfortable journey she had decided that if she was to survive the ordeal she would have to come out of it mentally and physically intact. She knew she would be all right if she could find within herself a tenth of the courage she had witnessed at the Central Remedial Clinic. The severely handicapped people she did voluntary work with had to deal with bigger problems every day of their lives. She could not afford to lose hope and knew that she had to funnel her anger and determination in a positive way rather than expend it fruitlessly. She was taken to a bedroom, handcuffed to Anthony Kelly, and told to lie on the bed with him beside her.

A few hours later, when her companion had fallen asleep, she was able to remove the wheel brace from under her jacket and hide it beneath her pillow. It was a mad risk to take, but it gave her some reassurance. She called to the other gang members and complained that Kelly was snoring so loudly that she could not sleep. Mickey Cunningham, called the 'Sergeant', pushed another bed over so she could move onto it, but the snoring Kelly was only an arm's length away.

Garda Headquarters was keeping an open mind on who was behind the kidnapping, but the scope of their investigation was narrowing fast. Paramilitary involvement had been ruled out fairly early on. The Special Branch had no intelligence that a kidnap was being planned, and while far from conclusive, it would have been extraordinary not to have heard a whisper, considering the number of informers recruited on both sides of the border. The kidnap gang also lacked the customary professionalism of terrorist groups; twenty-seven years' experience and court revelations of police techniques had transformed the main terrorist groups into formidable and skilled opponents. Finally, no statements had been issued admitting liability.

Detective-Superintendent Hubert Reynolds and the local superintendent, Tom McDermott, were heading the investigation. Reynolds, a former Co. Leitrim footballer, had been a detective for ten years and had worked on several notorious murder investigations. Telephone taps had been placed on a number of lines that the Gardaí considered could be used by the kidnappers when making contact. In other recent kidnaps the use of intermediaries had posed serious problems for the Gardaí. The Government stance was that no ransom should be paid to kidnappers and the burden of enforcing this decree fell on the Garda Síochána, a task not made any easier by companies that purchased kidnap insurance for their senior executives. The underwriters would send in representatives to negotiate with the kidnappers, making a successful resolution, arrest and prosecution by the Gardaí a much more complicated process.

Two leading Dublin criminals were considered as possible suspects. Martin Cahill, a prominent figure in Dublin's gangland, was the better known. One of his lieutenants, John Cunningham, fitted the physical description of the man his accomplices had addressed as 'Colonel'. Gillian Guinness had provided detectives with a vital clue: she had noticed that the 'Colonel' had a stiff finger. It was on Garda files that John Cunningham had been left with a permanently damaged finger after a serious burn to his hand. While he was setting fire to a car, burning petrol had melted the rubber glove on his hand. The car he had been intent on destroying had been used in the highly successful O'Connor gold robbery of July 1983, one of Martin Cahill's most spectacular operations. Cahill's large gang had got away with £2 million in gold and diamonds. The robbery had been executed with military precision, giving rise to Cahill's nickname of the 'General' and Cunningham's of the 'Colonel'.

But a second criminal, from the Santry area of Dublin, was also under the spotlight. Some of his associates were known to have carried out several armed robberies in the previous twelve months. It was thought likely that the kidnap was part of a continuing campaign to raise finance for a large drug purchase. At a strategy meeting held at Raheny, a decision was made to concentrate on the north-side suspects first. This was a disappointment to Gerry McCarrick, who felt certain the Cunningham brothers were involved. Five officers and forty gardaí were reassigned from other duties to assist in the investigation.

The gang members were in high spirits the next morning and appeared relaxed and confident. Things were going exactly as they had planned. Mickey did the cooking for the men and their hostage. Jennifer Guinness traded her silence for a radio and a selection of magazines. John Cunningham bought a chain and a padlock, which meant that she could be handcuffed to the bed rather than to Kelly. Despite their assurances that no harm would come to her, and that her husband would pay the ransom, she believed that her life was in constant danger. They had removed her hood and their own masks, which meant she could see their faces. Alive, she would always be a threat to them. She tried to talk to them and draw them out a little in an effort to form some sort of relationship, in the belief that it would be at least slightly more difficult for them to harm someone they knew. But she was not prepared to let them have it all their own way, and she insisted that she be allowed to wash daily. That night one of the men slept in her room but, to her relief, not in the same bed.

The news blackout was lifted on Thursday morning, the third day, after it became increasingly obvious to the Gardaí that it would be untenable to maintain it in the face of worldwide media attention. This decision sparked a disagreement with the Guinness family. The Gardaí issued descriptions of the men and announced that a stolen Toyota had been found in Swords, Co. Dublin. The car had been stolen from Coolock, but the Gardaí refused to confirm that it was the vehicle used in the kidnapping until further detailed forensic tests could be carried out.

At about midday the gang learnt that the media had been informed of the kidnap. Jennifer Guinness had known several hours before them after hearing a news bulletin on the 'Gay Byrne' radio show, but thought it prudent to let the gang find out for themselves. Their reaction was as she expected. John Cunningham ranted and raved and made threats to her and to her family. The others were equally unsettled. It was obvious, Cunningham said, that they could not stay any longer in the bungalow. The Gardaí were appealing for the owners of empty or isolated property to check their premises. Guinness was told to dress in her warmest clothes and even in her spare clothes too, because they were taking her into the woods to bury her. It was all her husband's fault, they insisted. Certain that she was to be killed, she struggled violently against being put into the rear of their green Opel Kadett. Cunningham explained that he meant she was to be hidden in the woods. He told her that they were taking her across the border. Her abductors remained very jittery, which in turn caused her constant anxiety.

They drove along minor roads for thirty minutes until they reached a wood. The gang led their hostage along a track into the centre of the wood and shackled her to a tree. They cut branches and gorse, with which they carefully concealed her. Anthony Kelly was ordered to remain with her. The next twelve hours were the longest of her life. She still thought she was going to die.

As the search for Jennifer Guinness continued throughout Ireland, reports from Beirut brought news of another kidnapping. An Irishman, Brian Keenan, had been abducted by Islamic fundamentalists (chapter 10).

The owner of the bungalow visited her property that afternoon. She spoke to two of the men she had seen before and was told that they were making a video for Bord Fáilte.

The media were making up for lost time. The sparse details of the kidnapping were being broadcast repeatedly on radio and television. Public opinion had been horrified by the abduction of a middle-aged woman. Speculation was rife about who was responsible. The whole country wanted to know who exactly John Guinness was, and what relation he was to the famous Arthur.

Guinness and Mahon, the merchant bank chaired by John Guinness, was one of the oldest banks in Ireland, celebrating 150 years of trading in 1986. Robert Rundell Guinness and John Ross Mahon had founded the bank. Guinness was the grandson of Samuel Guinness, a goldbeater of Crow Street, Dublin, and a younger brother of Arthur Guinness, the founder of the famous brewery. Descendants of the two founders had always headed the bank, and on Sir George Mahon's retirement in 1971 John Guinness replaced him. In 1974 the bank had merged with Lewis and Peat to form Guinness Peat. The bank had recently taken a serious knock when the management buy-out of the Nicholl Group of department stores had failed. Control of offshoots of the bank in Jersey, Guernsey and the Cayman Islands was switched from Dublin to London, greatly reducing the assets of the Irish arm. John Guinness had stepped down as chief executive some years previously and his position as chairman was largely a figurehead one. On the same day that the news blackout was lifted the vice-chairman of the bank, Des Traynor, announced his resignation. He confirmed that he was taking up a position as vice-chairman of Cement Roadstone Holdings.

Only a few minutes into the fourth day of her abduction Jennifer Guinness heard a whistle and the sounds of the Cunningham brothers tramping through the wood. They had found the hidden wheel brace and were furious with her. They released her, and she was led to the Opel Kadett and once again bundled into the luggage compartment. They tried to convince her that she was being driven across the border, but Guinness's methodical mind was having none of it. The border would have meant army and police patrols on each side, checkpoints and Special Branch patrols, helicopters and observation posts. The men would have been foolhardy to risk such a strategy now that the story had broken.

The gang's genuine destination was a grubby ground-floor bed-sitter at Rosemount Terrace, Arbour Hill, Dublin, that Kelly had earlier rented as a back-up safe house. The conditions were primitive: peeling wallpaper, a bucket for a toilet, no heating, and four of them in the cramped space. The men passed the time discussing the merits of their weapons and macho boasting that anyone who got in their way would be shot without a second thought. At one point there was a knock on the door, and Guinness did believe the men were prepared to shoot if the caller had not gone away. She continued her strategy of talking to the three men, playing along with their naïve pretence that they were now in Northern Ireland. While they were at Arbour Hill there was the sound of gunfire in the distance. Guinness remarked that it was to be expected now that they were north of the border. Mickey Cunningham said there was an RUC station nearby and the gunfire may have been directed at it.

The first communication purporting to come from the kidnappers took place at 10:28 a.m. on 11 April, when a call was made to Garda Communications in the Phoenix Park. A second call in the early afternoon was made to the offices of the *Evening Herald*. Superintendent Frank Hanlon of the Garda Press Office later declared both these calls to have been hoaxes. He also confirmed that three weeks previously, Jennifer Guinness's handbag had been snatched from the front seat of her car while it was paused at traffic lights in Dublin city centre, though it was too early to say if the theft was linked to the abduction.

The Gardaí were soon to encounter a serious distraction to their investigation. As thought likely, the Guinness family had called in a specialist firm to negotiate for Jennifer's release. Mark Sorby and Eric Westdropp of the London security consultancy Control Risks held discussions with John Guinness at his home in Howth. The *Sunday Times* Insight team claimed that Control Risks negotiated the payment of £2 million protection money from Associated British Foods to the Provisional IRA after Don Tidey had been freed by the Gardaí. The payment, denied by ABF, was to buy the safety of other senior executives. Sorby would remain at the Howth house until the kidnapping was resolved, while Westdropp would move to and from their London office as required. In the clandestine world of ransom negotiation it is considered a grievous mistake to consent swiftly to pay a ransom. It could lead the kidnappers to think they had underpriced their hostage and encourage them to hang on to their captive for a further ransom.

Control Risks' afternoon session with John Guinness lasted for a couple of hours, during which a number of strategies were put forward for consideration. Guinness confirmed that he could gather up £300,000, which he would gladly pay to free his wife. The Gardaí's primary concern with Control Risks' involvement was the firm's practice of keeping all activities with their clients strictly confidential. Their involvement put a further strain on the already tense relationship between the Gardaí and John Guinness. While both Control Risks and the Gardaí desperately wanted Jennifer Guinness returned unharmed, their contrasting approaches were bound to cause friction.

The three-day deadline was reached on the Friday evening, with no contact from the kidnappers. Superintendent Hanlon played down the significance of the expiry of the deadline. He said there had been a huge public response to appeals for information, with more than a thousand calls.

The Cunningham brothers were as appalled at the bed-sitter as Jennifer Guinness was, and on the Saturday morning they left to seek more suitable accommodation and also to catch up with the criminals' grapevine to ascertain whether the Gardaí had zeroed in on them as suspects. The quest for alternative accommodation was to prove a disaster.

Detective-Inspector Gerry McCarrick had learnt from inquiries that the Cunningham brothers had not been seen at home for some time. He ordered his men to keep a watch on places the brothers were known to frequent. One such venue was a bookmaker's in Middle Abbey Street, Dublin. Detective-Garda Jim Mitchell of the Serious Crime Squad spotted John Cunningham leaving the bookie's shop on Saturday afternoon and hopping into a green Opel Kadett. He was not able to make out the face of the driver, but it was the first confirmed sighting of Cunningham. The detective made a note of the car's registration number. The car belonged to Liffey Car Rentals, but, incredibly, as it was the weekend there was nobody readily available to say who had hired it.

John Cunningham met an associate, Brian McNicholl, a native

of Derry. McNicholl listened as Cunningham told him of the kidnap and the problems the gang were having over safe houses. McNicholl agreed to help in exchange for a cut of the ransom, stating that he might have an answer to the accommodation problem.

That evening Jennifer Guinness was informed that she was to be moved again. She was ordered to put an arm around one of the men and pretend she was his girl-friend as she was taken the short distance from the house to the car. They drove to 7 Orchardston, a quiet cul-de-sac off Willowbank Drive, Rathfarnham. Fergus Kerrigan, a former insurance broker whose business had collapsed, leaving him in dire financial straits, owned the house and lived there with his daughter Daryl. Kerrigan was a drinking buddy of McNicholl and had arranged to meet him and John Cunningham at the Tuning Fork pub in Rathfarnham on that Saturday evening. Down on his luck and too fond of drinking, Kerrigan had been easily persuaded to let the Cunningham brothers have the use of the house while his daughter was away. Daryl was not expected back until late on Monday night. The intoxicated Kerrigan was given £100 for a hotel room.

McNicholl turned up at the house a few hours after Jennifer Guinness had been moved there. Foul-mouthed and menacing, he appeared to easily intimidate the other men. Whenever he was present, the Cunninghams and Kelly, Jennifer thought, were much more aggressive and rougher. The northerner insisted she wear an extra hood and made a fuss about her never seeing his face. He wanted her to be locked in the garage, but Kelly intervened, and she was taken instead to an upstairs bedroom. The apparent obsequiousness the gang displayed towards McNicholl was probably dreamt up as a ruse to further convince Guinness that she was in Northern Ireland and that republican paramilitaries were involved. If so, they had seriously underestimated their hostage's intelligence.

All the men started to apply pressure on Guinness to provide them with the names and telephone numbers of trusted friends, someone she could depend on to relay a message to her husband without the Gardaí finding out. She prevaricated, believing that the longer there was no line of communication the more chance she had of being found. Trepidation also held her back. Should a ransom be paid, her usefulness to the gang would be finished. This unease had been greatly increased with the arrival of McNicholl. He grew increasingly short-tempered and abusive towards her. In one of his rages he took her watch and threw it against the wall. She eventually compromised by saying that her husband would require proof that they were the kidnappers before any ransom negotiation could be entered into. She gave them the name of a family friend whom they could contact. They could prove that they were genuine by quoting her daughter's nickname. There was no answer at the home of the first friend, so Guinness gave them an alternative, and Kelly made the call. It was the first verified communication from the kidnappers, the first confirmation John Guinness had received that his wife was unharmed.

McNicholl and John Cunningham were already making plans for the fourth safe house. It was decided that McNicholl would take his girl-friend for a few days' holiday, and the gang could keep Guinness at her empty house. Cunningham felt that a couple of days was all that was needed. He was so close to the ransom, he felt, he could smell the money!

On the Sunday evening, the sixth day, Guinness learnt that she was to be left alone with McNicholl. She was fearful for her safety. Again it was Kelly who came to her rescue when he warned the man not to harm her. Her policy of befriending the original three kidnappers was now paying dividends.

At a press conference given by the Gardaí that same evening Superintendent O'Hanlon confirmed that Jennifer Guinness's family was considering offering a reward for information concerning her whereabouts. Although he refused to speculate about what amount the reward might be, it was generally believed that £50,000 might bring results. O'Hanlon refused to be drawn about reports that Control Risks had recommended the payment of a ransom.

John Guinness had earlier denied that a rift had opened up between the Guinness family and the Gardaí. However, the reward could be interpreted as further criticism of the Gardaí, who had apparently made no breakthrough in their investigation, although they had raided the homes of a number of known criminals and made several arrests on unrelated matters. One of those arrested was the Santry criminal who had been an early prime suspect.

On the Monday morning, the seventh day, Jennifer Guinness realised she could stall them no longer, and she agreed to ring Control Risks' office in London. With the kidnappers listening at her side and a gun being held to her head, she made the call. She did not give a name but said she was ringing in connection with the kidnapping. She was put on hold, presumably to give the firm time to trace the call. John Cunningham cut off the call and made her dial again. The next three calls produced the same result. Finally, a representative of the company told her that they could not be of assistance. Guinness then gave John Cunningham the London telephone number of her brother, George Hollwey. He was to be their go-between. Cunningham made her make the call herself, but Hollwey was not there. She tried again an hour later, this time with success. Kelly took the receiver from her and spoke to Hollwey. Negotiations for a ransom payment and Guinness's release had begun; but an unforeseen development was to interrupt the process.

The Gardaí's now seriously strained liaison with the Guinness family was through Chief Superintendent Michael Maguire, head of the Central Detective Unit, and Chief Superintendent Ned O'Dea, head of the Special Detective Unit. O'Dea was used to operating in the spotlight: he had been the arresting officer of Neil Blaney before the 1970s Arms Trial. The involvement of Control Risks meant that any leads the Gardaí thought might prove fruitful could not be hinted at to John Guinness. The Gardaí knew that John Guinness intended to pay, though they advised him against it. It was as though the Gardaí and Control Risks were playing a game of high-stakes poker.

The Garda Síochána's reservations concerning Control Risks' strategy found support in Britain. An MP, Dale Campbell-Savours (Workington), asked during Prime Minister's question time, 'In the light of the news from Ireland that Mrs Jennifer Guinness has now been kidnapped, is it about time the government came forward with a statement telling the house and the country what they intend to do to stop these insurance policies being sold? They act as incentives.'

Inspector Gerry McCarrick had finally discovered someone at Liffey Rentals who could supply him with the name of the person who had hired the Opel Kadett: he was Anthony Kelly, a known associate of the Cunningham brothers. Kelly telephoned the hire company later that day and asked them to extend the hire for a further forty-eight hours. Details of the car were circulated to Garda patrols, and it was only a matter of time before it would be found.

Daryl Kerrigan and her boy-friend returned to Rathfarnham unexpectedly. She was surprised to see the blinds pulled down at 4:30 in the afternoon. Walking into her home, she found three strangers appearing simultaneously from the three rooms that opened onto the hall. The gang had been preparing to move once more. Daryl asked them what they were doing there. They told her that Fergus had allowed them the use of the house while she was away. The girl admitted that she had returned early and agreed that it sounded exactly like the sort of thing her father would do. After the failure of his brokerage he had started drinking heavily and would bring home his drinking buddies from time to time.

She said she needed to go upstairs, but the gang refused to allow it. She insisted, and one of them accompanied her. Jennifer Guinness was being held in Daryl's father's bedroom, and the man made sure she did not go in there. In her own bedroom she found a fourth man standing with his back to her. He was wearing a mask. She turned and fled downstairs in tears. John Cunningham told her not to worry, they would be gone soon, and she could forget that it had ever happened. He told Mickey to make everyone a cup of tea.

It was then that Fergus Kerrigan arrived home, full of bonhomie and whiskey. He soon sobered up, going to pieces when it dawned on him what he had got himself and his daughter mixed up in. Then there was a knock on the front door. The local Garda station had received a call from a neighbour about unknown men coming and going. The station had sent a patrol car round. Kerrigan assured the garda that the men were friends of his, and invited him in to see for himself. Mickey Cunningham acted as though everything was normal, even when Kerrigan stumbled over a coffee table. The garda left, apparently satisfied. If the Garda Síochána had been quicker to circulate round Dublin Garda stations the descriptions of the wanted men, the kidnap could have ended at that point. Fergus Kerrigan, Daryl and her boy-friend were ushered into a bedroom and told to remain inside for ten minutes.

Jennifer Guinness was on the move yet again. She was taken to the garage and placed in a large cardboard box, which was loaded into the back of the Kadett. It was a short drive to her fourth location, 61 Waterloo Road, in the Ballsbridge area of south Dublin. She was handcuffed and made to sit on the floor for a couple of hours. Later she was chained to a fireplace and remained there for roughly twenty-four hours.

After the gang left the house, Daryl Kerrigan discovered items of women's clothing in her father's room, but, wary of the consequences to her father, she did not phone the Gardaí until the next day. Fergus Kerrigan made a statement to the Gardaí, giving them the breakthrough they badly needed. Detectives and members of the Technical Bureau returned to the Orchardston house with Kerrigan. McCarrick and his men had been keeping discreet surveillance on Kelly's hired car. It had been spotted in Ballsbridge, parked in Waterloo Road. Thanks to Kerrigan's statement, they now knew the house in which the gang were hiding.

The kidnappers had been acting out of desperation when they obtained the use of the new house. They had to promise Brian McNicholl £100,000 for the use of it for a couple of days. McNicholl claimed he ran a demolition business but was better known as a small-time criminal and as an associate of the Dunne criminal family. He lacked the resolve and determination that leading criminals needed and was to prove it time and again over the following days. The Georgian two-storey-over-basement house belonged to

Clora Lenehan, his girl-friend. McNicholl was to tell her nothing; he just had to make sure she was out of the way for a few days. Lenehan, a totally innocent party, was taken by McNicholl to Kinnegad and then to Delvin, Co. Westmeath.

Late on Monday night John Cunningham received a phone call at Waterloo Road. A mystery caller told him that the Gardaí knew they were there and were about to seal off the street. He had to move fast. He told Jennifer Guinness to dress and ordered Kelly to reverse the Opel up to the door. Guinness's eyes were taped and she was told to wear dark glasses. Then she was brought downstairs and seated in the hall.

Shortly after midnight the last few details of a rescue plan were being settled at Raheny. When they received word that the car had been reversed up to the front steps, the doors left ajar, surmising that the gang was about to flee, McCarrick considered rushing the house but was ordered to hold back. Armed reinforcements were sent in and the area closed down tight. Detective-Inspector Bill Somers and Detective-Sergeant Dermot Jennings, with three other members of the SDU, cautiously approached the house. At 1:23 a.m. they knocked on the front door.

Inside there was pandemonium. The gang could see that the house was surrounded, and Kelly dived out of a basement rear window, Mickey Cunningham right behind him. 'Stop. Gardaí. Stop!' an armed detective shouted. Mickey Cunningham fired a shot at the detective, missing his head by inches. Detective-Garda Tony O'Donnell fired a single shot. Two of his colleagues fired bursts from their Uzi sub-machine guns. Kelly dived into a garden shed; Cunningham retreated into the house.

The brothers came running up the stairs from the basement, seized their hostage, and sought shelter in an upstairs bedroom. Jennifer displayed great presence of mind by rolling under the bed.

At the rear of the house Kelly realised that his situation was hopeless. The Gardaí demanded that he give himself up. He emerged from the shed with his hands raised and was taken into custody.

John Cunningham smashed a window and shouted, 'We have the woman up here, and we will blow her fucking head off if you don't get out of the house.' Somers, a trained hostage negotiator and a veteran of the Don Tidey kidnapping, replied that if they released the woman and gave themselves up he would guarantee their safety. 'No way are we going down for thirty years,' John Cunningham shouted. Somers asked that Jennifer Guinness be produced. She scrambled out from under the bed and approached the window. She said she was unharmed and gave the Gardaí the phone number of the house. Then she was abruptly pulled away from the window. 'You'll shoot us if we come down like you did our friend,' John Cunningham said. Somers told him that Kelly was alive and unharmed. Kelly was interrogated about the arms in the house. He said: 'Don't go up there. They'll blow you away. There are enough explosives to blow you to kingdom come.' He went on to say that Cunningham had a remote control switch for the bomb, which was now probably strapped to Guinness. Cunningham, he added, was mad enough to use it.

The negotiations were going nowhere, so at 3 a.m. Kelly was brought to the front of the house. John Cunningham asked him from the broken window if he had been bashed up. 'No, no, I'm all right. They didn't go near me,' Kelly said. 'I just want to say one thing to you: remember the pud.' This was a reference to John Cunningham's wife, Mary, who was heavily pregnant. Kelly was brought into the hallway of a neighbouring house, 63 Waterloo Road, and spoke to John Cunningham on the phone. 'I'm fucked. It was a fair cop, no other way. She would want you to do the right thing. No heroes. No heroes. I wouldn't like to be sending flowers to your grave.' Kelly went on to tell Cunningham that if he released Mrs Guinness it would go a long way.

The mood was tense inside the bedroom. John Cunningham was chain-smoking, holding the grenade and gun in his other hand. Guinness was allowed to phone her husband, and the Cunningham men phoned their wives. John seemed to be weighing his options. He did not want to die, but for a man who liked the finer things of life twenty years in Mountjoy Jail would be hard to swallow.

Somers kept talking to the Cunningham brothers, explaining about solicitors and which Garda station they would be taken to. He told them to put the guns and the explosives in the centre of the room and to come out. The first sign that he was getting through to them was when two bags of clothing were thrown from the bedroom window.

Inside, the Cunninghams emptied their guns and shook hands with Jennifer Guinness and each other. They returned a few pieces of her stolen jewellery. John Cunningham asked her if it would be okay, if his baby was a girl, to call her Jennifer. At 6:24 a.m. he smiled at Guinness and opened the door. 'Ladies first!'

Bill Somers led Jennifer Guinness away to be reunited with her husband. Michael and John Cunningham were arrested under section 30 of the Offences Against the State Act.

The news of the successful resolution of the kidnap was on the air in minutes. McNicholl heard it and assumed that Kerrigan had sold them down the river. During his trip in the country he had already let slip to one acquaintance that he expected to come into a lot of money soon. The next day he told the same man that he was in a lot of trouble, as he had organised the kidnap of Jennifer Guinness. On his way back to Dublin he phoned Kerrigan's house and a detective answered, posing as Kerrigan. 'We're coming to get you and you won't know until we're there', McNicholl threatened. When McNicholl brought Clora Lenehan back to her house, he was promptly arrested. He was deeply indignant that the Gardaí should think he had had anything to do with such a monstrous act.

Jennifer Guinness gave a press conference the day after her release. The courage and fortitude she had displayed during her ordeal astounded the public. She said she bore no hatred for her abductors, although she had been in no doubt that her life was in danger. An appearance on 'The Late Late Show' added to her reputation as a cool-headed, resilient woman. On 1 May, she set off for Plymouth to start an attempt at a sailing record in some of the toughest waters of the Mediterranean. Robin Knox Johnston sailed with her.

A further tragedy was to strike the Guinness family in February 1988 when John Guinness was killed while climbing a mountain in Wales.

On 24 June 1986 John and Michael Cunningham both pleaded guilty at the Circuit Criminal Court to the charges relating to the kidnap. They were sentenced to seventeen years and fourteen years, respectively. The judge heard that John Cunningham had twenty-eight previous convictions and his brother nine.

In November, Anthony Kelly, of Kingswood Heights, Tallaght, pleaded guilty to his part in the Jennifer Guinness abduction and received a sentence of fourteen years from Mr Justice Frank Roe. Kelly had thirteen previous convictions. The judge said that Mrs Guinness had been subjected to appalling treatment and that the kidnappers had threatened to kill her. A Garda source claimed that Kelly would not be extradited to Britain until he had served the sentence imposed in Ireland. However, the extradition was dropped when another suspect confessed to killing Sergeant John Speed. After his release from prison Kelly soon found himself in trouble again. In October 2000 he was jailed for six years for the possession of cocaine with a street value of £160,000.

Brian McNicholl pleaded not guilty at his trial, which began on 6 November. Jennifer Guinness gave evidence, as did her husband. McNicholl was found guilty and sentenced to twelve years and nine months.

John Cunningham served ten years of his sentence before escaping from Shelton Abbey open prison in September 1996. Despite a mammoth manhunt, he was not apprehended. Jennifer Guinness criticised the authorities for not informing her of his escape. As chairwoman of Victim Support, she said, 'there has to be a system where if something like this happens, the victim is informed.' She added that Cunningham's escape did not cause her any distress, because she had already put the 1986 kidnapping incident behind her. She regarded it as history.

John Cunningham was arrested four years later by Dutch police at a house near Schipol Airport. In June 2001 an Amsterdam court handed him a nine-year prison sentence, later reduced to seven years for his part in a multi-million pounds drug and arms smuggling operation between the Netherlands and Ireland.

Gardaí believe that Cunningham has been behind the importing of more than £20 million of drugs that reached Irish streets. The Criminal Assets Bureau is at present attempting to identify and confiscate property in Spain and Portugal belonging to Cunningham. It is expected that he will be returned to Ireland after serving the Dutch sentence, to complete the sentence imposed for kidnapping Jennifer Guinness.

10

Brian Keenan's Four-and-a-Half Years of Captivity

When violence is all around you, it soon becomes acceptable. So Brian Keenan from Belfast did not see his move to war-torn Beirut as a huge step. For him the decision that altered his life had been taken years before.

Growing up in Northern Ireland is an immersion in tradition. Few cultures can be as retrospective as the Ulster Protestant one. Under constant erosion, the dominant focus is conservative, to a time when their way of life was in the ascendancy. Almost every aspect of life in Northern Ireland reinforces the traditional, in particular the twin pillars of education and employment. The majority of schools were not integrated and, unlike its southern neighbour, this part of Ireland did not have to endure the forced economic emigration of its young. Generations of young men followed their forebears into the linen mills, shipyards and engineering works of industrial Belfast. Abundant job opportunities for the middle classes in the civil service and the public service generally helped underpin the values of a reactionary populace.

Young men like Brian Keenan were the exception—a working-class Protestant from the Woodstock Road area of Belfast who had dared to plough his own furrow. Leaving school at sixteen, he started an apprenticeship as a heating engineer but soon found that the work lacked challenge. He decided to resume his education. It was a courageous decision and the first step of a journey that would eventually take him to Beirut.

To pursue his interest in twentieth-century literature, Keenan chose to study at the New University of Ulster in Coleraine, a town built on the mouth of the River Bann in the north-east of Ireland. The Co. Antrim coast is a place of lonely, rugged beauty, as different from industrial Belfast as night is from day. Having shed the shackles of his background, Keenan repeatedly found himself in conflict with the majority. Plain old-fashioned cantankerousness was how some fellow-students described his attitude to life.

Stifled by the constraints of Northern Ireland, he sought new horizons. He took up teaching posts in Brussels and Spain. A few weeks before Christmas 1985, at the age of thirty-six, Keenan left Belfast once again, this time for a job with the American University of Beirut. In his book *An Evil Cradling* he describes having a last drink in the deserted Crown pub and being the sole passenger on a bus to the airport, portents of his coming ordeal in the Middle East.

Guards carrying automatic rifles and a police sergeant provided security for Keenan's new colleagues who welcomed him at Beirut Airport. For the next week he wandered the streets, familiarising himself with the busy, noisy city. Once the pearl of the Middle East, Beirut's croisette had attracted the jet-setters in the same way as Cannes. Now the luxury hotels were bombed-out shells, and the beach was pockmarked with shell craters.

Civil war had erupted in 1975 between the predominantly poor Shi'ite Muslims from the south of Lebanon and the wealthy Maronite Christians. This conflict was transformed into a Muslim revolution in 1982 when Israel invaded Lebanon to oust Yasser Arafat's Palestine Liberation Organisation. The Shi'ite fighters were augmented by the Hizbollah guerrillas, a group backed by Iran when Muslim revolution swept away the Shah. An early success for the 'Party of God' came in 1982 when a truck bomb killed two hundred American marines and prompted the American withdrawal from Lebanon. The strategy of taking Western hostages was to raise money, grab media attention, and seek revenge on the capitalist West.

Keenan moved into accommodation outside the college, a Turkish villa close to the 'green line' dividing Christian east from Muslim west Beirut, with a few fellow-teachers. It was the expatriates' habit to ring each other regularly to acquaint friends of their movements. Beirut at that time was a dangerous city to live in. Keenan was offered a handgun by one of his students, but he declined the loan. He saw no need for one in Belfast; why would he change his attitude now, even if circumstances might have dictated caution? The fundamentalist Shi'ite extremists had just before Easter 1986 stepped up the kidnap of foreigners. Apprehension among the lecturers was heightened when Leigh Douglas and Peter Padfield were kidnapped. (Abducted ten days before Brian Keenan's kidnap, they were murdered a month later.) Keenan's housemates agreed at dinner in their villa that, starting the next morning, the lecturers should travel to the college in a group. The Belfast man readily agreed but later in bed remembered that he had an early class at the Hariri Institute the next day. Any new security arrangements would have to wait for twenty-four hours.

At about 7:20 the next morning, 10 April, he left the villa and had taken barely a dozen steps before four men jumped him. Armed with automatic rifles and handguns, they pushed him into the rear seat of their old Mercedes. They forced him to lie across their laps as the car sped away. When Keenan told them that he was Irish, his kidnappers seemed puzzled. One of the men who could speak some English asked Keenan what he thought of Margaret Thatcher. Not a lot, he said. Clearly the kidnappers had assumed he was English. The car was driven to a deserted subway and he was pulled out. Keenan's knees turned to water. Had his kidnappers realised their mistake and decided to dispose of the only witness? Every muscle tensed as he waited for the shot. But they had only stopped so that he could be transferred to the car's boot. A further journey brought them to the covered car park of a building. Keenan was hauled out and rushed along a corridor to a cell.

The room's only furniture was a folding camp bed. After a brief interval, two men entered and made Keenan strip off his shirt, which was wound round his head as a makeshift blindfold. Money, his watch and a ring were taken from him. He was led down three flights of stairs. Having declined a cold shower, the prisoner was locked in another tiny cell. The room was 4 feet wide by 6 feet long, and without lighting. This time there was only a foam mattress on a concrete floor. Keenan's sense of isolation was brought home to him by the cries in Arabic of other prisoners. He chose to believe that his abduction was a mistake that would soon be rectified.

A guard came in and handed Keenan a bottle of Coca-Cola and two sandwiches made with coarse bread. The door was left unlocked for a few minutes before several armed guards entered, and behind them an older man. The white-haired man asked questions in English. Where was Keenan from? Could he prove he was Irish? After telling the prisoner he would not be harmed if he co-operated, the men withdrew and the steel door was padlocked. Many hours passed before Keenan lay down and fell into a troubled sleep.

The next day he was questioned again, mainly about the political standing of the university. This time his interrogator was the man who had questioned him about Thatcher. Keenan tried to answer as simply as possible and without incriminating himself. The names and addresses of fifteen other teachers were demanded from him; Keenan hedged by saying he had not been in Lebanon long enough to know. His briefcase was returned to him. An hour later the older man came and asked further questions, but refused to explain why Keenan had been abducted. It became apparent from the questions that the kidnappers had been following Keenan for some time.

Keenan's disappearance had not gone unnoticed. John Rowan, first secretary of the Irish Embassy in Beirut, arranged for notices to be placed in the local newspapers informing the kidnappers that Keenan was Irish and travelling on an Irish passport. It was hoped that the kidnappers would consider Keenan as of no great benefit to them and release him. Little should be read into the fact that Keenan was travelling on an Irish passport. Being from Belfast he was entitled to a British passport, but, like many young people at that time, his choice may have had more to do with economics than politics. Also, an Irish passport cost considerably less than a British one!

Five American and one French-run school began a two-day strike in protest against the recent kidnappings of teachers. The day Keenan was taken coincided with the freeing of a French teacher, Michel Brian, after a shoot-out with his kidnappers.

The days quickly became a monotonous routine for Keenan. In the mornings he wrapped a towel round his head and was taken from his cell and led ten paces to a cockroach-infested squat toilet, before being allowed to shower. Communication with the other prisoners as he was escorted along the corridor was strictly forbidden. Food would be waiting for him on his return: some bread, cheese, a hard-boiled egg, and a portion of jam. No plate or utensils were supplied, but a bottle of water was provided. These meagre rations were all he would be given for twenty-four hours. He was forbidden to look at his captors or at any fellow-prisoners, but inevitably as the weeks went by he managed to steal surreptitious glances at almost all of them.

Keenan named his jailer the 'Grim Reaper' because of the man's quick temper and his propensity for extreme violence, mainly directed at the younger Arab prisoners. One of the original kidnappers would make occasional appearances; Keenan gave him coaching in English and in return was allowed access to a larger room upstairs for exercise. This room was occasionally used for beatings and torture, as was evident from the bloodstains and a set of blood-smeared pliers that Keenan found there.

During this early period of his incarceration Keenan made plans to escape. His first attempt ended in comedy; the second almost killed him. Operation 'clean getaway' involved climbing pipes in the shower room to a ventilation hatch high on the wall. Unfortunately the plumbing wasn't up to bearing his weight, and he crashed to the floor with water cascading from the ruptured pipes. The second attempt, a few days later, meant removing a ventilation pipe protruding through a steel grille above his cell door. Keenan knew that the best time for this noisy enterprise would be in the small hours, when the guards were absent. He hauled himself up and reached out to grab the grille. He was knocked back with an elbow-jolting surge of electricity. The grille was electrified.

These failures plunged Keenan into a pit of depression. He felt abandoned and humiliated. Determined to maintain some self-respect, he would ignore fruit thrown into his cell as though he was an animal in a zoo. The surreal madness of his captivity was brought home to him when one of the jailers took to wearing an ET mask.

An overheard conversation was to bring Keenan joy and helped lift his dark mood. He heard voices. Someone asked another prisoner if he was English. The answer, 'Yes, I'm English. My name is John,' was in what is often described as BBC English. The next morning on the way to the shower room, gazing downwards from a gap in his towel blindfold, he saw a large portable camera in the corridor—a hint about the profession of the new captive, but no clue to his identity. Keenan did not know any of the foreign journalists or cameramen in Beirut.

The precarious nature of Keenan's captivity was demonstrated a few days later. The door of a neighbouring cell was marked with a skull and crossbones drawn in chalk. A little later there was some commotion and then the sound of a shot. On the way back from his shower the following morning Keenan heard the victim's cell being washed out by the guards and discovered in his own cell that he had been left double rations.

Unable to consume a morsel of the murdered man's food, Keenan embarked on a strategy that he had been mulling over for a few weeks. Imprisonment and hunger strike are tragically familiar in Irish history. Only five years had passed since twelve republican prisoners had starved themselves to death inside the Maze Prison. The electoral success of Bobby Sands had been a powerful enough epiphany for the Provisional IRA to commit itself to a twin campaign of 'Armalite and ballot box'. Keenan saw a hunger strike as one of the few rights he had not been stripped of. He started to put the daily ration of food in a corner and ignored it. He did not tell his captors of his plans.

Fearful that the mound of rotting food would attract the fearsome cockroaches, he began to smuggle it from his cell and dispose of it down the toilet. Enough of the food that was slow to decay was kept to convince the Grim Reaper that he was in earnest. Eventually he began to experience bouts of dizziness, and he asked the Grim Reaper to summon his boss. The next day the kidnapper appeared and relayed Keenan's comments to a superior. Through translation it was made clear that no doctor was available, and if the prisoner insisted on killing himself, so be it.

A further discussion the next day did nothing to lessen Keenan's determination. His rations were still brought, but he touched nothing except the water. The hunger strike ended with a victory for the Belfast man.

The kidnapper delivered copies of *Time* and *Newsweek* covering the bombing of Tripoli by the US Air Force and the targeting of Gaddafi and his family. The young kidnapper said, 'My boss, he say this why you here.' 'What the hell has this got to do with me?' Keenan asked. 'I am not American. I am not British. I am Irish.' 'Now we give you what you ask . . . Now you eat?' The loner from Belfast had become a pawn in a much bigger game than he had possibly imagined.

Keenan's sisters, Brenda and Elaine, were discovering much the same thing. In constant contact with the Department of Foreign Affairs, they were being provided with little concrete information. The power struggle in the Middle East was volatile, and most European countries were wary of upsetting the delicate balance of power. It is doubtful if the Irish Embassy could even have supplied exact details at this time, but the two sisters made it clear that they were not going to leave it at that. Their brother would not become another forgotten victim. Their public campaign for Keenan's release might even put their lives at risk. That their brother, a Belfast Protestant, had chosen to travel on an Irish passport was tantamount to treachery to some people in Northern Ireland.

⟨⟩⟨⟩

Weeks dragged by. The prisoner had to constantly create new ways to fill his time and to prevent himself from falling into psychosis from the isolation. He recalled films and books he disliked, rewriting and honing the plot and characters to improve them. He visited his childhood in his mind, but this brought with it the dread of perhaps never being a father. Slowly but inexorably his attention to hygiene decreased. Mosquitoes fed on his flesh. His hair and beard grew long. The Grim Reaper would clip his nails occasionally, because the hostage was denied any sharp tools. Keenan's body rebelled against the strict regime of a captive. His bowels moved when they had to, not always during the short session at the toilet. He became impotent. Then, as lethargy consumed him, he started to hallucinate and to hear music.

One day a bowl of fruit was left in his cell. This small act of kindness from the Grim Reaper intoxicated Keenan. The glorious colour and smell of the fruit swamped his senses. He determined not to eat it, not to lose such a stimulus for the sake of a few hours of satisfaction.

After three-and-a-half months of captivity, one day started differently. The Grim Reaper announced, 'Today you go.' Two men took him blindfolded upstairs and loaded him into a Volkswagen van with other prisoners. Keenan recognised the familiar note of the most popular vehicle in Beirut. As they were driven through the streets of south Beirut a fellow-prisoner reached out and touched his foot. Keenan was overcome at this small gesture of warmth and gently patted the touching hand.

Eventually the van arrived at its destination and Keenan was led to his new cell. He sensed that it was larger than the last one. After the guards left, he slowly raised his blindfold and was amazed to see another prisoner lifting his. 'Fuck me,' the prisoner said in an English accent. 'It's Ben Gunn.' Keenan's mind raced. For a few moments he forgot the famous characters in *Treasure Island* and tried to recall any staff member at the university with that name. The other prisoner produced a pack of cigarettes and introduced himself. He was John McCarthy, a Worldwide Television News journalist who had come to Beirut for a month to stand in for the head of the bureau, Ken Jobson. One of McCarthy's last jobs had been a story on Brian Keenan. McCarthy had been abducted on his way to the airport to catch a flight home. For days they talked inces-santly, exchanging news and exploring each other's background.

Treatment was better in the new prison, but underneath this much-appreciated improvement an ominous menace emerged. Their room was large enough to walk around, and meals were brought three times a day. One of the friendlier guards was called Abed, and they referred to their accommodation as Abed's Hotel. They were tempted into pushing their luck, making more and more demands. After they requested more cigarettes the door opened and a man's arm appeared holding a gun. 'Pray to God, pray to God,' the gunman urged. The arm withdrew, and the door was closed. If the intention of the gunman was to instil fear, he had been more than successful. No matter what sort of relationship Keenan and McCarthy built up with the guards, it was clear that their murder could come at any moment. On another occasion Keenan burst into song in the shower and was abruptly silenced by three shots fired blindly into the room.

These threats encouraged them to try an escape. One guard, who called himself the Joker, had a habit of leaving the key in the lock. McCarthy jiggled the key in the lock until it fell out onto a sheet of paper he had slid under the door. Unfortunately, when they pulled the paper in with the key they discovered that the lock could not be opened from the inside. Since there was no way of replacing the key, they could expect severe punishment when the guards discovered it was missing. McCarthy devised a method of swinging the key, sus-pended loosely on a thread, in an arc from a vent above the door, and then trying to drop it onto a table in the corridor outside. It worked, and the key landed on the table. A sudden snap was enough to part the thread yet still leave the key on the table.

Their joint captivity inspired a hope that their release might be imminent. This was dashed when new clothing—white shorts and blue T-shirts—was issued. Keenan saw the acceptance of the clothes as a submission that their ordeal had a long time to run. He announced that he would not wear the clothes of a prisoner, that he had done nothing wrong and did not deserve to be locked up.

He explained to McCarthy the thinking behind the 'dirty protest' of some republican prisoners in the Maze Prison.

For the duration of their stay at Abed's Hotel, Keenan wore only a ragged towel wrapped round his waist. The topic of the protest in the Maze sparked further long conversations between Keenan and McCarthy on their different backgrounds. The boarding school that McCarthy had attended contrasted with Keenan's Belfast secondary school. Keenan had exceeded parental expectations; McCarthy had failed to reach the targets his family had expected of him. Keenan was a Protestant nationalist, McCarthy a Catholic monarchist. A relationship began to develop that would prove to be an enduring mainstay in the lives of both men, one that was much closer than the bond formed by criminal lifers, for Keenan and McCarthy endured indignities and punishment that no justice system would tolerate.

Their stay at Abed's Hotel was to last a mere six weeks. Then, without notice, they were bundled into the boot of a car and taken on a twenty-minute drive. When the car reached its destination they were removed from the boot and lowered through a manhole-sized opening in the ground. A tunnel led to their new underground cell. A guard whispered, 'Hope to go home soon. Your friends from the other place at Rauché have gone to their home.' Keenan realised that the man was talking about Douglas and Padfield, the two men whose abduction had taken place ten days before his own. The ominous manner in which the news was passed on suggested that they had been killed.

The new cell, much smaller than the previous one, was painted white. John McCarthy was standing near the door. To be separated was a dreadful prospect, but it did not happen, not this time at least. 'Welcome to the house of fun,' McCarthy said of the purpose-built prison. A pair of shorts was thrown in, and Keenan put them on. The new guards did not know what the naked protest was about, and Keenan saw no sense in antagonising them until something was known of their disposition. Meals were provided three times a day: breakfast consisted of bread, jam, cheese, and tea; lunch was rice and vegetables; and supper was the same as breakfast. Any food the prisoners did not eat was thrown away, since unclean hands had been in contact with it, and religious rules forbade the guards to eat it.

It was not long before Keenan's obstinacy was to land him in more trouble. The guards decided to trim the prisoners' beards. Like Samson when shorn of his flowing locks, Keenan felt that the loss of his facial hair would rob him of strength, the power to resist. His face had been bearded all his adult life, and no kidnapper was going to remove it. When he resisted, a gun was pointed at him, and then the guards beat him. His eyelids were taped shut and the electric shaving began. They taunted him with chants that he was Jesus. Eventually he was taken back to his cell, shaven but unbowed.

The beating meted out to Keenan was the beginning of a period of abuse for him, McCarthy, and the other prisoners. An older American man in a nearby cell was marked out for especially rough treatment.

A transistor radio was hung in the corridor, tuned in to static and left at full volume; the 'white noise' drilled into every nerve. The only time the noise would be stopped was during the guards' breakfast. Keenan would cram his dirty fingers into his ears in a desperate effort to block out the screeching. Inevitably, in his weakened state, the dirt caused infection. The pain inside his ears was incredible, but repeated complaints to the guards brought no medical attention. One morning when he returned from washing himself, he discovered that McCarthy had been taken from the cell. His depression descended one more. The infection was showing no sign of improving, and now he had no soulmate to alleviate the long hours. Something drastic needed to be done. So Keenan broke a light-bulb and used a sliver of glass to cut the skin between his toes. He dabbed tissue paper in the blood and stuffed the sodden wedge into his ear. After five or six mornings displaying the dried blood to the guards, he was taken one night to see a doctor.

It soon became clear that there were new arrivals in the cells opposite. Signalling with messages written on tissues and tracing letters in the air, Keenan discovered that their names were Tom Sutherland and Terry Anderson. McCarthy was returned to their cell the next morning, and three days later Keenan was given the much-needed antibiotics. Companionship and the penicillin wrought a dramatic change in him With a new zest he set about inaugurating the 'Hamman mail', an exchange of information with the other prisoners by means of notes in a letter drop in the shower room. News of other prisoners was passed on. An American, David Jacobsen, was in a cell on the same side as Keenan and McCarthy's. Anderson and Sutherland brought fresh hope with the news that they had spent time with Ben Weir and Lawrence Jenco, who had since been freed. Sutherland was constantly being accused of being a CIA agent and had received some horrendous beatings at the hands of his captors.

The guard in charge of the prison was given the sobriquet 'Road Runner' after the cartoon character; he liked to patrol the corridors making the 'beep beep' trademark call of the cartoon bird. His real name was Said, and he held the rank of lieutenant. Like most of the guards, his judgment of a man's worth was the size of rifle he carried. Obsessed with sex, Said would often ask the prisoners about western women. He was fascinated by tales of uninhibited love-making, wanting to be told how the prisoners would have slept with three or four different partners in a week. Keenan and McCarthy obliged him with tales of lusty encounters!

After a few weeks the two prisoners were moved to a larger cell, which the guards, out of some sense of bridge-building, had furnished with a few small luxuries: new mattress covers, soap, and tooth-brushes. The effect on McCarthy was the same as when Keenan had been given new clothes to wear: he saw it as an affirmation that their stay had just begun. A birthday celebration on 27 November, which the guards had laid on for McCarthy to raise his spirits, illustrated the confusion of their relationship with the prisoners. In some respects the guards' religious zeal had made a prison for themselves, one from which there could be no release.

A new arrival, Frank Reid, was able to confirm that Leigh Douglas and Peter Padfield had indeed been murdered. The 'old lags' could only watch over the next few weeks as Reid went through the same emotional maelstrom they themselves had experienced: the days of false hope, the long nights of despair, the determination on the one hand to survive, transformed in an instant into a desire to take his life. Words of advice or counsel were of little solace: the new prisoner would have to find his own method of coping.

Reid escaped from his cell twice and ran amok along the corridors, shouting and banging on the cell doors. His punishment was a couple of life-threatening beatings, administered by Said. The other prisoners were interrogated to ascertain if they had assisted in Reid's escape, and unfortunately, as a result, Said started to spend most nights at the prison.

Without any warning, the guards entered Sutherland and Anderson's cell with fresh clothes and shoes. The Americans were told to dress and twenty minutes later were taken away. Sutherland felt there would have been no money spent if they were to be killed, so it could only mean they were being set free. The other prisoners were jubilant at their release. There was no envy. Sutherland and Anderson had been the longest in captivity, and it was seen as only right that they should be the first to taste freedom.

Keenan and McCarthy were still buoyant over the release when Said entered their cell and attacked McCarthy with the butt of a rifle. Then it was Keenan's turn. The beating of two unarmed, defenceless prisoners seemed to give Said some sort of sexual release. Keenan likened his attack to being raped, in that rape is not for the sexual act itself but has more to do with the ability to subjugate another person. This man, who days before had thrown a party for McCarthy and had talked to them like a friend, was now determined to abuse them. The beatings continued for days, if not from Said then from one of the other guards. They never inflicted injuries that would require hospitalisation, but Keenan's and McCarthy's bodies were covered in bruises and welts.

Keenan knew that his friendship with McCarthy was a rock of sanity that both men could cling to. The shared black humour and the constant teasing about each other's background would provide the vital catharsis for the punishments and trials yet to come. They had no way of knowing that a further three years of captivity lay ahead.

Efforts to free Keenan were still being made in Ireland and Britain. Both governments tried negotiating but were united in refusing to pay a ransom. Terry Waite, the Archbishop of Canterbury's envoy, travelled to Lebanon for negotiations. Members of Sinn Féin opened discussions with Middle East terrorist groups, and some Provisional IRA members travelled to Lebanon to make contact with the kidnappers. McCarthy's girl-friend, Jill Morell, was campaigning tirelessly for his release, using her knowledge of the media to prevent McCarthy's imprisonment becoming a forgotten story. Keenan's sisters made repeated television appearances, criticising both the Irish and British governments for not doing more. Jill Morrell travelled to Paris to speak to the French hostage Camille Sontag after his release but unfortunately was not able to see him. A chance meeting with a French journalist who travelled to and from Lebanon provided her with more information than she was able to obtain through eleven months of haranguing the British Government.

The two prisoners were moved once again, this time to an apartment, where they were to remain for six weeks. The beatings stopped, and their treatment improved. They were given books and other small luxuries. But there were crushing disappointments too. The Americans, Sutherland and Anderson, had not been released but were being held in the same apartment block. A chance news bulletin overheard on the guards' radio brought them the news that Terry Waite had been kidnapped. At night they could hear shelling and gunfire as a battle raged near by. Amal, a Shi'ite paramilitary group, was attacking Palestinian refugee camps.

Their next move involved the longest journey so far. They were loaded into a coffin-like compartment under a lorry for a journey lasting four or five hours. The conditions were appalling. Dust and fumes choked them, the heat making the claustrophobic compartment feel like an oven. Said was waiting at their journey's end to welcome them. They were kept at a farmhouse for forty-eight hours before being moved again, in the boot of a car, to an outhouse or farm building. From then on a guard, Mahmud, was their overseer twenty-four hours a day. A fresh 'refinement' to their captivity was introduced: shackles were fastened and padlocked round their ankles and wrists, then attached to the wall with chains. Their objections were ignored, and the shackles were to remain until Keenan's release three years later.

It appeared that many of the hostages had been the subject of some sort of transfer between Muslim factions. Although Said was still there, the captives recognised none of the other guards and were subjected to fresh interrogation. The interrogator was genuinely angry at the stories of beatings and torture that had been inflicted on the men. Efforts were made to improve the conditions. Books, magazines and even a television were provided.

A flimsy sheet suspended on string acted as a barrier between the prisoners and their Muslim guards. This meant overhearing the religious ritual that the guards observed three times a day. Taped chanting and recitals from the Qur'an soon became an endurance for the prisoners. Reruns of 'The A Team' on the television were almost as bad!

During their time together McCarthy and Keenan were moved to seventeen different places in the hills of south Lebanon, sometimes to houses within the Israeli-occupied zone. The other hostages would have been moved around approximately the same number of times and in the same manner. The routine grew repetitive. Their captors would bind their hands and feet with tape and place a hood over their heads before putting them in large sacks with drawstring necks and carrying them to whatever vehicle had been selected. Accommodation would be other farm outbuildings or apartments. High in the hills the temperature would plummet, and it required five or six blankets to keep warm at night. The metal of their shackles would feel like ice in the sub-zero conditions. Frank Reid was continuing his campaign of disobedience, and they often heard him being punched and kicked. Some of the guards from earlier in their captivity reappeared, including Abed who had beaten them badly in the past. It was not long before he was doing it again, taking every opportunity to cause them pain and frequently beating the soles of their feet with a broom shaft. After Keenan had dared to fight back he was subjected to a session with the broom shaft and was left suspended upside down. After an hour Abed returned and released him, protesting, 'He made me do it, he made me do it. He bad man, he bad, bad man. He made me do it.'

Their bodies, weakened by beatings, would succumb to other problems. The prisoners were fed meat of questionable quality from time to time, with stomach cramps and diarrhoea the inevitable result. Avoiding bouts of 'Beirut belly' was almost impossible in the unsanitary conditions. Plates were left unwashed, and the prisoners were forced to use their hands as utensils. The only cure available to them was fasting, and they took it in turns to nurse one another. Over time Keenan and McCarthy developed a deep compassion for each other, which added another weapon to their armoury of resistance.

A further trip in the coffin-like container in May 1988 delivered them to a hide-out in the Beka'a Valley, the bread-basket of Lebanon. When they were removed from their container they were placed in a cellar of a building not far from the Roman ruins at Ba'albek. When the hoods were removed they saw Anderson, Sutherland and Frank Reid next to them. Soon the hostages were busy exchanging information and telling 'war stories'. The beatings were a common denominator between the five, though techniques and perversions differed. One of Anderson's tormentors would stroke his face with a gun barrel, saying, 'I am Dracula. Tonight I kill you.'

Anderson had spent time in cells with Jacobsen, Jenco, and Weir, all of whom had since been freed. Sutherland had received the worst beatings, because his captors persisted in the belief that he was a CIA spy. A natural comic, Sutherland amused the others with his stories, then lapsed into contemplative silence as he gazed at a newspaper photograph of Salomé, the daughter he had never met. Frank Reid had suffered a lot and probably endured more solitude than the others. He had become further withdrawn than his fellow-Americans and had to be dragged into conversations.

After watching a film on Christmas Eve, about the killing of Israeli athletes at the 1972 Munich Olympic Games, a guard, Ali, inflamed by the film, smacked Keenan's head. Keenan dared him to do it again, and Ali duly obliged. Keenan jumped to his feet and Ali ran from the room. He returned with his automatic rifle and set about hammering Keenan with the butt. When he had exhausted himself he hunkered down beside him and whispered that he would be back the next day. Keenan was to receive a special Christmas Day present.

The next day the prisoners refused food. After some threats, Terry Anderson was taken from the cell, and a few moments later the sound of a shot reverberated through the building. The prisoners might have believed Anderson had been murdered if it had not been for a long moan from one of the guards. His ham-like performance gave the game away. Anderson was returned, unharmed, a few minutes later. When it was made clear what had provoked the protest, Ali was replaced, and the hostages declared the hunger strike over.

The ending of the Iran-Iraq War in 1988 brought improved conditions for the quintet at Ba'albek. Magazines, mainly *Time* and *Newsweek*, were given to them. Heavily censored, they still contained enough information for the prisoners to deduce what political changes had taken place. There was much discussion about the *Vincennes* incident, the shooting down of an Iranian passenger jet by an American naval vessel in July 1988, and its possible ramifications for their well-being. A guard gave them a radio, and for six weeks they had a window to the outside world. Not everything they heard was good. A bulletin announced that the Islamic Jihad had vowed to kill the American hostages if their demands were not met. This was the cause of the radio and magazine privilege being rescinded as unexpectedly as it had started.

Frank Reid was the first of the group to be released. The guards asked for his shoe size and measured him for clothes. Although the prisoners were told he was being freed, they were reluctant to believe it. They had fallen for that story before, and the radio threat made them seriously concerned for Reid's safety. The guards returned the radio for twenty-four hours so the prisoners could hear confirmation of Reid's release, but, as luck would have it, no mention was made of it. The guards were concerned that the prisoners might rebel if they thought they were going to be killed and had nothing to lose.

A few weeks after that, Terry Anderson was taken from the cell. Once again the remaining prisoners had no definite proof that he was to be freed. Tom Sutherland was next, leaving McCarthy and Keenan. The prison regime was relaxed slightly, and the two men comforted each other with assurances that their time could be just months away.

Nine months after Reid had been taken from them, the two were chained, hooded and bagged in the usual manner for moving. This time the sounds heard from inside the car boot were different. The trip was a long one, and the vehicle appeared to be travelling in convoy. The horns of other vehicles blared continually and there were no stops at security checkpoints. Keenan has always been convinced that the Syrian army had been their escorts on this trip.

On their arrival in the suburbs of Beirut they were taken from the vehicle and chained to a wall in an upstairs room. There was another prisoner in the room—Frank Reid. He had been held there in solitude for the whole nine months and had been treated abominably. His mental state had deteriorated, and he had become even more withdrawn. Keenan realised that he would have been in a similar state if it had not been for the company of John McCarthy. Pleas to the guards, supported with a show of iron will by McCarthy, brought about a change of Reid's treatment and he slowly improved. The macho-driven guards respected anyone who had the courage to stand up to them, while showering contempt and abuse on any prisoner displaying weakness.

Their food was much improved here; they were also given a television and the chance to watch a video film every couple of days. Requests for medicine or for luxuries such as chocolate were granted almost immediately. Mahmud, the guard with the best English, would come and chat with them, bringing news of world events. It was from him that the trio heard of the fall of the Berlin Wall in November 1989.

Reid was taken away once again, but this time his release was confirmed when Keenan eavesdropped on the guards' radio. Their exuberance was tempered by the arrival of another prisoner in the room next to theirs. The new arrival was Terry Waite, hungry for news. The Archbishop of Canterbury's envoy spent his first few weeks relaying messages back and forth by a system of taps on the wall. A slower mode of communication would be hard to imagine, but it was all that was available. During breaks the two would stuff a sock with rags or paper and throw the 'ball' back and forth, reminding them of scenes of Steve McQueen bouncing a baseball against the wall of his solitary confinement cell in the film *The Great Escape*.

The end came without warning. Guards entered their cell and ordered Keenan to stand. He was hooded, led to another room, and chained to a wall. Keenan dreaded separation from McCarthy, but one of the guards laid a hand on his shoulder and whispered in his ear, 'Brian, you go home.' 'Home! You mean another place?' asked Brian. 'You go home. Family. Dublin!' the guard stressed.

It started to sink in. Keenan was really to be released, after four years and four months of captivity. Obstinate as ever, he insisted on speaking to McCarthy. He was given an assurance that he would have a chance to say goodbye after a few hours. Keenan was determined not to leave without his friend. But was he being fair to his loved ones, who had waited for so long? He owed them a debt of gratitude as well, especially his sisters, who had battled so tirelessly for his freedom. For most of the time left he frenetically measured the pros and cons in his mind. He finally reached a decision. To deny his freedom now would be to diminish his friend. To walk unhooded and unshackled, to see the sky and feel the sun on his face, would be to claim freedom for them both. Feeling that a limb had been torn from his body, Keenan showered and had his hair cut. He sat still while the scissors clipped, trying to send a tele- pathic message to John McCarthy.

Keenan's abduction had taken place in a Mercedes car, and so it was with his release. They drove through the back streets of Beirut until eventually the car stopped and there was a brief discussion with some men. He was driven for another quarter of an hour before the car stopped and he was told to go. 'Yallah, yallah. Go, go. Good luck, good luck.'

An old man took Keenan's hand, and they walked slowly for- ward. Like a spy exchange scene in Cold War films, a car a hundred yards away flashed its lights, then left them on. The Mercedes lights were also switched on. Keenan walked along this floodlit path. Two men emerged from the shadows, one of them carrying an automatic rifle. The four men met in the middle, and greetings were exchanged. The old man placed Keenan's hand in the hand of one of the men. No other word was spoken. The old man walked away.

'You are Syrian?' Keenan asked. 'Syria,' one answered, with a nod of his head. Keenan looked back, but the lights of the Mercedes blinded him. He was ushered into another car. 'You, nationality?' the driver asked. 'Irish,' replied Keenan. 'How long?' 'Four-and-a- half years.' The driver whistled appreciatively and turned back to the wheel. The car moved off.

Keenan was taken for a short meeting in a Syrian diplomatic building, then driven through the hills of Lebanon to Damascus. He spent two nights in Syrian army intelligence headquarters for debriefing. They told him about the Iraqi invasion of Kuwait and were keen to hear what his views were. He recalled advice once given to him in Belfast: whatever you say, say nothing. His pig- headed silence did not seem to trouble the Syrians too much. He was supplied with new clothes, and when showered and dressed he joined them at a celebratory banquet. The food was too much for Keenan's fragile stomach, but he found the smells, colours and tex- tures exquisite. That night, his liberty restored, he went for a walk around Damascus.

Seven days after his release, Keenan gave a press conference in St Patrick's Hall, Dublin Castle. Before he started he reminded the assembled journalists that there were still many hostages held in Beirut and asked them to exercise sensitivity and restraint in their reporting of his comments. He thanked all those who had never given up on him, especially his family and friends. When asked what it meant to be a hostage, he said, 'A hostage is crucifying aloneness. There is a silent, screaming slide into the bowels of ultimate despair. A hostage is a man hanging by his fingernails over the edge of chaos and feeling his fingers slowly straightening. A hostage is the humiliating stripping away of every sense and fibre of body and mind and spirit that makes you what you are.'

He later talked of holding a newborn baby in his arms in the Cock Tavern in Howth, Co. Dublin. The simple cradling of the infant had made him feel more free and alive than any other experience since his release.

It was to be another year before John McCarthy was released. When he flew into the British air force base at Lyneham, Wiltshire, Keenan was there to greet him. Keenan was awarded a CBE along with John McCarthy in 1992. The two have remained close friends, making a trek together through Chile and publishing a book, *Between Extremes*, about the trip. A film, *Blind Flight*, based on Keenan's book *An Evil Cradling*, is in production. Ian Hart will play Keenan; Joseph Fiennes will play McCarthy.

11

The John O'Grady
Kidnap and Mutilation

John O'Grady, a prosperous Dublin dentist, was a keen horseman and a member of a local hunt. So when on 13 October 1987 he became the substitute kidnap victim of a terrorist called the Border Fox, the black irony did not go unnoticed among members of the press. Details of the kidnap were scarce, but the story that eventually unfolded dominated the headlines for six weeks. Little was known about O'Grady, but the same could not be said about his kidnapper.

Dessie O'Hare, the Border Fox, could rightly have been described as mad, bad, and dangerous to know. In his short career of three years as an active terrorist for the Provisionals, the Irish National Liberation Army (INLA) and finally as self-proclaimed leader of the Irish Revolutionary Brigade, his personal tally of murder victims was over thirty. The oldest was Iris Farley, the seventy-year-old mother of a UDR soldier.

O'Hare grew up in the beautiful drumlin countryside of south Armagh. Dark, small, and of slight build, he often found himself the target of bullies and would fight back with a violence that shocked his adversaries. A quiet and brooding youngster, he seemed to prefer his own company. His murderous rampage started when he was still in his teens. A seven-year term in Portlaoise Prison for possession of an automatic rifle brought a welcome respite to his killing, but on his release in 1986 his career quickly resumed. Having abandoned the 'tame' Provisional IRA during his time in Portlaoise, O'Hare pledged allegiance to the INLA, an offshoot of the Official IRA. The INLA leaders recognised in O'Hare a cold-bloodedness that would be an invaluable asset in their internecine feud with the 'Irish People's Liberation Organisation'.

Clashes between paramilitary factions were reaching epidemic proportions in the late 1980s. Terrorist organisations dependent for their survival on secrecy and absolute loyalty proved fertile breeding grounds for paranoia, suspicion, internal conflict, and division. Whether schisms arose from ideological and financial differences or were engineered by counter-terrorism efforts, the result was inevitably a high body count. A carcinogenic fear of betrayal led to paramilitaries adopting an active policy of torturing suspected collaborators until suitable confessions were forthcoming. These would be promptly rewarded with a couple of rounds fired at close range into the back of the skull, and the body dumped by the roadside as a warning to other would-be informers. Anybody dispensing this type of summary justice to former comrades in arms could not expect to survive for long. Only a madman would want to take it on. In O'Hare, the INLA command knew they had such a man. He was set to work.

Undeniably ruthless, O'Hare had something else that any successful avenger needed: more than his fair share of luck. He was a survivor, not something that could be said of those who volunteered to stand shoulder to shoulder with him. Staff at Monaghan County Hospital near the border were used to patching up O'Hare's wounded comrades after his latest foray into the North. Some were not so lucky: Peadar McIlvenna and Anthony McClelland both ended up on slabs in the mortuary after shoot-outs with security forces.

Tony McCluskey and Gerard Steenson were among O'Hare's victims. McCluskey was suspected of setting up two INLA leaders for assassination at a Drogheda hotel. In an interview in Portlaoise Prison, O'Hare admitted that he wanted to give McCluskey a 'hard death'. He used a bolt-cutter to remove part of McCluskey's ear and the tip of a finger, a *modus operandi* he had used before and was soon to use again.

Eventually the feud sputtered to a halt. Keen to wash their hands of O'Hare, the INLA expelled him. Insisting that he had jumped before being pushed, O'Hare quickly formed the 'Irish Revolutionary Brigade'. On 11 September 1987 he and his gang robbed an Ulster Bank branch in Castlepollard, Co. Westmeath, of £3,000. Other raids that autumn, none of them very lucrative, were also blamed on O'Hare. Desperate for funds and thinking that his reputation would help a kidnap and ransom succeed where others had failed, he hid in a house near Malahide, Co. Dublin, and began to cast around for a suitable target. Several prominent figures were considered and rejected. Finally he selected Dr Austin Darragh. A very successful businessman and consummate self-publicist, Darragh had made his millions from clinical research and in 1985 had floated his company, the Institute of Clinical Pharmacology, on the New York stock exchange. Darragh, O'Hare decided, would be an ideal kidnap victim. Ransom money was readily available, and, unlike Herrema, only minimal public sympathy would be felt for the victim. The financial excesses of the eighties, encouraged by Thatcherite policy, with the advent of the Porsche-driving yuppie and the 'greed is good' culture, had barely touched Ireland. There had been no comparable boom in the Republic: the 'Celtic Tiger' economy was still in the politicians' imaginations. Darragh's company had received a lot of bad publicity over an unsavoury incident in its recent history, when, in 1984, a student had died while taking part in a drug-testing scheme.

O'Hare allowed his gang into his plan. Fergal Toal was another of the 'boys from the County Armagh'. The third northerner was a Belfast man, Tony McNeill, though his family had moved him to Dublin for his own safety in the 1970s. Eddie Hogan was from Cork and had served time with O'Hare and Toal in Portlaoise. An acquaintance of McNeill, Gerry Wright, had a house in Cabra and a barber's shop in Parkgate Street, Dublin, which the gang could call on. The three men were not of the calibre O'Hare would have wished for, but after his bloody exploits of the previous twelve months, few wanted anything to do with him. It showed poor judgment on O'Hare's part to entrust such an ambitious undertaking to relatively inexperienced men. As if to prove the point, on the

Sunday before the kidnap Toal killed a man outside the Imperial Hotel's night club in Dundalk during a dispute over the dead man's former girl-friend. It is not known to what degree this senseless killing contributed to the débâcle that occurred less than forty-eight hours later.

It was 9:30 at night when O'Hare and his gang, having donned gloves and balaclavas, used a sledge-hammer to break through the outer wooden door and the inner glass door of the six-bedroom Tudor-style house in Brennanstown Road, Cabinteely, a south Co. Dublin suburb. Upstairs, John O'Grady and his wife, Marise, had retired to bed early and were watching television. The house belonged to Marise's father, Austin Darragh, who had vacated it some four years previously, neglecting to remove a brass nameplate at the gate.

O'Grady, his wife just behind him, came face to face with the masked and armed intruders on the stairs. The gang ordered them to retreat to the landing. Two of the O'Gradys' children were in their rooms, six-year-old Louise already asleep, her thirteen-year-old brother Darragh reading. Twelve-year-old Anthony was in the bathroom and had a gun held to his head when he emerged to find out who was causing the rumpus. O'Hare, making a quick reconnaissance of the bedrooms, found Darragh taking cover behind his bed with a phone in his hand. 'You little bastard!' O'Hare roared, tearing away the phone.

The family was ushered into Louise's room, which the kidnappers, clearly rattled at finding their target absent, had not checked for a telephone. Marise quickly placed a call to the 999 operator, but O'Hare burst in and ripped the extension from the wall. Toal was left to watch the family as the rest of the gang took John O'Grady downstairs for interrogation in order to throw some light on their foul-up.

With his family at risk, O'Grady had no option but to answer O'Hare's questions. He explained that he was Austin Darragh's son-in-law, but could not be certain if Darragh was then in Ireland. After helping themselves to tea and biscuits, the gang discussed their next move. Would it be possible to lure the millionaire to his former home? Perhaps some feigned sickness with one of his grand-children would do the trick, or, alternatively, a story that Marise had fallen downstairs and injured herself. The O'Gradys convinced them that Darragh was unlikely to respond to such appeals. The gang set about ransacking the house for valuables. Jewellery and private papers were taken. Determined that his plan would not be a total wash-out, O'Hare, on discovering a video camera, decided that a video demand should be made to Darragh for £300,000 for the release of John O'Grady and one of his children. The tape was recorded with a masked gunman standing on each side of O'Grady. When Marise pleaded with him not to take a child, O'Hare relented. It was not the first time the notorious INLA killer had displayed compassion. He once stopped the car of the Unionist politician Jim Nicholson but refrained from firing when he saw that the car was being driven by Nicholson's wife.

None of the house's nine occupants slept that night. Next morning, after listening to the radio news, the gang blindfolded O'Grady and bundled him into the boot of a car. They gave him some fruit and a drink. The car was driven across the East Link toll bridge to the north of the city.

Shortly after noon the two gunmen left behind in the O'Grady house, to ensure that nobody alerted the Gardaí, received a series of coded telephone calls. Ninety minutes later, after leaving detailed instructions about what they expected Marise O'Grady to do, the gunmen left in the family's car. Shortly before five that afternoon O'Hare telephoned and told Marise the car was parked at the Fairways Hotel, Dundalk. She immediately contacted her father, who alerted the detective unit at Harcourt Square, Dublin.

John O'Grady was on the move again, this time in the back seat of a second car. His destination was 41 Parkgate Street, the barber's shop owned by Gerry Wright. It emerged later that Wright was assisting the gang in return for the promised killing of the man who had murdered his brother Billy more than a decade before.

O'Grady was fed and spent the night in a sleeping bag in a dingy basement, one arm handcuffed to a chair. At the same time as he was eating his evening meal of hamburger and chips, washed down with a Muscadet, his wife was picking out Dessie O'Hare's face from police photographs, he being the only gang member who had removed his mask at her home. Having identified the ring-leader, it was still difficult to put names to the other three in the gang. Some consideration was given to the theory that O'Hare had teamed up with a Dublin gang for this operation.

News of the kidnap reached the media on the Wednesday, but a news blackout was soon ordered. A decision to lift this was made locally on Thursday by Dún Laoghaire gardaí. This error of judgment was the first of many that would plague the investigation and delay the subsequent capture of the gang. Four days after the abduction, almost certainly in response to heightened public awareness as a result of media attention, O'Grady was moved to an isolated shed in Co. Cork, not far from Carricktohill. It was an area of thin rocky soil, thickly coated with gorse and brambles.

The mercurial nature of O'Hare's character, exacerbated by the severe and constant stress, was demonstrated. One minute he would be pandering to O'Grady's comfort, the next would have him beating his victim with a chain. These violent mood swings forced the intelligent O'Grady to comply with his captors. But even this submission would prove not to be enough against the psychopathic O'Hare.

The next few days passed slowly for the victim. He found himself drawn to Tony McNeill. At times there was a surreal quality to the imprisonment, with games of chess in the gorse, and watching a masked gunman patrolling the perimeter of the bracken in the dentist's cashmere coat.

On Thursday 22 October, before being moved to another new location, O'Grady was made to write a ransom note. The demand had leapt to £1,500,000, this fivefold increase prompted by media reports on the extent of Darragh's wealth. The note also contained instructions on how contact would be made. A courier would be paged at a hotel and given further directions.

O'Grady's new hide-out was a container that had been salvaged from a box van. Farmers often placed these containers in outlying fields as makeshift storage for hay bales. The new location was Ballymacsliney, Co. Cork. Like Carricktohill, it was an area covered in heavy gorse and brambles. Conditions were primitive. The sole source of heat was a single-bar electric fire powered by an extension lead from a nearby cottage; the only light was that thrown off by the small fire. The toilet was a choice between a bucket or al fresco at the edge of the field. Hogan, Toal and McNeill were left to guard the prisoner while O'Hare departed to rendezvous with his wife. Clare O'Hare's flat in Castleblayney was under round-the-clock Garda surveillance, yet she managed to disappear with minimal effort. It would be a month before she was to surface again, and then under the most extraordinary circumstances.

The gang miscalculated if they thought their presence would go unnoticed. By the Monday afternoon the Midleton gardaí had been informed of armed men seen near the container. A Garda patrol drove out to Ballymacsliney and took a snoop around, imprudently walking up to the container and rapping the door. Fortunately there was no response, but they saw enough to arouse their suspicions, and when they reported back it was decided that the field should be surrounded. The superintendent in charge had sixteen armed gardaí at his command and requested army support from Collins Barracks, Cork. While waiting for the reinforcements, three units were despatched to set up four roadblocks in an attempt to isolate the container. A few minutes before five that afternoon the detective-inspector leading the men on the ground radioed headquarters to report that they had arrived and were taking up position. He had barely broken off communication when he was back on the air announcing that they were under fire.

The three terrorists and their hostage had been moving along one of many tunnels through the gorse—formed by small animals and foraging sheep and goats—when the gardaí had made their ill-advised foray out to the container earlier that afternoon. The kidnappers remained in hiding and dithered over tactics until the arrival of the larger body of men forced their hand. Charles and Theresa Terry were returning to Kilva from visiting Theresa's parents when two armed and masked men jumped in front of their van. 'Get out, get out!' Hogan roared, training his gun on them. Theresa had trouble releasing her seat belt and was slow to climb out of the van. A second vehicle pulled up, the Renault of Michael and Mary O'Brien with their daughter Patricia driving. The kidnappers decided to take the faster Renault. One of the armed gardaí, only yards away, witnessed this confrontation but did not have a clear shot. A gunman aimed his weapon and fired at the garda, the bullet raising a clod from the grass beside him. More shots were fired as O'Grady was manhandled into the car.

'Get down, you fucking scum!' one of the firing gunmen screamed above the noise of his shots as he backed towards the car. Toal smashed out the rear windscreen of the car and continued to cover their escape by firing through it. Lying across the rear seat, O'Grady was Toal's shield against any return fire as the car accelerated away. The detective-inspector caught a glimpse of the unmasked driver and recognised Eddie Hogan. A garda fired his sub-machine gun at the wheels of the car, and another fired two pistol shots from closer range. A round grazed Hogan's head, but the terrorists made good their escape.

Recriminations soon started to fly. Why, Garda Headquarters wanted to know, had Midleton not informed them? It had taken two hours to gather the men together, arm and equip them, yet not a word to the detectives co-ordinating the hunt. It was not the Garda Síochána's finest hour; and worse was to come in the next few days.

The gang hijacked another car on the Waterford road, and as night closed in they headed north-west along a succession of back roads. Another stop was made at a house near Mallow, the residents tied up and their car taken after Hogan had attended to the bullet graze on his temple. After making a stop for petrol, the gang headed towards Dublin and Gerry Wright's house in Cabra. O'Grady was put in a small space beneath the stairs of 260 Carnlough Road. The next day he was allowed out of his cubby-hole to attend to Hogan's wound. He was given three newspapers, which reported the shoot-out in Midleton. It was only then that O'Grady knew where he had been held.

Dessie O'Hare turned up at Cabra, where he bought some beer from an off-licence. Tuesday night was a time for celebration, and the terrorists recounted tales of the events in Midleton. The next two days passed quietly, Wright shopping for provisions and videotapes. O'Grady was given propaganda leaflets to read and memorise. One contained the writings of the hunger-striker and MP Bobby Sands.

Hilary Prentice, a solicitor and one of O'Grady's patients, received a phone call from O'Hare instructing her to contact Elizabeth Doyle-Kelly, O'Grady's aunt, who in turn was to travel to Limerick Cathedral and retrieve instructions for the payment of a ransom from under a statue of Our Lady beside the thirteenth Station of the Cross. These were to be handed over to Austin Darragh's wife. Doyle-Kelly complied with O'Hare's instructions, but not until the Serious Crime Squad had been briefed. The only message she found was a prayer to Our Lady of Perpetual Succour.

On Saturday evening O'Hare contacted the *Sunday Tribune* and told them O'Grady had not been hurt in the escape from Midleton, but if any member of his gang was killed their hostage would be executed at once. It was a threat the Gardaí took very seriously. The Garda Technical Bureau had discovered many items of interest abandoned in the container at Midleton, not least the fingerprints that linked one of the kidnappers to a murder outside the Imperial Hotel, Dundalk. Of lesser interest was an admission card to the Guinness leisure centre, which was set aside for later investigation.

It was widely rumoured that Austin Darragh had called on the services of Control Risks Group, a British firm retained by many multinational companies to advise them in the event of corporate kidnap. A former Commissioner of London Metropolitan Police, Sir Kenneth Newman, had a seat on the board. At this time the O'Grady family still understood that the ransom was £300,000, not having retrieved O'Hare's latest demand in Limerick Cathedral. The Taoiseach, Charles Haughey, declared that the Government was totally opposed to paying ransoms to terrorists. The Control Risks

Group was reported to have been actively involved in negotiations in the Don Tidey and Jennifer Guinness kidnaps.

Five days after the first phone call, Hilary Prentice received a second from a somewhat baffled O'Hare. He had no knowledge that Doyle-Kelly had failed to find his ransom instructions, his confusion arising from his having just discovered that the hotel he had selected as the courier's starting point had been closed for renovation. A series of phone calls followed, deepening the misunderstanding and throwing O'Hare into a rage. He returned to Cabra, convinced he was being messed about by the authorities and determined that he would send them a message to prove he was not to be trifled with.

O'Grady was told to write a letter saying that a courier should be sent to the Silver Springs Hotel in Cork with the money and a car phone. When O'Grady had finished writing, O'Hare gagged him, put two pillowcases over his head, and laid him on the floor. O'Grady described what happened next in a written statement for the Special Criminal Court:

> My left hand was taken and the finger spread out on what seemed to be a board put under my hand. He then told some-body, whom I presumed to be one of the three raiders, to stand on my hand. Then I felt something on my little finger and then there was a bang like a hammer coming in contact with a chisel. Then I felt excruciating pain in this hand and I realized that he had cut off my little finger. I could feel the blood flowing.

The carpet tiles were stained with blood. O'Grady was to endure fresh agony when the wound was cauterised three times with a red-hot knife blade. The primitive amputation was repeated on the little finger of his right hand, with further cauterisation. He was untied and made to pose for three Polaroid photograghs. O'Hare took his time with the pictures, taunting the dentist: 'Think of the seasons. Think of spring and summer.' O'Hare left McNeill and Hogan to dress the wounds and give O'Grady some basic medication.

Hilary Prentice received another call from O'Hare just before five that afternoon. He told her that he had given orders to his men for a couple of O'Grady's fingers to be cut off. He demanded her home number so he could call her later with the whereabouts of the fingers and fresh instructions.

It was seven o'clock when O'Hare phoned the Prentice home and told her that O'Grady's fingers could be found in Carlow Cathedral. He tried to pass the blame for the mutilation on to Doyle-Kelly, threatening to cut O'Grady into bits if he didn't get some co-operation this time. Still not knowing that the first message had not been found, a befuddled O'Hare made several references to a Kilkenny message. Prentice asked him if he meant the Limerick message. He rang off but called back a few minutes later saying, 'I made a mistake there when I said Kilkenny. I meant Limerick.' Later that night gardaí found a package wedged behind a statue of St Teresa in Carlow Cathedral. Inside were three envelopes. They contained a ransom note, a Polaroid photograph of the mutilated victim, and two severed fingers.

The Government made a U-turn and declared that if the family wanted to pay the ransom, the Government would not prevent it. Austin Darragh started planning to buy the release of his daughter's husband. Father Brian D'Arcy was chosen as courier to take the money to the Silver Springs Hotel at lunchtime on Thursday 5 November. Peter Elliot, Darragh's chauffeur, drove to Limerick Cathedral on Wednesday and found the original ransom note under the statue of St Teresa. For the first time the family knew the full amount of the ransom.

Sergeant Henry Spring and Detective-Garda Martin O'Connor, stationed at Dún Laoghaire, were given the Guinness card to follow up. On Thursday morning they called at the Parkgate address of the card's owner, Paul O'Sullivan. The card had been lent to a neighbour, they were told, Gerry Wright, who had the hairdresser's shop a few doors away. Wright knew he was in trouble as soon as the gardaí arrived in his shop. He said the gardaí were welcome to search his house at Cabra without a warrant. They would find nobody there. Even if the gang had vacated the house it was likely that there would have been incriminating signs of their recent occupation, so Wright's decision to invite the two gardaí back to his home must be viewed as a bluff.

Father D'Arcy was still an hour's drive from the Silver Springs Hotel when the two gardaí and Wright pulled up outside 260 Carnlough Road, Cabra. Sergeant Spring was forty-five and an intelligence collator, rarely working in the field. His colleague, O'Connor, was thirty-six and carried a detective's firearm.

There was pandemonium inside the house when Wright opened the front door. Hogan hid in the space under the stairs with O'Grady. McNeill dived into bed and pulled the bedspread over him. Fergal Toal remained in the kitchen and was the first to be found. McNeill was discovered next, fully dressed in a stone-cold bed. O'Connor told him to go downstairs, unescorted. The two gardaí knew they needed more manpower. O'Connor went outside to the car to radio for urgent back-up. Wright, who followed him out, overheard the short conversation and ran back in yelling that the game was up. McNeill turned, aiming a pistol he had concealed in his clothing at Spring's head, and shouted, 'Get down, you bastard!'

Hogan chose that moment to emerge from his hiding-place. The garda was kicked in the head and stunned. McNeill rushed outside and pushed his gun into O'Connor's chest, ordering him out of the car. O'Connor wrapped his hand around the barrel and struggled with McNeill. Toal came to McNeill's assistance and started raining blows on O'Connor. Witnesses assumed that a car hijacking was in progress. Hogan emerged from the house carrying a pump-action 12-bore shotgun. He was pushing O'Grady in front of him. Spring, left in the house with the unarmed Wright, seized the chance and escaped into the back garden.

Hogan pushed O'Grady into the back seat of the unmarked Garda car, aiming the shotgun at O'Connor. 'Stand back. Stand back!' he ordered Toal and McNeill. 'I'll blow his knees off!' Even though the young detective stood up and backed away from the shotgun, Hogan still fired into O'Connor's abdomen from a few feet. O'Connor bravely pulled his weapon and fired, missing his target. He cocked his weapon for a second shot but received a handgun round in his shoulder. He collapsed onto his back. Hogan kicked the stricken detective and took his weapon.

McNeill hijacked a van, but before O'Grady could be transferred the first armed gardaí arrived in response to O'Connor's call. Detective-Garda Gregory Sheehan took up position and shouted, 'Armed gardaí. Drop your weapons!' Several shots were fired at him in response. He aimed his revolver and fired all six rounds at the three gunmen. As he reloaded, they took off. Sheehan was about to give chase when he saw the wounded O'Connor. He stopped to give assistance and called for an ambulance. In the confusion O'Grady slipped away, oblivious to the fact that he was headed in the same direction as his kidnappers, tearing off the blackened glasses he had been made to wear.

He had no idea where he was, but he knew to run from the sound of gunfire. A neighbour closed the door on him when he asked for shelter.

The three fugitives tried to hijack another vehicle further along Carnlough Road. There was a brief volley of shots at another unmarked patrol car arriving at the scene, then Hogan and Toal ran off along Kilkiernan Road, while McNeill commandeered a car at gunpoint.

Gardaí were chasing Toal and Hogan along Kilkiernan Road. The gunmen were taking it in turns to cover the other's retreat. Toal's knee was grazed by a shot from a garda. Two newly arrived gardaí saw a man running along the road before he disappeared into an overgrown garden. They instinctively followed and found their quarry huddled behind a bush. 'Don't shoot,' the dishevelled man pleaded. 'I'm John O'Grady.' With minimum delay he was on his way to Blackrock Clinic to have his wounds attended to.

Hogan and Toal were reduced to hijacking a slow-moving road-sweeping vehicle. It may have resembled a stunt from a Mack Sennett comedy, but it worked. They gave the following gardaí the slip. Several other errors would allow the three fugitives to pass through the net of roadblocks. Twenty miles from the Silver Springs Hotel, Father D'Arcy's car was pulled in by gardaí. O'Hare had had his prize snatched from him at the last minute.

Hogan and Toal abandoned the road-sweeper near the Phoenix Park and hijacked a series of cars, finally ending up in Clondalkin. They coolly rang the doorbell of Una Dermody's house and pushed their way in. Dermody happened to have a friend in the house, Maria Hennessy. Hennessy, at gunpoint, dressed the wound to Toal's knee while the two fugitives took time for a snack. They used Dermody's car to flee Dublin. Both women were taken on the drive to Limerick, where the gunmen released them three hours later and the car was handed back to them. The women were amazed as the gunmen waved them off.

Toal and Hogan dumped their weapons, walked to Limerick railway station and took a taxi to Hogan's sister's house in Tipperary. The taxi passed through four checkpoints on the journey—even receiving directions at one! But their luck was not to hold for much longer.

Meanwhile Detective-Garda O'Connor was undergoing life-saving surgery at St Laurence's Hospital. The most serious wound was the one to his abdomen. His intestine required a resection. Surgeons painstakingly removed dozens of lead pellets. Meanwhile at the Blackrock Clinic, O'Grady's wounds were also being attended to. Unfortunately, his fingers could not be re-attached.

At the fifth roadblock outside Tipperary, Toal's reluctance to identify himself to a garda aroused suspicions. The unarmed garda was sufficiently curious to have an armed patrol car follow the taxi. When the taxi stopped at traffic lights, the armed gardaí took the opportunity to question Toal and Hogan further. Doubting the validity of their driving-licence identification, they took the two into custody at 8:30 p.m.

Outside the station the fugitives, not handcuffed, were being escorted from the Garda car when Hogan ran off. One of the gardaí gave chase, while his two colleagues took Toal into the station. 'Hold him,' they instructed the gardaí inside. 'There's another fella gone away.' They hurried out to assist in the chase for Hogan. While Toal was being booked in, he took advantage of a moment's distraction and fled. One of the gardaí grabbed and tore Toal's shirt as he tried in vain to prevent his escape. Two of Ireland's most wanted men had evaded custody and took to their heels.

A heavy fog had descended on Tipperary. Hogan was last seen running across the Clanwilliam Rugby Club ground. Members of the club assisted in the search, but once again Hogan evaded capture. Toal waved down a car and climbed into the front passenger seat. 'Keep going. The cops are after me,' he ordered the driver, Michael McCarthy. Realising the identity of his unwelcome passenger, McCarthy drove only a short distance before ordering him from his car. Toal ran off into the fog and soon commandeered another car and took the driver hostage. He was then waved down at a checkpoint, but he accelerated through it. The car's owner, Catherine Ryan, was terrified. She thought the gardaí would open fire on the car and hit her.

Outside Borrisoleigh a patrol, which had been alerted to the car crashing through the checkpoint, spotted the car and gave chase. Toal clipped a ditch and rolled the car onto its roof. Both he and Catherine Ryan were hanging upside down by their seat belts. The gardaí fired warning shots into the air as they cautiously approached. 'Keep back or I'll kill her,' Toal shouted.

Garda Pat Phelan circled behind the crashed car, and when Toal eventually extricated himself and Ryan he was on hand to stick his sub-machine gun in Toal's back. 'Let her go and nobody will get hurt.' This time the gardaí made sure to handcuff the prisoner.

Hogan was recaptured fifteen hours later. A report had come in to the gardaí at Caher, Co. Tipperary, about a strange man seen walking along the Ballydrehid road. Hogan ran off when a Garda car pulled up beside him. He was quickly caught and gave up after a brief struggle. But it was a ruse. The prisoner broke free of the arm-lock, and a more ferocious struggle started. With nothing to lose, Hogan kicked, butted and bit Garda Lynch and Garda Seery. He managed to get a grip of the barrel of Seery's gun, and two shots were accidentally fired during the tussle for control, fortunately not hitting the combatants. With Hogan's teeth clamped to his crutch, Seery managed to pistol-whip Hogan and, with his colleague's assistance, eventually handcuffed him.

O'Hare was the next of the gang to surface. Early on the Sunday evening he and his pregnant wife stopped at a chip shop in Dunleer, Co. Louth. Julie-Ann, their seven-year-old daughter, was in the car. He entered the shop and placed an order. Outside, his wife got out of the car and was attempting to escape, leaving her daughter in the car. Dessie O'Hare pulled a gun, pushed his way through the line of customers to the door of the shop, and fired at his fleeing wife, shouting, 'Stop, you bitch!' He went to his car, removed a shotgun, and fired again at his wife. He then turned and blasted out the window of the chip shop. He climbed into his car and drove after his wife. Clare O'Hare, wounded in one leg, sought refuge in the Mill Race pub. Her husband skidded the car to a halt, blocking most of the road in front. The owner of the pub had stepped out to see what the commotion was about. O'Hare fired at him, then got back into the car and raced off, his daughter screaming in the rear seat. Clare O'Hare was arrested at the scene. She denied ever having been in the Cabra house, but several fingerprints found there proved her a liar. The following day a special meeting was held of the Government ministers with responsibility for security. A reward of £100,000 was offered for information leading to O'Hare's capture.

The morning of 11 November brought the arrest of the final member of the trio who had shot their way out of Cabra. A tip-off led gardaí to a house in Ballyfermot, Dublin. They caught McNeill asleep. It appeared he had intended to take his own life if faced with arrest: a farewell note to his loved ones had been written.

Three weeks were to pass before the reward produced dividends. The gardaí received a tip-off that O'Hare would be driving through the Minister's Cross area outside Urlingford, Co. Kilkenny. This time there would be no mistakes. A force of fifty armed gardaí and soldiers was assembled shortly after noon and an apparently routine checkpoint set up with a strongly manned roadblock further along.

Vehicles for a secondary roadblock were hidden beyond that, should O'Hare's BMW crash through. It was an hour and a half before O'Hare's car slowed to a halt at the checkpoint. There was a second man in the passenger seat. Detective-Sergeant P. J. O'Rourke invited them to step out of the car. The passenger, Martin Bryan, raised a handgun and aimed at Inspector Pat Moriarity.

The two gardaí threw themselves to the ground, and O'Hare gunned the engine, burning rubber as the car surged away. Soldiers hidden behind a wall opened fire. A bullet tore through the passenger door and others shredded a rear tyre. A marksman at the roadblock fired at and burst both front tyres. A hail of bullets rained down on the car. It struck a Garda car and swung sideways. O'Hare raised Bryan's gun and fired at the soldiers behind the roadblock. The soldiers fired again, thirty bullets in all striking the car. Bryan was already dead. O'Hare had been hit five times but stopped firing only when a round jammed the breech of his semi-automatic. The sound of firing died away, leaving an ominous silence.

Detective-Garda Harry Mulhaire volunteered to check the car. Moriarity and O'Rourke joined him. Bryan's body tumbled out of the opened passenger door. When asked to identify himself, O'Hare said, 'Agh, you know who I am.' Moriarity went in the ambulance with O'Hare. The most feared man in Ireland fiercely gripped the inspector's hand for the whole trip. On the wrist of the Border Fox, and covered in his blood, was John O'Grady's gold watch.

Five months later the Minister for Justice, Gerry Collins, approved an extensive reorganisation of the Garda Síochána. Ministers had been horrified and amazed to learn that senior officers in the ordinary crime sections were not informed for eight days that the security section had identified O'Hare as O'Grady's kidnapper. Other breakdowns in communications within the Gardaí hindered the recapture of O'Hare's gang. The Garda Síochána had seen little change since the foundation of the Irish state in 1921. There would now be increased exchange of intelligence between the security sections and the ordinary crime sections. Training procedures were to be revised and new strategies implemented for dealing with kidnaps and other serious crimes. Deputy commissioners were to act as senior force managers. The changes were supported by Éamonn Doherty, the Garda Commissioner.

In April 1988 the Special Criminal Court sentenced Dessie O'Hare, who had pleaded guilty, to forty years' imprisonment, twenty years for the kidnapping, and twenty years for the mutilation to John O'Grady's hands. Determined to send a clear message to terrorists, the court also jailed Hogan for forty years, twenty years for the kidnapping and a further twenty for the shooting of a garda—the longest sentences in the history of the state for a non-capital crime. Fergal Toal was sentenced to twenty years, Tony McNeil to fifteen years, and Gerry Wright to seven years. Mr Justice Liam Hamilton, the presiding judge, described the O'Grady kidnapping and mutilation as barbaric acts. O'Hare showed no remorse and made a ten-minute statement from the dock blaming Britain, Ireland, the Provisional IRA, prison officers, the Gardaí, and Dr Austin Darragh for his brutal treatment of O'Grady. Clare O'Hare appeared in court a month later. She was acquitted.

O'Hare is now forty-three and has spent more than half his life in prison. He claims that he is the only prisoner eligible for release under the Belfast Agreement who is still in prison. He claimed membership of the INLA when captured; membership of the 'Irish Revolutionary Brigade' would not have guaranteed him political prisoner status and, as events unfolded, early release under the Belfast Agreement. In April 2002 O'Hare was granted leave in the High Court to seek a judicial review of his forty-year sentence. On the same day as the High Court reserved its judgment on O'Hare's application his victim, John O'Grady, cancelled a lecture he was to give at a stress conference at Dublin County Stress Clinic. A deeply private man, now separated, O'Grady said that he was not aware that the conference would become the subject of media attention. He was reluctant to talk about the kidnap, even to close friends, preferring to gloss over his ordeal with an anecdote about trading stamps, being saved for a garden strimmer, disappearing from his car!

In December 2002 the Minister for Justice, Michael McDowell, approved an order for O'Hare to be transferred from Portlaoise to Castlerea Prison in preparation for his release. No date for the release has yet been fixed. Chief Superintendent Bill Herlihy, who led the O'Grady kidnap investigation, said that O'Hare was entitled to be released, having served fourteen years in prison.

12

Deirdre Crowley and the Murder-Suicide by Her Father

The abduction of children is universally abhorred, not least because it can frequently lead to something much worse. The abduction and murder in August 2002 of Holly Wells and Jessica Chapman at Soham, Cambridgeshire, was one such appalling incident. For months afterwards, children throughout Europe received cautionary warnings from their parents about 'stranger danger'. But children can be at risk within the family. Even in a small country like Ireland, tug-of-love incidents that end in tragedy occur with regularity. Michael Burke drove off the pier at Howth, Co. Dublin, killing himself and his partner's child, Miriam. Eight-year-old Karl Murphy's mother was placed in psychiatric care after he was found drowned on the beach at Greystones, Co. Wicklow. Jack Everitt Brennan, eighteen months old, was found drowned in a quarry at Drogheda, killed by his eighteen-year-old uncle, David Brennan, who was suffering from a psychiatric illness.

The Deirdre Crowley tragedy differed from all these in one significant respect: the much greater length of time that had elapsed between the abduction and the final tragedy.

Christine O'Sullivan worked as a computer technician at the Cork Institute of Technology. She had a great love of life and enjoyed the outdoors, camping and hiking being two of her many interests. In 1994 she met, through mutual friends, Chris Crowley, a teacher who shared her passion for the outdoors, and she soon found herself falling in love. Unlike most of the other men whom

Christine had dated, Chris was sensitive and caring, did not smoke, and drank little. Christopher Crowley, thirty-seven years old, was tall and lean, a keen mountaineer, who also had an interest in the arts. He had been married to Ursula Nagle, but the relationship had broken up before he met Christine. He had taught French and maths for fifteen years at the Loreto Convent School in Fermoy.

A dream trip to India for Christine with Chris confirmed that they were made for each other. They bought a house in Glounthane, Co. Cork, and on 11 August 1995 Christine gave birth to a baby girl. They named her Deirdre, and the three of them settled down to normal family life. By the time Deirdre was three she had a head of shoulder-length blonde hair and was full of impish mischief. She was a bright and inquisitive child and everyone who knew her said she had a smile that could make the greyest day light up. Like a lot of little girls, she loved playing with her doll and would experiment with her mother's make-up when her back was turned.

Unfortunately the dream turned sour for Christine, and at Christmas time 1998 she and Chris split up. The problem was Chris's obsession with his daughter, to the exclusion of herself. Men can sometimes feel excluded when their wife has a new baby and her affections for him are transferred to the child. In Christine's case it was the other way round. She tried to work it out, but after four years she reluctantly admitted defeat. Christine took Deirdre and moved to a new house in Douglas, Cork. It was an amicable enough separation, and visiting rights were agreed for Chris. He was determined to be a good father, never failing to pick Deirdre up for her regular visits at his house. He had taken her on her first camping trip during the summer. Christine was happy that as a single mother her child could still remain close to her father.

A few weeks before Christmas 1999, Christine and Chris agreed arrangements for the holidays. Deirdre would spend Christmas Day with her mother and Christmas Eve, St Stephen's Day and New Year's Day with her father. He had promised his daughter that they would do something extra special to celebrate.

On Saturday 4 December 1999 Chris collected Deirdre from her home at 10 a.m., as she was to spend the weekend with him. They failed to return at the agreed time of 5 p.m. on Sunday, and Christine at first thought that they may have been in a car accident. She rang around the local hospitals and, when she found no trace, contacted the Gardaí. They soon discovered enough to suggest that her former partner had been planning for some time to abduct his daughter. He had cleared out his bank accounts and had taken a week off sick from his school. He was also in the final stages of selling his house, having told Christine that there were too many memories in it for him to remain there. The more they investigated, the more the Gardaí were convinced that Deirdre's father had absconded with his daughter.

A nationwide search was started for the missing schoolteacher and his four-year-old daughter. Relatives and friends were interviewed. Guesthouse and hotel owners were asked to report anybody fitting Crowley's description seen in the company of a child. The Gardaí issued an appeal for Crowley to contact them. Christine took annual leave from her employment but rarely moved far from her phone. Relatives and friends took it in turns to stay with her and to offer what solace they could. An early report was of a sighting at a shoe shop in Midleton, Co. Cork, where a man resembling Crowley was seen buying a pair of pink trainers for a young blonde-haired girl. Christine spoke to the *Irish Examiner* and said, 'She probably would have been excited at first, thinking they're just on a holiday, but I know she'll be getting very agitated not hearing from me all this time.' The teaching staff at the Loreto Convent School was still finding it difficult to comprehend what their mild-mannered former colleague had done.

Christine had been left devastated by the abduction but knew that she had to remain strong for her daughter's sake. She immediately launched a vigorous campaign to find her. Her appearance on the television programme 'Crimeline' ten days after the abduction was an attempt to jog the memories of possible witnesses and to alert people throughout Ireland. Unusually for the programme, the feature on the Crowley abduction did not generate a single response. Christine used her computing skills to put out details of her missing daughter on the worldwide web with a special web site. A personal message to Deirdre was included: 'Deirdre, wherever you are, we want to let you know that you are dearly loved and missed by your family, especially your mother.'

In a more immediate move, she applied for an injunction freezing the proceeds of the sale of Crowley's house. The two-storey detached house had been put up for sale in the autumn and had been sold for the asking price of £200,000. The court order was not expected to bring about Deirdre's return; rather, its purpose was to hamper Chris Crowley's efforts to establish a new life for himself somewhere else.

Mary Banotti MEP, the mediator for the EU Parliament on transnationally abducted children, became involved with the Crowley case at an early stage. Founder of the Irish Centre for Parentally Abducted Children, Banotti offered advice and support to the distraught mother. She believed that Christine had done all that was possible, and stressed that a breakthrough in these cases often came after two or three weeks. It took that long for the reality of a life on the run to sink in with the abductor. Then, realising the enormity of the undertaking, the abducting parent would surrender the child.

Two weeks after the abduction, Christine made a second televised appeal for help in tracing her daughter. She told the Gardaí that although she had Deirdre's passport, she was afraid that Crowley could take her past international ports of entry with a copy of her birth certificate. This time her television appearance produced a result, with a confirmed sighting of Crowley in Mitchelstown, Co. Cork. Unfortunately, the lead petered out and the Gardaí were back to square one. Christine's worst fear appeared to be confirmed when, on Christmas Eve, Crowley's car was found in Co. Wexford, near the ferry port of Rosslare, and it was thought likely that the two had gone to France. Crowley was almost fluent in French, and that country may have seemed an ideal place to move to. Staff at the ferry terminals in Rosslare and Cork had been given photographs of the Crowleys, but no-one fitting their description had been reported boarding ar ferry. Interpol was called in to help with the hunt, as were the American authorities. Eventually more than 250 police forces around the world would be informed of the abduction.

Christine kept her daughter's room exactly as it was when she was abducted: her toys neatly lined up, the bedspread turned down waiting for the young girl's return. She had embarked on a lonely vigil, expecting news to come at any moment. At Christmas she bought presents for her daughter, and in the new year they were put aside, still wrapped in the Christmas paper.

A few months after Deirdre's abduction it was reported that a shotgun belonging to the Loreto Convent School's caretaker, Patrick O'Flynn, had gone missing from his house in Fermoy. However, there was nothing to link Crowley to its disappearance, because the Gardaí could not ascertain when it had been stolen. The caretaker felt certain he had seen it in the new year. If so, then Crowley would have had to take an enormous risk by returning to Fermoy to steal it.

In May 2000, Christine travelled to Wales after the Gardaí had received an anonymous tip that the child had been spotted there, but again the lead appeared to be groundless. The Gardaí appealed for the caller to get in contact with them again, but no second call was received.

On Deirdre's fifth birthday, Christine arranged a quiet celebration at her home, though still making very public and emotional appeals in the hope that some spark of remorse would be kindled in Crowley's psyche and he would return Deirdre to her mother's arms. The British women's weekly magazine *Take a Break* published an article about Deirdre in the hope that if a woman was helping Crowley she might see the article and realise the pain and hurt Christine was suffering.

Another year went by without any breakthrough. As the hours, days, weeks and months passed, Christine remained confident, never once giving in to the growing scepticism of others that her daughter would not be found. Shortly before Deirdre's sixth birthday

Christine appeared on the television programme 'Would You Believe?'; but although the feature generated a huge response, there was still no definite news of Deirdre. On her sixth birthday Christine once again bought presents and held a private celebration. She made a fresh appeal for information on the 'Pat Kenny show' on radio. One listener, Mary Horan from Coleville Road in Clonmel, heard the programme and was touched by Christine's heartbreaking story. She was surprised to hear that there were so many children missing in Ireland.

In October 2000 a man going by the surname of Allen rented Croan Lodge, Coleville Road, near Clonmel, Co. Tipperary, from Billy and Ann Molloy. The Molloys had lived there until recently and the dormer cottage was in pristine condition. They thought Allen was a quiet, respectable man and would make a good tenant. Their opinion of him seemed to be vindicated in the following months, as the new tenant kept to himself and neither the Molloys nor their former neighbours had cause for complaint. Many of the local residents did not even realise the cottage was occupied, much less that a young girl was living there as well. The wall of the cottage that faced the road had no windows, so passengers in passing vehicles would not have been able to see into the house.

The first real sighting of Allen by a neighbour came when a young boy who lived in a nearby house kicked his ball into the yard of the cottage and the newly arrived occupant returned it. The man, in his early forties, was bearded, had a slight tremor in one hand, and seemed polite. There was no sign of anyone else on that occasion.

The young girl was not enrolled at any local school and remained inside the house like a modern-day Rapunzel, locked inside her tiny room, never going outside to play with local children. Allen set up a mini-classroom inside the cottage, with just one pupil on the roll. When he left the house to go shopping the young girl would rarely be with him. Even these trips to the shops were few and far between, because he had his milk and vegetables delivered to the cottage.

Curiously, he would practise his language skills on the numerous immigrant workers from eastern Europe who were temporarily in the area. With his heavy beard and the baseball cap he habitually wore pulled low over his eyes, it would have been difficult for Clonmel people to describe him accurately.

On his shopping trips he would go by taxi, and he had the unusual habit of making each leg of the journey with a different taxi company. He always wore his baseball cap in the taxis and would say little, other than to grunt an answer to any question asked. The Coleville Road milkman, Dick Murray, who delivered a litre of milk three mornings a week, thought his customer a meticulous man. Because small birds used to peck the foil tops off the milk bottles, Allen left a biscuit tin on the doorstep so that Murray could place the bottles underneath it. Without fail, the biscuit tin would be there on the mornings the milk was to be delivered. The milk was paid for six months in advance, and Allen would open the door only slightly when passing out the money. At no time during his occupancy did Murray suspect there was a child in the house. However, occasionally Allen was seen walking with a young girl along the banks of the River Suir on the outskirts of the town.

What sort of life could the young girl have had inside that cottage? We can only imagine the fear and loneliness she endured. The sounds of neighbours' children playing in the sunshine must have been particularly hard for her to bear. Naturally she would have pined for her mother, and presumably she had been told some tale to explain why she could not see her. Allen's behaviour meant that the young girl missed most of the landmarks of a child's life. There was no first day of the new school year; no birthday party with her friends all there; no presents from her grandparents, uncles and aunts left under the tree at Christmas; no trips to the zoo; no visits to the cinema to see the latest Disney cartoon; indeed, not even a visit to the local doctor when she was ill or needed a vaccination. Her father had become her jailer.

One of the few times she was seen in town with Allen was at a local hotel in early August. A local newsagent, Eddie Kelly, saw the

man and child sharing a cup of coffee at the coffee dock in Hearn's
Hotel. Kelly formed the opinion that money must have been tight
for the father and daughter, as the man drank most of the coffee
before passing the cup to his daughter to finish. As they sat there, the
girl pulled out a purse and counted the coins in it before shaking her
head and closing it. Kelly considered offering to buy them breakfast
but was afraid his gesture might be misinterpreted. He thought the
young girl had a sweet, very pretty face, and that there appeared to
be an unusual tenderness between the two. Allen looked at his
daughter with a great deal of affection. The child was well behaved
and had obviously been taught to act in a mannerly fashion. When
leaving, she returned to push her chair fully under the table. The
next time Kelly was to see the girl was when Deirdre Crowley's
photograph appeared one day in a newspaper.

At about three in the afternoon on 31 August 2001 two local
gardaí in plain clothes were carrying out house-to-house inquiries
along Coleville Road in Clonmel. Scraps of information the Gardaí
had received suggested that Chris Crowley may have been hiding
out in that road. The Gardaí, keen not to alert anyone in case it
would prove a genuine lead, concocted a cover story about an
investigation into some cowboy builders touting for work in the
area. They knocked on the door of the rented Croan Lodge, and a
man dressed in a red T-shirt and track-suit trousers, answering
Crowley's general description opened the door. The Gardaí asked
his name, and the man gave it as Allen. There was no sign of a
young child.

The Gardaí felt that Allen had acted oddly and seemed uneasy.
They returned to their vehicle and reported their conversation,
requesting further instructions. They were advised to return to the
house and put further questions to the occupant. As they arrived at
the front door they heard the muffled sound of shots from inside.
They tried to force the front door but could not break it down. They
ran round to the back and broke a window to gain access. Inside the
house, in a toilet-laundry area, the gardaí discovered the body of a
young girl who had been shot in the face, and a badly wounded

Allen partly slumped across her. The young girl was wearing a worn vest and blue shorts, with sandals and socks on her feet. The man's left hand was on the barrels of the shotgun, the thumb of his right hand wedged inside the trigger guard. He was still alive but died within moments of being found. The shotgun he was clutching had had its stock shortened, and two layers of sticking plaster were wrapped around the stump. It was all too clear what had happened: the man had shot the girl before turning the gun on himself. The gardaí called an ambulance and then informed the local Garda station. A criminal investigation was immediately launched, but it seemed likely that the detectives would not be looking for anyone else in connection with the incident. A preliminary identification of the bodies was made. They were Chris and Deirdre Crowley.

Christine O'Sullivan was shattered that the 21-month search for her child had ended in such a tragic manner. Her distress was exacerbated because she had been at first told by gardaí that her daughter had been found, only to be told later of the terrible news. The next harrowing ordeal for Christine was the identification of her daughter's body at the hospital mortuary. Through her sister, Mary O'Sullivan, Christine asked for privacy so she could grieve for her dead child and time so that she could come to terms with what had happened. Christine's sister thanked the public for their message of support and the gardaí for the work they had done in tracing Deirdre. She also thanked the media for all their assistance since her niece's abduction.

Angela Crowley, sister-in-law of Chris Crowley, said: 'The family is devastated by what has happened. We never thought it would end like this.' Veronica Whyte, principal of the Loreto Convent School, said that all their thoughts and prayers were with Christine at this time.

The Gardaí received a barrage of criticism for their handling of the final stage of the Crowley case. Many thought the two gardaí should have forced their way into the house immediately their suspicions were aroused. Faced with this criticism, the Gardaí were unwilling to discuss it publicly. A press conference, due to be held the day after the shooting, was cancelled, though a Garda spokesperson said there would be no internal inquiry and that the two gardaí had acted in accordance with procedure. Alan Shatter of Fine Gael condemned the cancellation of the press conference, claiming that it showed the lack of transparency in Garda procedures. He said: 'It is important that the general public is made aware of the extent to which gardaí planned the approach to be taken when the visit took place.'

Inside the cottage the state pathologist, Dr John Harbison, found that food had recently been prepared in the neat and clean kitchen. A child's toys—teddy bears and dolls—were stored in cardboard boxes. Crayons and a child's cough mixture were on the mantelpiece. Two live magnum shotgun cartridges lay on the sofa. Deirdre had been shot in the face from very close range and had died instantly. Chris Crowley had then turned the shotgun on himself. Dr Harbison found four finger bruises behind one of the young girl's knees and two semicircular marks on her neck. He could not account for them. In the pocket of Crowley's trousers, there were several bobbles that would have been used for ponytails. Later, forensic tests on the bodies revealed no traces of alcohol or drugs.

Christine O'Sullivan had contacted Mary Banotti on Thursday afternoon before the story of her daughter's killing broke. Banotti later spoke to the press, saying that the tragic killing of Deirdre Crowley emphasised the need for the authorities to act swiftly in cases of domestic abduction. She added that she was distraught for the grief-stricken mother and angry at how Crowley had managed to evade detection for twenty-one months. She thought it highly probable that Chris Crowley must have received help from someone. She described Christine O'Sullivan as an extremely impressive woman, serious, who never gave up. Deirdre's mother knew that Chris Crowley loved their child and obviously hoped he would never hurt her, but had to live day to day with that worry. People have a tendency to regard a parental abduction as a domestic row between partners and outside involvement as unwise. 'Surely,' Banotti stressed, 'you would have to accept that someone hiding for over twenty-one months with a small child has to be obsessional or dangerous.' She urged the authorities to learn from the Crowley case and accept that they must act swiftly, regardless of whether a parent from Ireland or another country was involved.

The Irish Centre for Parentally Abducted Children, the charity Mary Banotti helped found, offers information packs to parents who think they may be vulnerable. It provides practical advice on having recent photographs of the child or children and of the potential abductor. In the case of infants it suggests that fingerprints and a DNA profile be obtained and kept in a secure place. Calls were made for photographs of missing children to be printed on milk cartons, as is done in the United States and some Continental countries.

A psychologist, Anne Marie McMahon, was asked what could have sparked the murder-suicide by Chris Crowley after such a long time. She said it was difficult to know what was going through his mind when the gardaí confronted him, 'but we have to recognise that there are people in this world who have mental problems who are not capable of minding children.' She continued, 'In modern society, with the separation of parents, the child is increasingly in the middle and becoming the victim.'

The day after the shooting the Garda Commissioner, Pat Byrne, appointed a senior officer, Detective-Superintendent Martin Callinan of the National Bureau of Criminal Investigation, to examine the circumstances surrounding the deaths of Crowley and Deirdre. The completed file was to be sent to the Co. Tipperary coroner, so that an inquest could be initiated. The Garda Síochána announced that it intended to investigate with a view to prosecution any persons who may have colluded with Chris Crowley, supplying him with money or other resources.

One immediate suspect to emerge was a woman in her early thirties, believed to be a former pupil of Loreto Convent School, whom Crowley had taught. She walked into Fermoy Garda Station and gave herself up after she had heard about the tragic events in Clonmel. Dublin detectives questioned her at length. It was believed she helped Crowley rent Croan Lodge and had visited him there regularly. The Gardaí were keen to set a precedent in the Crowley investigation in the hope that people assisting similar abductors might come forward so the cases could be resolved without bloodshed. The Gardaí are also still examining the possibility that Crowley may have had assistance from other sources, very probably another former pupil. The spokesman stressed that no stone would be left unturned in finding out if anyone else was involved in assisting Crowley to evade detection.

The principal of Loreto Convent School, Veronica Whyte, urged anybody with information to contact the authorities. She said the staff and pupils were in a dreadful state of shock following the double deaths. It was alleged that the past pupil of the school who had been assisting Crowley had become infatuated with the teacher some seventeen years previously, when she was a sixteen-year-old pupil. Crowley did little to discourage the girl's feelings and may have rekindled them when he went on the run. It is thought that it was she who had driven Crowley to Dublin after he had abandoned his car in Co. Wexford, creating a false trail for the Gardaí. A woman had made a mystery telephone call some months after the abduction, suggesting that Crowley was in Wales. The telephone records of several suspects have been examined. The Gardaí believe that Crowley may have evoked sympathy and support by claiming that Christine had joined a cult and that Deirdre was in danger. While it is true that Christine had become a Baptist, Crowley may have put whatever spin on the story best suited him.

Deirdre was buried on 2 September 2001 after a Requiem Mass at St Patrick's Church, Ballydesmond, next to her grandfather, Eugene O'Sullivan, in a plot at Kiskean Cemetery, Co. Cork. Placed next to her were things she loved most during her short life: her Barbie doll and her black patent-leather shoes. Christine, choking back her tears, told the congregation that God had answered her prayers. She had asked him to bring Deirdre safely home, and he had done so. 'But just not to my home.' Christine finished her emotional message by saying, 'I trust in God. I know that I will see her again.'

Father Michael O'Reagan, a friend of Christine and former chaplain in the Cork Institute of Technology, told the large crowd of mourners that Deirdre was as perfect as an apple-blossom, but she is now an angel in Heaven, touching our lives with mystery. He read out a short message from Chris Crowley's family: 'We, the Crowley family, are devastated by the loss of little Deirdre and ask that you convey our heartfelt condolences to Christine and her family at this time. Both she and little Deirdre will always be in our hearts and prayers.' Pastor Terry Price of Cork's Baptist Congregation delivered the homily. After the service, Christine and her four sisters carried the small white coffin out of the church.

Chris Crowley was laid to rest the next day. Four hundred people attended the service, and wreaths and flowers lined the driveway of the Church of the Way of the Cross in Togher, a Cork suburb. Christine O'Sullivan attended the service and sat behind the Crowley family, just a few feet from the coffin of the man she had once loved. Her presence at his funeral was an act of forgiveness. On top of the coffin sat a small wicker basket with a child's china tea set inside.

Whatever mistakes Chris Crowley made, there were many who remembered him with affection. His former teaching colleagues at Loreto Convent School sent one of the wreaths. The Gardaí were represented by Superintendent Brian Callinan. A local TD, John Dennehy, also attended. Father Michael O'Riordan conducted the service. 'Chris Crowley was motivated by tremendous love,' the priest said. 'Some might say that love was excessive, but that is not for me to judge.' He expressed admiration for the tremendous love Christine had displayed for her daughter during her abduction. The whole Crowley family had asked him to thank Christine for attending the funeral. Crowley's sister-in-law, Angela Crowley, also thanked Christine. She said that her brother-in-law had acted out of love. After the Requiem Mass, Crowley was interred at St Finbarr's Cemetery.

The Crowley case was in the news again on 9 September 2001 when two hundred parents burned legal access orders outside the

GPO in Dublin as a protest against a legal system that fails to safeguard their rights. The demonstration was organised by the Parents' Defence Campaign, which wanted the judiciary to recognise the damage inflicted on children when one parent deliberately obstructs the other from seeing them, even when they have been granted access. The chairman of the campaign, Peter Coleman, said that when a couple break up, the children can often be used as a weapon by one parent against the other, and this should be considered a form of abuse. Seán Mac Suibhne said that the emotional damage inflicted on the child in these cases was being ignored by the courts.

The inquest into the death of Deirdre Crowley opened on 20 May 2002. Christine O'Sullivan confirmed to the coroner, Paul Morris, that she had identified her daughter's body and that of her former partner in St Joseph's Hospital mortuary, Clonmel. Derek Crowley testified that he had identified his brother's body. Dr Harbison, state pathologist, described the scene inside Croan Lodge as he had found it. Superintendent Dick Burke requested that the inquest be adjourned, pending possible criminal prosecutions in the matter. He confirmed that a file on the case was still with the DPP. The coroner approved an immediate adjournment.

The Crowley abduction is without doubt one of the most appalling to have happened in Ireland. It is easy to imagine a love so strong that a person would rather die than live deprived of that love, but it is impossible to comprehend a love that can be expressed only by depriving others of that love. All we can do is try.

Bibliography

Arnold, Bruce, *Jack Lynch: Hero in Crisis*, Merlin Publishing, Dublin, 2001.

Boyd, Andrew, *The Informers*, Mercier Press, Dublin, 1984.

Connolly, Colm, *Herrema: Siege at Monasterevin*, Olympic Press, Dublin, 1977.

Coogan, Tim Pat, *The Troubles: Ireland's Ordeal, 1966–1995, and the Search for Peace*, Hutchinson, London, 1995.

Dillon, Martin, *The Dirty War*, Hutchinson, London, 1988.

Edwards, John, *Fools and Horses: The Mammoth Book of Unsolved Crimes*, Robinson Publishing, 1999.

Harnden, Toby, *'Bandit Country'*, Hodder and Stoughton, London, 1999.

Holland, Jack, and McDonald, Henry, *INLA: Deadly Divisions*, Poolbeg, Dublin, 1994.

Keenan, Brian, *An Evil Cradling*, Random House, London, 1992.

Kerrigan, Gene, *Hard Cases: True Stories of Irish Crime*, Gill & Macmillan, Dublin, 1996.

McCarthy, John, and Morrell, Jill, *Some Other Rainbow*, Bantam Press, London, 1993.

McKitrick, David, Kelters, Séamus, Feeney, Brian, and Thorton, Chris, *Lost Lives*, Mainstream Publishing, Edinburgh and London, 1999.

O'Callaghan, Seán, *The Informer*, Bantam Press, London, 1998.

Ryder, Chris, *The RUC: A Force under Fire*, Arrow, 2000.

Smyth, Sam, *Thanks a Million, Big Fella*, Blackwater Press, Dublin, 1997.

Sutton, Malcolm, *An Index of Deaths from the Conflict in Ireland, 1969–1993*, Beyond the Pale Publications, Belfast, 1994.

Taylor, Peter, *Provos: The IRA and Sinn Féin*, Bloomsbury, London, 1997.

Walsh, Liz, *The Final Beat: Gardaí Killed in the Line of Duty*, Gill &
    Macmillan, Dublin, 2001.
Williams, Paul, *Gangland*, O'Brien Press, Dublin, 1998.

BBC Sport

RTE

Belfast Telegraph
Daily Telegraph
Evening Herald
Irish Examiner
Irish Independent
Irish News
Irish Press
Irish Times
Limerick Leader
News Letter
Pacemaker Magazine
Times
Sunday Times